STARLUST

STARLUST

The Secret Fantasies of Fans

FRED VERMOREL

faber and faber

This edition first published in 2011
by Faber and Faber Ltd
Bloomsbury House, 74–77 Great Russell Street
London WC1B 3DA

Printed by Books on Demand GmbH, Norderstedt

A CIP record for this book is available from the British Library

ISBN 978-0-571-28076-6

Contents

Introduction

This book, at first glance full of the fantasies of maniacs, is really full of the wonderful dreams of people just like you and me.

Put more celestially, when we pursue perfection, in ourselves or in others, we are searching for God. A perfect father or mother, brother or sister, son or daughter – all are dreamed of in the demand for a psychotherapeutic placebo, often embodied in the image of a chosen star.

What made me enjoy this collection of fantasies and letters was not that I thought, 'Hey, all these people are like pawns, I feel superior.'

Rather I found myself identifying with the fans, not their heroes or heroines.

There is always danger, however. I have had letters from fans that have scared me a little, usually because I have found that my importance to the writers seems out of all proportion with my own opinion of my real worth.

But that could be my ego at work. What I think of myself doesn't really matter, what matters is that I have made myself available as what Jung called a symbol of 'transformation'.

Lennon's tragic death illustrates how disastrously this can sometimes end for both subject and object.

Thank God that such misfortunes are relatively rare, for we all need to have heroes that are of this world, as well as spiritual figures that we put above or beyond it. That makes us all potential 'fans'.

This introduction will probably add to the apparent perversity of the star-system in pop music as observed by the outsider. But such a system exists at every level of life, in every arena of the arts, performing arts and political life.

The *Henry Root Letters* showed how easily public figures of all kinds are flattered or misled by sycophancy and criticism.

But the letters collected here are benign, heart-warming and occasionally erotic. It's good to know that ordinary human beings are capable of such passion, imagination and creativity.

If I sound like a manipulative star who is patronising fans, then I should point out that every star feels patronised by his or her fans.

It is quite sobering to realise that someone who writes to you as though you are the most important person in the universe doesn't need you to be *alive* in order to eulogise you.

Pete Townshend

Foreword

THE FANS IN this book are typical pop star fans as we found them in over four years of research. For every story told here there were dozens of similar ones. There are fans like these in every classroom and every suburban street.

We have highlighted three major categories of fan: rock, teeny pop and MOR, through fans of David Bowie, Nick Heyward and Barry Manilow. Many other fans are represented, however, and the overall selection is balanced to present the characteristic moods and shades of pop fanhood in general.

The material was distilled from about 350 hours of interviews, 20 hours of ansaphone messages, and over 400 written accounts: fantasies, replies to questionnaires, diaries and dreams journals. We also read about 40,000 letters written to every kind of star and made a content analysis of 1,200 letters written to the showbiz column of the Sun newspaper.

We contacted fans through editorial appeals and ads in the music press and by hanging around ticket queues, concert venues, signings, auctions of memorabilia, etc, and by visiting fan club conventions, etc. We also sent out questionnaires to several fan club mailing lists.

Not all these people wanted to speak at first, and many were reluctant to express the full extent of their feelings. Some we corresponded with and interviewed over a period of three years.

Slaves are people who cannot speak their thoughts
Euripides, 4th century BC

Passion

Joanne: what love should be

When I make love with my husband I imagine it's Barry Manilow. All the time.

And after, when my husband and I have made love and I realize it's not him, I cry to myself.

It's usually dark when the tears flow and somehow I manage to conceal them.

It happens to an awful lot of people, too. I didn't realize how many until I got involved with Barry fans. A lot of them are married and around my age and they feel the same way and they do the same thing. It's comforting to know I'm not the only one.

But it's still not easy sometimes. It can be very, very upsetting. 'Cos sometimes, besides everything else, I've got this terrible guilty feeling.

But I can't help the way I feel. There's no one can change the way I feel. Not me, or anybody. You can't just press a button and hope it will change.

I always say you can't make yourself love somebody and you can't stop loving somebody. It's just something that happens and you've got no control over it. You don't particularly want it to happen but it does. There's nothing anyone can do about it.

It can cause a lot of problems sometimes.

And I do feel guilty sometimes, very guilty. But mostly I go along with it because it's easier to.

I suppose it's the same kind of thing people get out of religion. I can't really explain it more than that. But they obviously get something from God to help them through their lives. And Barry is – maybe I shouldn't say it but it's the way I feel – he's the same sort of thing. He helps me through my life.

But also it isn't just that, because I'm attracted to him as well. I am definitely attracted to him. It's what I describe as a one-sided love affair. He's my lover in my fantasies. He's my friend when I'm depressed. He's there and he seems to serve as something I need to get through my life.

He's my friend and he's my lover – mostly he's my lover!

I've been married 20 years. My husband's used to me being a fan because he knows what I am now.

But when it first happened it frightened him and it frightened me too because neither of us knew what was happening.

This was over——in 1965. And I was terribly in love with——at the time.

I saw him first on TV, and then I got to see a concert.

And it became more and more an obsession with me. So that nothing else mattered but him.

And I found this girl who felt the same way about him as I did. And we used to send each other these letters.

Then one day I got really upset and obviously my husband realized that what I was upset about was something I was keeping to myself. So he decided to find out what it was.

And there was this case I kept with all these letters this girl had written to me and one I was writing to her – all locked up in a case.

So he broke the lock open and read them all.

He never knew I was in love with——to that point.

When he found out he said it all had to stop, that I couldn't go on like that and I just had to pull myself together and get rid of all the pictures I'd put up – 'cos at that time he just thought it was pictures of pop stars and there was nothing in it – it was just something that everybody did.

I can remember him raising his voice and we had a real row. I was crying. I went hysterical and I said: 'I don't love him, I hate him. I hate him for what he's doing to me. He's ruining my life. I really hate him.'

I didn't really. Well, I suppose I did. Love and hate can be so close. I did sort of think: What is he doing to me? He's absolutely ruining my life.

be so close. I did sort of think: What is he doing to me? He's absolutely ruining my life.

And that's when I really did nearly go out of my mind. I really couldn't see any way of feeling any different. I would never feel any different. I thought: If I can't have him, I can't live without him. So I was on the point of suicide.

But I had children, and the children kept me from doing anything stupid like that.

Though if it had been only me I would have. I mean I was that much in love with him.

My husband said I could keep the records – he said the records were different, but I had to get rid of all the pictures and I wasn't allowed to keep scrap-books or anything like that.

I said: 'You can't dictate what I can do.'

And so it went on, rows, mainly over me looking at the pictures.

Because he didn't understand what was going on, what was happening to me.

Somehow we did get through it. Things eased off. But it was very, very gradual. I mean it went on for about 15 years.

But somehow——faded.

I actually got to know him and I got very close to his family. I visited them in the States and I remember sleeping in his bed and having a shower in the same shower! And I thought that was the biggest thrill ever. And I joke about it to people now. I say: 'I've slept in——'s bed – but he didn't happen to be in it at the time!' And having a shower in the same shower was a turn on as well.

But the years went by and this fire had gone, the fire I'd felt for him. It became just a gentle kind of love feeling for him and it didn't cause any problems. The sexual thing faded off.

At the time I'd been frigid to my husband because I wanted——and not my husband. And I hadn't discovered this fantasizing thing so much then.

Now I find it helps. A lot.

So now with Barry I can cope better because I've been through it all before.

When I felt it coming on I thought: I'm older now, I can cope with it. I couldn't cope with——because I'd never felt anything like it before.

And although there have been times when I've been very depressed and I have the crying fits where I can't stop crying over him, I've never got suicidal over Barry.

It helps too that my husband accepts it – he accepts Barry.

This time it's easier for him to accept.

I don't know what the outcome will be. It may fade in the future as it did with——. I mean I still love——, the same as I love my husband, if you know what I mean. But it's a different kind of feeling.

I've gone over that, trying to analyse it time and time again. I *do* love my husband, very much. And I love——and I'll always love——. But Barry at the moment is something that excites me and he's the be all and end all of this moment in my life.

My husband's away quite a bit, so Barry kind of keeps me company when he's away.

I imagine he's composing at the piano and I'm just there and I'm his girl-friend. And he is so deeply involved in composing his music he doesn't take any notice of me whatsoever. I bring him a cup of coffee and he kind of says: 'Put it there', and carries on. And then he's angry because something won't go right with the piece and he's angry and in this terrible mood. And I'm just sort of there, but I don't interrupt him. And then suddenly he realizes what he's like and he comes out of it and sympathizes with me, apologizes for being that way. And then we make love and everything's fine.

Usually we make love on the settee or on the floor – or anywhere. Not very often in bed. Usually where we are.

He's very passionate, very gentle, considerate. I can't imagine that there's any aggression there at all. He's not that aggressive sort of love-maker. Very passionate, very romantic.

Sometimes I imagine us having a shower together. It's beautiful. We're caressing each other and kissing under the shower, our bodies are pressed together and oh, it's heaven. Always so gentle and loving he appears to be.

Touch plays a big part in it, it really does. Touching each other is really important. It's all done so romantically and gently. Not just for sex. It's love more than sex. And it's a bit like it's all in slow motion.

I love his lovely, long fingers. I can imagine being caressed by his hands all over my body.

Usually it's in subdued lighting, and in the open air ones it's under the stars.

And it really does help me through my life. It makes life, you know, worth living.

He's the type of man who would buy me flowers. He would be considerate and treat me like a woman and not like a mate, you know, like making me help him shift the settee.

I like to be treated like a woman sometimes and have flowers bought for me. So I imagine Barry would be very tender and loving.

And I think that's probably what I'm in love with. Although I'm also attracted to his looks and his body – I'm very attracted to his body!

I love touching him all over, every part of him, and running my fingers through his hair.

And I'm particularly attracted to his neck. I think he's got the most gorgeous neck I've ever seen. I kiss his neck.

And, I'm also attracted to his arms. People laugh at me because he's got thin arms but I find them so attractive. I've got pictures of him in a sleeveless T-shirt which shows all his arms.

And he seems to have such soft skin – it's a real turn on that is! I imagine putting my hand inside his T-shirt and his body would be very soft. I would love to touch his body.

I do get wet thinking about him like that, but I don't ever orgasm. It can be very frustrating.

It's handy having a husband!

I think Barry has improved our sex life if anything. To be quite honest, definitely, he has improved our sex life.

I was quite frigid before but now with this fantasizing it's better for me and it's better for my husband. And luckily he never says no, he's always ready for it.

Often I look at a poster and that will start it off. I think he's got the most beautiful body. And certain posters turn me on more than others. Some just make me happy and others I find sexually attractive.

I like to lay in bed at night before I turn the light out and look at them.

That's when I start to fantasize.

He comes into his dressing room. I'm aware of him shutting the door and locking it. There's nobody else there. And he's all excited and sweating from his exertions with the concert. And there's just me and him in his dressing room. And there's no place to lay down so we usually do it standing up.

Sometimes he unzips his trousers, sometimes I do.

Then there's the one in front of the fire, on a fur skin rug. That's after the wine and the soft music and the talking.

I imagine that we would talk an awful lot beforehand but not actually when we're making love.

He becomes silent.

He French kisses me and kisses me all over and on my breasts and he touches me here, between my legs.

I've got no appetite whatsoever whenever I'm about to see Barry. It completely goes. I just don't want to look at any food. I've always got this feeling I'm going to be sick, going to spoil things. It's an odd feeling. It always affects me in that way, the excitement.

The first time I saw him was at Blenheim.

And when I actually saw him I thought: He's real, that's him. Especially when he stood there after all these fantasies and looking at pictures and videos and things. He was actually *there*.

I could have burst into tears. In fact I did, but that was at the end when he'd gone. It was an emotion that made me want to cry – that he was there after all the waiting and fantasizing and staring at his pictures. I mean, his pictures are plastered all over the bedroom walls. And it was just something that made my heart beat faster.

I kept thinking: Oh God, when he goes – what's it going to be like when he goes?

And at the end when he'd gone it was dreadful. I

thought: I'll never see him again. I felt: This is it. He's gone. I was really, really upset.

I kept saying over and over again: 'I can't stand it. When am I going to see him again?' And my friend said: 'The Festival Hall.' I said: 'Ridiculous! What, at £50–£100 a ticket?!'

That was awful. That really hit me more than anything – that money comes between me and Barry. 'Cos I hate money anyway. It embarrasses me. I'm not interested in having it unless I want something.

So I got this job delivering coupons. I delivered 5,000 coupons to buy one concert ticket! I nearly dropped but I did it. I worked it out – it was 5,000 coupons to buy one concert ticket, and that was the cheapest one.

And when I arrived there I was right up the back row of the balcony. For £50!

And I just felt like crying. I just wanted to go home. I thought: I can't bear it. To be so far away from him was almost worse than not being there at all.

But I thought: I'm not giving up. I don't give up that easily! So I managed to borrow another £50 and I went down to see if there were any returns.

I stood there for two hours waiting. Then suddenly they said they were going to open the press seats at the side of the stage. And they said that they had a restricted view. So I said: 'Well, how restricted?' And they said: 'You just get the side face of him instead of the front one. I said: 'I don't care!'

And I sat there.

It was like a nine foot drop to the stage, and there was his piano. It couldn't have been more than nine feet away from me. I thought I was dreaming. Now *that* was one of the most exciting moments in my life, to know that he was going to come on and be stood there in front of me. And when he came on – oh!, the excitement I felt! My stomach was going over like a washing machine and it was wonderful to just see him stood there.

And he kept coming over and shielding his eyes from the lights and looking up to where I was. At one point, he actually looked right at me. Just that once. Whether he actually saw me . . . but he actually caught my eye at that precise moment. It was wonderful.

I felt shaky and *happy*! I felt so happy. I was so wound up too and I was shouting for him and everything. Usually when I go to concerts I sit and listen. I don't scream or do anything like that normally. But I was shouting ir Barry all the time with all the others.

And there's one point in his concert act where he plays the synthesizer and his whole body ..!

Well, he did that with his back to me, about four or five feet away. I nearly went over the balcony! The girl next to me pulled me back. She said: 'Don't fall over.' I said: 'I don't care.'

Just to fall at his feet. . . .

It's the body movements. He does these suggestive hip movements with the music when he's playing the synthesizer which really get me going.

That is a really sexual thing. I couldn't believe how excited I got.

I've never known such a sexual element with any other star as there is with Barry. Because the fans all go for these photographs we call 'bum shots'. It's a sort of race for who gets the most bum shots.

When he was last over here he caught on, because he said: 'Since I've been over here I've seen more photographs of my backside than of my face!' And he sees the funny side of that.

With all the photographs that get passed around, the more disgusting ones the better. Like one particular photograph I got hold of called 'the headless wonder'.

A girl took this photograph of him in a fantastic black satin outfit and she was so thrilled with her efforts because it showed up his manly bulge to a treat!

She was so pleased with this photograph it was three weeks before she noticed they never printed his head.

She had it pointed out to her: 'Yeah, it is very nice, but where's his head?' She said: 'Oh, I hadn't looked up that far!'

And that is the kind of fans he's got. I reckon 99 and three quarter per cent of his fans are like that. They do get a great thrill out of that kind of thing.

But it isn't only that.

Because I've been to lots and lots of concerts but I've

never felt that kind of atmosphere and that kind of closeness.

Complete strangers catch hold of your hands. And you are all united, united as one.

And to think that one man can do that to so many people.

I mean, he must be special to be able to do that, to create this atmosphere and this special feeling. He can't just be ordinary, can he?

So many people can't be wrong.

I rarely dream about him. And when I do it's not what I'd like. I rarely dream romantic dreams. They're usually troubled dreams.

I often dream I have this concert ticket and I can't get there. There's always something stopping me and by the time I get there it's all over.

When he was due to come on TV the other day and I was planning to tape it, I had this dream where it had been on the day before and I'd missed it, completely.

I was glad to wake up and find it was only a dream.

That is a thing I dread anyway. I always make a point of buying two tapes and I have my friend make a copy in case something goes wrong with mine.

I'm a neurotic when he comes on TV. I never enjoy it, not the first time I see it. Not until I play it back and know I've got it.

Last Christmas Eve my husband was away and I was alone and when midnight came I thought: It's Christmas Day, I'm going to spend it with Barry.

I'm going to open my presents now and I'm going to have Barry for company.

So I sat here all on my own and I opened my presents and played Barry on the video. He was like my friend that was with me, because I was alone.

Him being there on television is like he's in the room with me. I don't go as far as thinking he's actually here. But his spirit's here with me.

When I watch him I sit right up close – I've always got to sit up close. I get a pouffe and sit right up a few inches away from him. The closer I am the better. I get frustrated if I'm not close. Because I feel otherwise I'm going to miss something.

I didn't have any of that back in the '60s with——. I'm so lucky that nowadays with the video I can just press a button and see Barry when I want to.

With——I remember having a camera on a table and taking black and white pictures off the television in a darkened room.

I often wonder whether I would actually give up my life that I'm leading now to go with Barry. It's difficult. I don't really know. You see, I can't hurt people. I find it very difficult to hurt anyone. I tend to put other people before the way I feel myself. I don't think if he came in here now and said: 'Come on', that I would go.

Even though I love him so much, I couldn't leave my husband to go with him.

But I often think that I would give up my life for him.

If it was just me, if it was just me to think about, I would give up my whole life for him. I would die.

I always say: 'If I could spend one night with Barry I would happily die tomorrow.' That's how much I love him. I just know I would be quite happy to give up everything for him. Just to know what he was like, what he was really like.

I suppose it does sound over-dramatic really, but it's not something I've just thought up on the spur of the moment. I've thought about it a lot of times, many times.

That's how deep I love him.

I don't know whether it is love. It feels like love. But then I've never met him. So how can you love someone you've never met? It's incredible really. It's something I don't really understand.

But then I wonder if we ever know what love really is. I mean, there's so many different kinds of love. There's the love I have for Barry, the love I have for my husband, the love I have for my children.

But this, what I feel for Barry, feels like the biggest love affair ever. I don't know whether it is or whether it isn't but it certainly feels like this is what love should be. It's quite hard to cope with sometimes, this passionate feeling, this ultimate of love.

Some people might say they fall in love, but I wonder if they really feel what I feel. Do they feel the type of love that I feel? I don't know. I think there's different degrees of love in different people. I don't think many people would say that they'd give up their life and die to spend one night with one man.

They might be very passionate about a man but I don't think they'd be prepared to die for him.

[*Joanne is 42. Her husband is a travelling salesman and she has three children.*]

Stephen's fantasy about Bruce Foxton

My name is Stephen. I am 16 years old and I am a homosexual.

After reading your advertisement I decided to write and tell you about my secret sexual fantasy. It is with Bruce Foxton of The Jam and it is as follows:

I attend a modern comprehensive school and I always imagine going to the toilets during the lessons and finding Bruce there, facing the wall, apparently having a piss. (He would be dressed in uniform: black trousers, grey jumper, shirt and tie.) Anyway, as I have always liked Bruce Foxton, that sexy-looking fifth-former, I decided to stand next to him to get a good look at his prick. As I do, I discover he is wanking himself and what an ace dick he has. It is seven inches long with a big red knob and I can see his brown hairs peeping through.

'Having good fun?' I said to him.

'Yeah, there's nothing like a fucking good wank, is there?' At this he walked over to the door and said that we'd better lock the door in case anyone came in. 'Wouldn't want our wanking session disturbed, would we?' he said as he walked across the floor, dick in hand, until he rested against the wall and continued wanking.

By now my nought inch prick was rock hard and I was enjoying a great wank. Facing Bruce, I watched him slowly pull his foreskin back and forth, revealing his lovely moist red knob. Bruce started moving his blazer pocket and brought out a pack of cigs. He handed me one and we both had a smoke and a chat whilst wanking off.

After a while he said: 'Oh balls! I'm going to take these bloody things off, they're aggravating me to death.' And so he quickly pulled his trousers off, revealing long, masculine legs. Then he took the undies off and everything he had showed – his long seven-inch cock stood upright, just asking to be sucked. In between his legs was a massive pair of really fleshy balls (they were the largest balls I have ever seen) and then his thick bush brown prick hair – loads of it. He was fantastic!

'Why don't you take yours off?' he asked. So with great speed I did and it wasn't long before we were both completely naked. He turned round for a minute, revealing his bum. It was ace. It was as smooth as silk and just the right size. He looked over at me and said to me: 'Will you wank me for a change and I'll wank you? It feels a lot better.' So we did so.

I put my hand round his dick and felt its thickness and warmth as I slowly pulled it up and down, getting more and more turned on as he was slowly wanking mine off. The next part just more or less happened. I felt him slip down my body and take hold of my cock. Then his mouth opened and with his tongue he licked all round my solid dick until he reached my knob when he fully opened his mouth and put the last inch of my dick into his mouth. He moaned softly as he slowly gave my cock an expert sucking. His tongue was right into the skin at the side of my knob and this was fantastic.

After a few minutes he withdrew and licked his lips. He sat on the floor, legs open, and said to me: 'It's your turn now.' So I placed my head in between his legs and started to kiss his dick and lick his hair. I opened my mouth and put his balls inside. His balls were so big, really a mouthful, and I could feel the flesh on the walls of my mouth. As I explored his balls with my mouth, his hard dick was lying against my face and a quick glance at his prick made me want to suck his knob. So I pulled away and his balls came into view (wet and warm from being in my mouth). I then started to kiss his knob before taking it into my mouth and sucking at the beautiful thing. He was now so excited I could feel his spunk ready to shoot out so I decide to let him bum me, as there is nothing better than someone shooting their load into your bum. So I told him, and I kneeled down while he got behind me and I felt his hand opening my bum as with his other he slowly guided his weapon into my bum. When after some lovely forcing he was fully up me, he started to let my bum wank him off and all the time he was biting my neck and his hands were groping round my dick and balls until finally I felt the spunk shoot up, out of him into me, and I heard him moan in sheer ecstasy.

Then he withdrew and I fingered my bum to feel his warm, milky spunk and I licked my fingers as I had got them full of his ace-tasting juice. His prick was now limp and our love-making was nearly over, except he wanted me to come in his mouth. So I got over him and lowered my knob into his wide open mouth. He started sucking me until finally I could not hold back any longer and let my spunk shoot into his mouth until there wasn't a drop left in me. And he smiled at me and showed me his mouth full of fresh spunk. He then indicated for me to kiss him which I did, and we swopped the spunk about in each other's mouths until finally he swallowed it. Both our cocks were now limp and we lay together, naked on the floor, holding each other, both totally satisfied.

This was my secret sex fantasy with Bruce Foxton – I hope you enjoyed reading it.

What strange feelings! – letters to David Bowie

Dear Bowie,

I am writing to ask you a question. How does Angie Bowie know what to give David for his birthday? After all, what do you give the man who *is* everything?

Yours,
Jane

Dear David,

Sometimes I am so afraid that something will happen to you, that I can't breathe, I am so afraid.
Please come to me soon!

Dear David,

I will wait for you forever, for you are my heart and I would rather die then live without it.

Take care of yourself.

Mr David Bowie/David Jones,

Pretensions aside, here is another letter trying to reach you among the thousands.

It would be useless to try and explain how I feel about you. All I have are albums and photographs and a place in my mind that holds all the inspiration you've been in my continuing struggle with my ideas of life.

You are my vision of man, the original beyond all the rules we've ingested to control our thoughts and actions. The words you supply me with give me strength, a foundation to stand on in my self-inflicted alienation.

It is hard knowing you're out there creating to even try to be presumptuous enough to think I have something worthwhile to say, but it will consume me if I don't.

I doubt this letter will get to you, I've written so many before.

An endless stream of love, awe, appreciation, respect has poured from this mind to hand to pen to paper, sometimes to the point of loneliness thinking you could care less about this human existence I still manage to enjoy so much.

I assume I will always try to reach you.

Peter

Dear David,

My greatest fantasy is to meet you in person. You are one of the greatest examples of humanity I ever thought there could be.

Sue

Dear David,

I am a big fan of yours, my name is Cosima. I am Spanish but unfortunately I live in the USA from four years.

I am sorry if I am telling you things you are not interested in, but for me is very difficult express my feeling for you.

The truth is that I am in love with you from a long time. I know it may appear ridiculous and I wonder what you will think if I should confess to you how deep are my feelings for you: please don't think I am crazy, I really love you!

This makes me feel so sad, especially when I see you on television. During the transmission I feel so happy seeing you so beautiful, but then after it is over, inside me there is a loneliness and it hurts me and makes me cry for the rest of the day.

It is very difficult to explain. People won't understand me. Every time somebody dates me I say no because I can think only of you. You are the only boy I have fallen in love with and I am afraid this crush will stay inside me for a long time. Everything seems an unreal dream.

How many times have I tried to communicate with you so I could know you better! What I feel for you is not just a physical attraction, it is more, something very deep and strong inside.

Every time people say bad things about you I feel the duty to defend you and sometimes I become violent.

David, I am begging you to understand this situation.

At least try to understand that these words come from me and that my heart is broken.

I remember when I was in Spain I had a good friend who was homosexual and I used to tell him my problems. He could understand my sentiments for you, but my parents found out about our friendship and they beat me and stopped me seeing him.

From that day I didn't have more news about him and I don't know where he is or if he is alive or dead.

Now my life is miserable. I never have a good time, so I spend all my days listening to your music. It makes me happy to hear your voice.

Oh David, please forgive me if I am disturbing you, but

you are my central life. I wish I could be in your arms and forget who I am and feel protected and secure with your love. What a dream!

What strange feelings!

I love you with all my heart.

You are the most important thing in my life, the only human being for who I would be capable to do sacrifice. You are always in my thoughts and in my soul.

I love you. I need you.

Cosima

PS An enormous kiss with affection for you

Lucille (16): fantasy about Robert Plant

Many a time have I thought about how passionate Robert Plant of Led Zeppelin looked. So many times I had Sat in the middle of my room (which is covered with pictures of him), and imagined that he was lying between my legs, with his lovely blond locks covering my stomach. His beautiful mouth embracing my cunt as my fingers drifted through his hair. He then mooves up my body pausing at my chest to circle my tits with a magical tongue. Whilst fondeling my tits very softly he kisses me, sort of searching for something.

Then we covered ourselves in Joy Jelly (passion fruit flavour) we rub up and down each other, sliding smoothly over each other. He teases me rubbing his gorgeous cock over my cunt, but not actually in it. I gently carres his

27

swelling prick which is wet
with joy jelly and my honey.
Soon neither of us can bear it
any longer, groaning with yearning
he rolls on top of me. He thrusts
cruelly into me, whilst bitting my
neck, my nails tear at his back,
the sides of my cunt are throbing,
and my honey drips onto the
floor. He's like a huge, golden, lion
conquering me. My legs
cling around his waist as we rise
and grind into each other. As
we reach a hot climax my legs
untwine themselves from his
waist, and spread themselves
as far as they can, tense
with excitment. Every muscle is
taught as we both cum. A lovely
warm, fulfilled sensation fills
me. We lie together parting and
holding each other close. He pulls
out and his wet swollen prick
rests against my thigh.

Not just a foolish child – Nick Heyward fans

Dear Nick,
  When I first saw you, my eyes filled and tears ran down my cheeks.
  These tears were tears of happiness and love.
  It was the best experience in the whole of my life.

Dear Nick,
  You may think this is a schoolgirl crush, but I assure you it is not, as I am nearly 16.

Dear, Sir, Madam,

I am really desperate to meet Nick Heyward.

I have tried many times to get myself knocked over just wishing that I would be hurt bad enough to be put in a coma.

I know this may sound stupid to you but I thought if I was hurt bad enough, my mum would write to Nick and ask him to pull me through. I thought that would be the only way that I would ever meet him.

Please help me before something really bad happens to me.

Dear Nick,

I think of you all the time, wondering where you are or what you are doing.

I get so frustrated, knowing that your life is happy without me, but mine is miserable without you.

Please don't laugh at this letter and throw it away, thinking a foolish child wrote it, because I'm not a child.

Julie (16): I'm an only child, and earlier this year my father died. He knew how mad about Nick I was and even when he was dying he asked about Nick. He meant the world to me, and I never knew something could change your life so much. I still haven't got over it but I only have to look at my posters or play Nick's records to feel a little better. My mum says I'm in a world of my own, as I'm involved so much with Nick.

Dear Nick,

To put it bluntly, I find you absolutely fascinating. Your virile voice sends shivers down my spine. You seem to be a perfect man who has everything a woman could possibly desire.

When I go to bed I leave the lights on and sit staring at the pictures of you that cover my bedroom walls.

Most nights I end up crying myself to sleep.

It deeply disturbs me knowing you will never belong to me.

Linda (11)

my dream

I'd like to go to nickos studio and star in his video I'd like to go on a boat ride and drink champayne in the sun I'd like him to sing to me. And then go to the opera. Then we go to a pub. Then to bed together.

Alison (14): Sometimes when I see him perform on television I hold my heart because it feels as if it's going to burst.

I carry him around in my purse in a little framed wallet and if I sit down in a beautiful place I take him out and look at him. Then I feel I'm alone with him.

When I get bored or get upset about something I go in my bedroom and lie on my bed and as soon as I set eyes on Nick it's like magic. I actually go all weak and have a wonderful feeling.

I just go into a thoughtless happy dream.

Casey (14): I dreamed once I found his house. I went in and up some big stairs and someone was telling me this was the door of his bedroom.

So I opened it and saw his bed.

Then suddenly I was in bed with him (with all my clothes on) and he seemed very happy.

I said: 'Can I just have a look?' and pulled the sheet away from his chest. There were no hairs on it and his skin was quite pale and very smooth and beautiful.

We moved closer together and he kissed me. It was so wonderful being close to him. I don't think I'll ever forget it and I'd love to have that dream again. I felt so good I can't explain it.

But when I woke in the morning, there was a tinge of sadness because it was all over.

Nick, I cant sleep at night
thinking about you I just lie
awake gazing at my posters and
thinking about you all the time.
My walls are absolutely
covered with posters of you
and I also have folders full
of you I even collect your
name no matter how small its
written. On my dressing table I
have a framed photo of you
which my mum took its so
gorgeous. Nick please come to
Nottingham again very soon
because I just cant live
without seeing you again. Nick
I'm just so crazy about you.

I LOVF YOU NICK. please,
please, please, please, please
will you write back to me
as I would really really really
love a letter from you. If it's
at all possible would you

please, please, please, please, please, please, please, please ring me up as I just love you so much and would do absolutely anything to just talk to you and I dont know what I would do to meet You again but I would do alot. Even if in a magazine there is just a little picture of you I dont care how much it is I just buy it even if it means sacrificing other things. I will do anything for you Nick. By the way my telephone number is

Hi Nick!

Remember me? How could you ever forget. It's Janet from Southend. How are you and how's life?

I will never, ever forget you – and I hope that soon you will reply to one of my letters. It's a terrible feeling when you're ignored, you know!!

Don't get me wrong – I don't follow any fella around – but you are so special.

You've got to be special though, haven't you? You were the first fella that I slept with (remember??).

Anyway please don't break my heart in two – it's cracked too many times already.

Love Always

Janet

Oh you bastards! – phoned fantasies

Young boy: My star is Sheena Easton. This is a dream I had about her. I was out walking and met Sheena. I was only out for an hour – I'd told my parents I'd be back.

Sheena said: 'Come back to my hotel room.' I told her I had to be back. Then she touched my hand and said: 'It's all right, I'm not that much of a modern girl.'

I went back with her to this big posh hotel and then she goes: 'I'll put the kettle on.' And she went out of the room.

And she came back wearing a low cut black bra and a suspender belt on with knickers and black stockings and a black see-through nightgown.

She said: 'Isn't it awfully warm?' and I said: 'I think I better be going now.'

She said: 'I haven't put the kettle on yet.'

So I says: 'Oh, OK, I'll wait.'

I'm waiting there and a few minutes later I heard like running water. I thought: What's that? And then she called: 'The kettle's boiling. Could you switch it off?'

So I opened the door into the room where I assumed the kettle was and she was having a shower, naked.

And she says: 'I don't know about your kettle but mine's just blown over.'

She says: 'I'm on heat.'

So then I ripped all my clothes off and got in the shower.

We had a shower and never got dried but went and laid down on the big double bed in the hotel room and then I made love – with Sheena Easton.

Young boy: My main fantasy is with Siouxsie from Siouxsie and the Banshees. Every night, you know, I lie in bed and rub my foreskin up and down my knob, my throbbing purple knob. I just can't get her off my mind. You know, just to go out with her, just to think of her existing and everything. Oh, it would be so good. You fucking – God, you're so fucking immature, you really are. [*Heavy breathing for about a minute, then climaxes.*] What a beautiful orgasm! Oh, you bastards!

Carol (15): I kiss the mirror

I picture Boy George on the wall. I just make a face appear and he talks to me. He tells me what it's like being in the pop business and what's it's like being who he is.

I lie in my bed and he sits at the end of it. He smiles. Then I drop off to sleep.

When I'm on my own I dress up like him and dance and the cat sits there watching me in the front room.

And I put a mirror on the sofa to see if I'm doing it right.

I kiss the mirror. It leaves a lipstick mark. And sometimes I talk to the mirror: 'Hello, George!'

At school I sometimes fall asleep. I fall right asleep. It's just something that happens, I can't control it. Usually in History. The teacher's going on about the plains or the Indians and I just think it's so boring and just fall asleep. I tell my best friend I've been dreaming about him. She goes: 'Oh, not again!' But I don't tell her that he was making love to me.

Sometimes I listen to his records and I start crying. Like when I got a letter signed by him I started crying. I just couldn't read it. I didn't think it was true – I thought it was another day-dream. I felt all faint and ready to drop down. And sometimes I go hysterical – I don't know whether to laugh or cry. My mate tries to calm me down.

I just keep feeling I want to meet him – so I can kiss him and see what he's really like.

I dreamt once that he fell out with his girl-friend. And he couldn't find anybody else he really loved and so he tried to murder himself. He was trying to jump into a waterfall. And I just caught him in time. And he fell in love with me and everything was all right.

Jordan (15), Boy George fan: he whispered in my ear

My craze started when I was watching Top Of The Pops and this person came on dressed in a frock with a hat and dreadlocks. I just sat there puzzled and amazed.

I have lots of day-dreams about him. I'm usually at

school sitting chewing my pencil. I go into a sort of trance and think I'm with him, eating caviar in a romantic little restaurant and we sip wine from each other's glass and he looks at me and I stare back.

He then takes me in his arms and kisses me gently on the lips.

I gasp and shrivel.

When I fantasize about him I nearly cry because I want to see him so much.

In my heart his fire burns and my love grows so strong that I think my heart is going to shatter in little pieces.

I'd love to go to bed with him.

In one of my dreams I dreamt I'd bumped into him and he fell in love with me and asked me for a date. I jumped at the chance and said yes.

One day he took me to the pictures and we sat in the back row where it was dark. I felt something warm and soft on my thigh and looked down to see his hand stroking my leg. He moved his hand up and down my leg and then he kissed me with his tender lips.

Afterwards he took me back to his flat and offered me a drink. I said yes.

He opened the bottle and poured it into a glass. I watched as his big hands fastened the lid back on the bottle and tightened it. I was very nervous as he offered me the drink. I shook all over. I took the drink and sipped it slowly.

After a while he took the drink from me and put it on the table. He then kissed me tightly on my lips. As I shivered he whispered in my ear.

I lay back as he undid my shirt and we made love on the sofa.

Lashings of Manilust – letters between Manilow fans

Dear Lisa,

Hope you like the photo (I'll have taken more by Sat, I know. I can feel my finger itching to press the shutter and capture him on film again (and again & again!)) Mind you, that's not the only thing I'd like to get my hands on!

Thanks for those 'lovely' piccies. The one where you can't see his face has other rather good attributes, you've gotta agree. Wow. I've come over all hot. Phew!!! Excuse me while I get a fan. And the other one looks so luscious – even at that time of the night.

Yes, I've had B/W 10 × 8 glossies from the Daily Mirror Group and I know the one your friend's got. I've got one in his dressing room taken at the same time and he's got his face in his hands. Lovely. Makes you wanna go up to him, cradle his head on your shoulder (hang on, I've come over all weak), and say, 'There, there.' The number is 6421/21Z.

You naughty girls, you – touching up that five foot poster when you know he can't defend himself. Ought to be ashamed of yourselves. Lovely feeling tho', ain't it?

Oh, Lisa, look what you've gone and done – you've made him all wet!

Lotsa love from your pal who Manilusts like hell for 'you know who',

Pamela

Dear Pamela,

So you're going to be a grass-widow from the 19th of March for a month then – eh!! God, what a pity Barry won't be over here then. Well, you never know, he could have accepted your invitation to put him UP!!! for a month. Now then, what's that filthy laugh for? What I meant was to 'STAY' with you for a month. Not even Barry could 'STAY UP' for a month, could he??? Wonder if we'll ever get the chance to find out. Kenny may think it's hot in Malaya but it would be *sizzling* over here!!

But I do relate to how you feel when you look at those posters of Dear Barry as you lie there alone in your bed, with tears running down your cheeks, because you only have pictures of him, and not his warm, beautiful body with that heart beating inside of it lying there beside you.

I could break my heart knowing that he is not there with me, and that I can't give him any of that love that's burning inside of me for him. Oh why does the flame of love hurt both of us so much? Oh God, please let Pamela and I make love with Barry just once. That's all we ask, dear Lord, to know the joy of his wonderful love for just

36

once in our lives, and through that union with the man we both love so dearly would be born the two most beautiful babies you have ever created. Please God, hear our prayer.

All my Barryhugs & Manilove and of course Mountains of MANILUST!!!

Lisa

Dear Lisa,

Lately, some of the fans have been going a little crazy it seems to me. There is a lot of bickering and dissension lately for some reason. I wonder why. I just don't understand getting all worked up over little things. After all, Barry's music is forever, so what's the use getting crazy and fighting among each other? Some of the girls really compete with each other for things like who has been backstage; who knows some of Barry's staff or members of the band; who has met Barry at the airport; who has been to the most concerts; who has met and talked to Roberta Kent; etc, etc, etc. If I were these girls, I would be ashamed of myself for acting like fanatical little groupies.

Take Care,
Love,

Corinne

Dear Lisa,

The party was to take place in the Cellar Bar, so I asked the barman if he would give me the key to the Cellar Bar so we could go and see how they had decorated it for the party.

We could see that all the three girls had been working very hard. It was decorated beautifully with posters, cardboard cut-outs, plastic tacky palm trees, etc. The bar was supported by pillars, one of which had the full-length poster of Barry on it. On one of the tables was a pink twisted candle!! Myrna and I looked at each other. Were we thinking the same thought?

We found some blutak and sellotape and stuck the candle at the appropriate place on the poster and supported it with a cardboard cut-out and chair. Then we wrote on a piece of paper: 'GIRLS, HAVE YOU SEEN

BARRY'S 12 INCH——?!!!' It looked hilarious, especially with the chair and cut-out of Barry giving it support.

The barman was very nice to us and told us that he would not say anything to anyone about what we'd done.

When we arrived back at the bar at around six o'clock to prepare refreshments, Sally said: 'Oh, no, just look at what that stupid barman has done to my poster. I'll kill him!' Myrna and I managed to keep a straight face, and I said to Sally: 'Wait till Kate sees it!'

All my love and lashings of Manilust as ever,
Pamela

Dear Corinne,

Well, have you recovered from Saturday night yet??? Wasn't he just terrific? My God, Corinne, I was just a heap on the floor with steam pourin' out of my ears – I swear. And if that wasn't enough, him singing R.E. & W. in that SEXY!! white outfit, he had to come on again later, wearing his tuxedo and looking so tall and handsome. Oh gee, wasn't I in a state. Why can't he be on telly EVERY WEEK?!!

Oh God, didn't he look beautiful!! – and I just couldn't get to sleep 'cos I was aching so much for him. God, Corinne, my love is getting deeper and deeper for him, and I just don't know how to cope with it.

Lots and lots of Barryhugs, Manilove, and as always Manilust.

SEE YA SOOOOOOOOOOON!!
GOD BLESS,
Judy

Dear Monica,

The fantasy of yours *really* got me going – (*God* – clean knickers were needed that day). Isn't it great that 'Read 'Em & Weep' is doing so well? I'm so happy for him, & us.

I hope you have everything you dream for in 1984 –
Much Manilove *always,*
Pamela X

Dear Monica,

Thank you so much for telling me all about Barry in Holland. I really enjoyed reading your account – I appreciated all the detail – you're really great to put so much into your letters – I love getting them. Yes – I too cried for days after Barry left – & I'm still crying now – this craving for him – this intense love is just too much – it's more than I can cope with at times. Yes, Monica – why does true love have to hurt so much. It's not fair to be given this ability to love somebody to distraction & not be able to fulfil that love.

Much Manilove as always,

Pamela

Dear Sally,

Isn't it a shame that Barry only got to No 17 in the Charts – everyone thought that it would be the *BIG one* (the record I mean). That last sentence was nothing about Barry's . . . Oh! Sorry, Sally – back to the letter, I really musn't let my mind wander like that. . . .

Much Manilove,

Kitty XXXX

Dear Pamela,

Mani-hi! How ya doin'? I'm fine, I guess! It was lovely to hear from you and to hear all your Barry-news. Did ya see the 'DIVINE MR M' on 'Superbowl' in January? God! he was absolutely 'GORGEOUS'——he looked so fit and healthy and in fine voice too, although I heard on the 'Barry-vine' that he mimed to the words, in case he forgot them – mm! Cute!! oooh! the way he had his collar turned up of his leather jacket and the wind blowing thru his hair – oohh! RAPE! RAPE!! (Dora, control yourself! Kindly keep your composure!!!) It was lovely how everyone stopped to listen to him. . . . I did what I usually do best on these occasions . . . I cried!! 'Oh what a clutz!!' To cry over a ballad, sure, but the American National Anthem?!!!

Yes, about the 'Read 'Em & Weep' video, I've heard that at the end Barry takes a shower, and you can see his heavenly boddddy! thru the cabinet thingy——oh RAPE! RAPE!! If that's true no wonder the BBC & ITV didn't let us see the ending!! rotten spoil sports!! (I bet that rotten old Mary Whitehouse stuck her two-penth in!!!)

Mountains of Manilove

and

Lashings of Barry-lust!

Dora XXX

Dear Julie,

I had more negatives of the Festival Hall but a certain member I loaned them to has not returned them – one of the members who only thinks of *herself* WE HAVE ONE!! I shall have to approach her myself, then I can send them to you but she will have some excuse.

Our raffle was fantastic but all our money has gone on printing and expenses.

Barry hugs and Barrybye,

Dorothy XXX

Dearest Monica,

I just *loved* your fantasy – what a long one (the fantasy – what else?). I really enjoyed reading it – it was so beautiful. I know exactly how you feel, & what you are going through. If only our fantasies would come true – I cried when I read it.

Much Manilove & Peace *always*,

Suzanne XXXX

Dear Anna,

MANI-LEGS GO ON FOR EVER

I'll follow that tush *ANYWHERE*

THE MIRACLE

is

BARRY

MANILOW

BARRY'S GOT A 12 INCH. . . .

. . . .RECORD

Karen

Dearest Lisa,

Thank you for your lovely newsy letter. It's always a great day for me when it arrives. I do so enjoy your letters – I don't know what I'd do without them. I'm glad you enjoyed the tape I sent you – especially the 'hot night with Barry'. I *knew* you would appreciate it and I'm really glad that you will keep it to yourself. You have to know some-body really well to let them hear it I think. You're the only one who has heard it apart from my two friends who compiled it. I guessed you'd get through all your spare pairs of knickers after listening to that. God – I wonder what *he* would think if he heard it? Probably enjoy it – knowing the way his mind works – good ole Baz.

Fred is in Gibraltar & I have been alone for a week. I have my full length poster of Barry on the back of the door in the sitting room – usually it's at the bottom of the stairs – but I want him right here with me while I'm alone. Isn't it *beautiful*, Lisa, and don't his legs look sexy – and his hips – I just can't take my eyes off them. I love him more than ever – if that's possible. Like you, I ache with love for him – and I just don't know how to control it sometimes. I *want* him so desperately – and we don't even know when we are going to see him again.

Well, now I've got *that* off my chest, I feel better.

Manilove as always.

Also, Manilusting, Manigropes, Manilegs.

Forever.

Millie

Dearest Monica,

Your lovely letter came this morning – thank you *so* much. I spent a very enjoyable time reading it – you sure know how to write letters – you made me laugh & cry at the same time. I will answer it carefully just as soon as I can but in the meantime I didn't want you to have to wait for the enclosed tape. Play it when you are alone – *please*. It's guaranteed to blow your mind – (& everything else). You'd better be sat down (or layed) before listening to it. If you've ever wanted to know what a hot night with Barry sounds like – this is *it*. (Clean knickers needed afterwards.) But, Monica, please don't let anybody hear it who's likely to be offended. A friend compiled it & I asked her if you could have a copy & she agreed – but for God's sake go careful – I don't want to get anybody in trouble. I *knew* you would appreciate it. Now sit back &——enjoy.

I'll be back with you again soon.

In much Manilust (more than ever now) *always*,
Judy XXX

Hot night with Barry – an unofficial Manilow tape

Let's do it, you're looking hot tonight, let's do it, you're
looking hot tonight . . . [Spoken] Can I do this without
my jive hat? . . . Mm! mm! . . . [Sung] Let's get on with
it . . . Ain't that beautiful, ain't that beautiful . . . Uh, uh
. . . Uh! uh! uh! . . . [Spoken] I could have done much
better . . . [Sung] I want to get it, ah haaa, ah haaa . . .
Can't you feel that something's coming up . . . uh! uh!
uh! uh! . . . ah! ah! ah! ah! . . . [Spoken] It's breathtaking
. . . I wanted to, I really wanted to . . . Please! . . . Oh,
man, I just love that thing . . . Oh! oh! oh! oh! ahh! . . .
OK . . . [Sung] And here we go again . . . Ahhhh, ahhhh
. . . [Spoken] Oh, God! . . . Uh! uh! uh! uh! . . . [Sung]
it's dark, it's hot . . . Ohh, ohh, ohh . . . I want to get it
. . . uh, uh, uh, uh . . . urh! urh! urh! huh! huh! . . . ah!
ah! ah! . . . Work it out . . . Oh, God! . . . Uh! uh! . . .
Even now I wonder why I can't go on . . . How does it
feel? . . . ah! ah! . . . Mm! mm! . . . Oh, man, I just love
that thing . . . Ah! ah! ah! . . . Uh! uh! uh! uh! uh! . . .
Ah! ah! . . . Oh, God! . . . Aaaaah! . . . God! . . . Ah! ah!
. . . Oh, God! . . . Ah! ah! ah! ah! ah! . . . Come on! come
on! come on! come on! . . . One more time . . . And here
we go again . . . You pulled me down and gave me . . .
Oh! oh! ah, beautiful! . . . Gets hard, gets hard, hard, hard
. . . I want to do it . . . Now, now, now, now . . . Ohh,
ohh . . . More, more, more . . . Ah! ah! . . . More! more!
more! . . . ohhh, ohh . . . huh! huh! . . . Uh! uh! uh! uh!
uh! uh! uh! uh! uh! uh! uh! uh! . . . Oh, God! . . . Uh! uh!
uh! . . . Ah! ah! ah! ah! . . . Lonely boy, lonely boy . . .
Ah! ah! . . . God! . . . Come, come, come, come . . . Ah!
ah! . . . All my life I would miss her dynamite . . . Ahh-
ahh-ahh-ahh-ahh-ahh! . . . [Spoken] Do I get it? . . . Now
I just wait for it to go down . . . Ahh-ahh-ahh, ahh-ahh-
ahh-ahh . . . [Sung] I know I'll never love this way again
. . . We made it . . . aahhh-aahhh-aahhh-aahhh-aahhh-
aahhh-aaaaaaah!!! . . .

[*The tape was made up with extracts from Manilow releases, interviews and bootlegs, cleverly dub-edited onto cassette for (highly selective) distribution on a fan to fan basis. No money changes hands.*]

My darling Nicky – Amantha's letter to Nick Heyward

My Darling Nicky, you really, really, turn me on. I love you very, very, very, very, much. I know you feel the same way about me.

I'll never ever forget the day we met. Eyes staring at each other. Your eyes in Astonishment. My eyes sultry and a grin across my face.

I hope you have enjoyed reading all my letters so far.

Are you coming round tonight? I could do with a warm-up. Now it's winter.

I'm going Red – Rosy cheeks. Cherry Red. Give Rosy cheeks Manty a kiss. I want to watch you bloom and breathe.

I've got Rosy cheeks, Small breasts, and a Podgy bottom; and you ain't going to pinch it or I'll suck your prick! at a party under the table. (Ha! Ha! Ha! Ha!) I must be really Abracadabra and sultry.

You'll go just right in between two slices of cheese spread. Your sperm'll be oozin' out! Don't come all over my face will you? or I'll make you lick it off!

If I was at a party and you saw me would you take me upstairs? I wanna see you in the Raw!

You can lick me out if you wish! But don't blow me inside or I'll get a chill. I want a thrilling sensation not a cold virgina! I've got a good mind to throw a custard pie in your face!

Could you possibly send me a photo with you lying down on a white rug in your Kew flat? Every time I think about you I get excited. Sexual orgasms keep coming on!

Seeing as you're 5'10" tall I expect your prick is just as long Donna Summers song, 'love to love you baby' is 16 min and 50 sexs long. How long would you screw me for at a party?

I think you have got an incredible and sexy body. I love melting into your eyes. Um, I imagine your kisses are as sweet as candy! your sperm would last me through Breakfast, lunch, dinner, tea and supper!

I'd love to think one day that it would be possible to see what sex with you is really like. Let's hope one day it comes true eh? Thinking of you, Yours lovingly,

Amantha

xxxxx

P.S. I love you.

Mystery

Colette: looking for Michael Jackson

To me the most personal thing I can think about is the moon.

The moon. I mean, it's just so weird. When you look at it it's just so incredible to think he might be looking too. At that very moment.

And I do that every night.

Sometimes my brother takes the dog out with a friend and I go with them. They're chatting away but my mind's on my own thing. I look up to the moon and I think to myself: This very second he's alive somewhere, and he's breathing.

And when I close my bedroom window of a night I look for the moon and if it's there I look at it for about 15 minutes thinking: What's he doing now?

It seems unreal but it's not. It's reality. Because he's living at that moment. He's alive that very second. And I think: What's he doing? And then it really gets to me.

It makes me cry because it's so impossible.

And I know what it is to never be able to talk to him.

When I look at posters of him I look beyond the posters.

You fix your eye on the poster but you don't really look at it, you look beyond. You just use it as something to fix your mind on.

And then you look beyond.

I don't really look at his face or his clothes – it's into his eyes I look.

I mean, there's nothing there, obviously, but your imagination runs wild. And then anything can happen. You look into his eyes but your eyes go beyond and then it's up to you – whatever you want to think.

Like you think of a nice, close, warm relationship.

Having his posters, having his records is not really as good as the real thing.

It's like you see someone on TV and you look at them, only it's not really them. Or someone on the radio. They're not in front of you and yet you're listening to them.

So the posters, they're great posters and everything, but they're still not the real thing. They're not the real thing, and the music's not the real thing. And you can't really do anything about it.

That's what upsets me.

When you walk into the bedroom it's his face all over the place.

And sometimes it's depressing because you think that although he's in the bedroom as such, you're never going to meet him in real life at all.

Plus the fact that he's famous and it just wouldn't work.

You think to yourself: Could it work? Could I ever get to meet him?

But even if it was utterly fantastic and I did get to meet him I don't think it would work.

Much as I'd like it to.

I'm too young for a start. I'm only 15. And I'm not as rich and wealthy as him. I live on a skimpy council estate out here in Cardiff, miles and miles and miles away.

And there's nothing I can do about it, nothing in my power.

I read an article about some fans who climbed over his fence. And he came out of a room and this family were touring round the house. I was imagining it could have been me. I could just picture it. He would say: 'What are you doing here?' And I can picture all sorts of things – like him inviting me to stay.

I can picture us being good friends as well.

Because while he is an idol obviously – he's a pop star and he's fantastic – I don't really want him to be that, and that's what really sticks in my mind.

I think we could be great friends and just sit down and talk and discuss music and things like that – not formally but in a friendly, close way.

Sit and talk and have coffee and do things.

I'm happy for him with all his money and he's famous and he's got lots of fans.

But I'm also sad because I don't think they really respect him. I think they think he's there to rip open. And I don't think that's right at all.

I've never really been in love before but this is like being in love – I think. In fact, I'm sure.

To me he's just the perfect person.

I can't put it into words, but I know I must really, really, really like him because you can't sit and listen to his music practically all day and all night without loving him, and I do. I love everything about him.

And you can't really describe love, it's what you feel inside.

So when I go to bed at night it upsets me because I think: I've got his posters all over the place and for what?

And I know I can't get annoyed with him. But it upsets me to think he doesn't even know about me, you know, I'm just one of many, many fans.

My grandad died when I was about six months old so I never saw him except in photos. And once I dreamt that me and my grandad were in this store and there was a bomb scare. We ran out and got into this car. And my grandad got in the driving seat and we were driving along and this taxi passed us. And Michael Jackson was driving the taxi. He sort of waved at us. So I said: 'Quick! Turn the car round.' And then there was this long journey with all these names – where I was born and where I was living, all places and everything about me – all flashing through my mind. Then I took over in the driving seat. But I never got to him.

In my dreams something is always in the way. It's like when you dream that you seem to be running for ages but never quite get there.

And there's never any bodily contact, not even in my daydreams. I can't even hold his hand.

I mean, I'd like to put my arms around him and do nice things to him. And share my feelings with him.

But there's always this blockage and it's really upsetting.

It's like when you go to touch a person and there's nothing there.

And whenever I dream about him I'm there but not there.

And he's there but he's not there.

I think: If I go near he'll probably disappear.

Every sight and sound – Heather's letters to David Bowie

Dear David,

I've just read 'Your Stars' in the Evening Chronicle. Further bushel to the fire, yeh?

This whole situation, if I am to believe it, leaves Cinderella standing. I mean simply doubt that this is all happening to me and you. Are the oblique references wafting across the radio/contemporary songmakers and in newspapers just my warped mind? My head spins trying to work out if I'm twisting or not. I have no experience of the lead you say you must take. I can only follow obediently in humility. I thought I didn't owe a fig to anyone until the overtures of 'Scary Monsters' penetrated the slow receptacles of my mind. You're right – it's a shock – a daunting prospect.

If this sounds clinical it's because I've spent hours writing letters that continually had to be revised for one reason or another and I'm drained. I was angry with the suspicion that you've had my family's phones tapped or mail opened due to the LEO message. I hope I'm wrong. The mixture of uncertainty and suspicions of being watched throws me – I have to ask myself am I cracking up? I was so angry I ate nearly a whole cake in exasperation but that's an extreme example of my mentality recently.

Am I living in the real world? What do I know? I love you, in doubt that you may be a shadow of me – not really there at all.

Love Heather

Dear David,

Don't rip this up in despair please. Read on. Of course I would come to London, or anywhere else if the need be (i.e. where you are).

I want to say more than 'sorry'; I admit I don't know what 'love' is yet but I'm prepared to persevere to find out. I was kicking against exposure but I now accept your all-knowing embrace. This change kills all those hateful and resentful thoughts which produced poisonous lies to hurt you, you being the only viable attack open.

Just one thing though, I find decoding the stars a bit time-consuming. Do you really write them all yourself? Do you think they could be less frequent or quicker to work out? I'm sure everyday that you will run out of things to say.

I'm glad you're with me and I'm sure I love you.

Heather

Dear David,

You seem to be every sight and sound to me. Sensations become blurred but the central spirit moves me

love you always

Heather

Dear David,

Due to the general character of your messages I'm forced to take surface readings and add a pinch of hype. If I go deeper they always contradict themselves totally. Also I know you can hear me through the radio but can you see me? I often surmise that you already know things you don't probably.

Your face on the sleeve cover seems to change day by day in expression. I watch it as a symbol of relating. Perhaps I should rip it up?

Love Heather

PS No one in the world except maybe you can have been subjected to such mental confusion. If you really do want me to fade away, please don't carry on so.

Dear David,

Please give my apologies to John Peel the other night

for my idiotic behaviour. I didn't realize he could hear me though I know you can.

I don't want us to fly at each other's throats straight away – or have I got it coming? I won't blame you. The less publicity the better as far as I'm concerned but maybe that doesn't fit your plans. I mean the possibility of you wrecking me with your next album and leaving me aside in the lurch – is that an alternative I have to prepare for?

Love Heather XXXX

Psychic

Bowie fan: It's always the same. I feel we have some kind of special link. Whenever he's on the radio it's as if something shouts inside me: 'Turn on the radio!' and there's his voice.

Or: 'Turn on your TV', and there he is.

I feel I may be 'psychic' as far as he's concerned.

It may sound whacky, weird, crazy or whatever you would want to call it but it's gone on for years now. It's as if he or someone or some silent voice or a force inside me thinks it's important that I know about him and makes certain everything that's written or played or shown on TV about him I get to read, watch or hear, whether it's good or bad.

I'll flick on the radio or TV and it's always just in time. I never miss a glance – it's just perfect timing for me.

Mick Karn fan: I can always predict articles or any text in magazines and newspapers about Mick Karn. I think about a certain magazine and I know I have to go and buy it. Sometimes I turn directly to the page the text is on, before anything else.

The Cassidy family: touching another world

[*The Cassidy family (Marc Bolan fans) live in a small Welsh village. Present are Lorna (54), her son Ewan(30), her daughters*

*Sheila (34) and Anne (20), two nieces Jan (18) and Maggie (20),
Pat the daughter-in-law (29) and Lorna's three grandchildren
Deborah (4), Clare (9) and David (11).*]

Lorna: Really it was Ewan got us all hooked. He used to play his records so loud the kids used to stand on the corner of the street and listen to him.

Sheila: It wasn't a question of hooked – you could hear nothing but him in the Terrace!

Anne: As far as me and Maggie were concerned, we were seven at the time and he used to take us into his room and shut the door and sit us there on the window sill. And we were stuck there for the rest of the day. In the end we just started singing the songs.

Pat: Brainwashing.

Anne: Yeah, it was. We just got hooked on him, didn't we?

Lorna: At first it was just a noise and I thought: Ewan do you have to keep on playing that?

And he said: 'Come in here, Mum. Sit down and listen. Just listen.' And I did and I got hooked.

And after that I just kept playing him. I still do. I mean, if I don't play a track of his some time during the day it's not right. It's like withdrawal symptoms from cigarettes – I can feel there's something wrong: I haven't played Bolan today. Isn't that true, Anne?

Anne: Yes, it is.

Lorna: This is the thing nobody can explain. Only another Bolanite can understand.

I mean, Ewan – he's not poetic in any way – I don't think I've ever known him write a piece of poetry, but he wrote – what was it he wrote?

Anne: In the deep dark corners of my mind
    I still see you bop and grind. . . .

Lorna: Marc, they tell me you've gone to a far better
    place.
    Where you can dance in a wide open space.

Anne: Dancing with your red shoes on
    Dancing all night long.

Lorna: And he put all his love he had for him in that
    little poem.

Lorna: People say to us: 'How come you *love* Marc?' Because even boys, I mean butch boys now I'm talking about, not gays, they really love him. They don't just like him, they really love him. And girls can't understand it. I know Bolan fans who've lost girl-friends because they can't figure it out, you know. And you can't explain. It's just *different*. It's a totally different affection.

Marc ignites people. He really does.

There's a magic about him. I don't know what it is.

[*There is a special room in the house set aside for Marc.*]

Q: How did Marc's room come about?

Lorna: Well, Ewan had him everywhere. He had him on the ceiling, on the walls, you name it.

Sheila: It was purple, the room, wasn't it?

Lorna: Psychedelic. And Marc was everywhere.

Ewan: Purple and green.

Pat: Errrr!

Lorna: And when he got married Pat said it all had to come off. Because. . . .

Sheila: [*whispers*] Pat doesn't like him.

Pat: I don't *dislike* him. . . .

Sheila: Actually the reason it was redecorated was because Ewan was moving out to get married and Dad thought: Well, this is the end of Marc now, so he thought he'd decorate it.

Anne: We left it like that until '77. And then when the crash happened in '77 it all went back up again.

Lorna: Now kids who can't put stuff up because their parents won't have it send it to me and I put it in Marc's room so at least it's up somewhere.

It's known as Marc's room. It's never the spare bedroom – it's known as Marc's room.

And it's funny, all the girls who sleep in that room have a most beautiful night's sleep.

Pat: Boys don't though, do they?

Lorna: No. They toss and turn.

Lorna: When we heard about the crash, I think it was on the five o'clock news and it came on and I said, 'Oh my God, no.'

It just felt as if the world had come to an end.

It was crazy. Here I was a grandma with all the kids, all the family, plenty of other people around that I love, but it just felt as though the world had crashed, you know? It was just disastrous.

And then Ewan came through the door looking white as a sheet and then Anne came home from school and threw herself in my arms.

The day of the funeral I stood there and I cried nearly all day. Father said: 'Oh come on, we'll go out and buy some wallpaper.'

Sheila: That's father's answer to everything.

Lorna: We went to buy the wallpaper and then he bought me a rose tree, same as Marc's at Golders Green.

But it wasn't only then, I mean it's *now*. I can be up in Marc's room playing a record and I just look around me and I say: 'Oh, God.' And I just start crying.

And you think to yourself: Well, this is crazy. [*To Anne*] And it still happens to you, doesn't it?

Anne: You can't explain it. Unless you're a Bolan fan you can't explain what the love is. It's not any love you can explain.

Lorna: It's not sexual.

Anne: It's not like a family love. If family died and was buried in Golders Green and we went to see their grave it still wouldn't be the same feeling as going to see Marc.

Lorna: But it's not a feeling that drags you down. I mean, you have a cry but then you're up again, aren't you? There's an elation. Oh, I can't explain it. It's impossible to explain.

Q: How many times have you been to Golders Green?
All: Every year.

Lorna: Every year since he died. And we go every year to the tree, the tree his car crashed into. We go to the tree to be there for the dreaded five to five. That's when it happened. His fans come from everywhere: Japan, Germany, France, Canada, Israel, Switzerland. . . .

Anne: They walk, don't they?

Lorna: The ones from Japan actually walked and hitch-hiked all the way from Japan just to be there. I mean, they couldn't speak a word of English but they didn't have to.

We stay there all night, just playing his music and what have you. Then when five to five comes we go to the tree.

Some of us pray. Or you do whatever you want to.

And people come out from the houses nearby. One old lady comes out every year and says: 'Why do you do it? Why do you come all this way and just stand by this tree. Because this is the tree that killed him!'

I try to tell her it's the only thing that we can identify with. Because if you go to Golders Green you can't put anything by the rose tree. Everything has to be put down the bottom on the cement.

And anyway the rose tree, well, it's just a rose tree with a little tiny thing with his name on – it's ridiculous!

There's nothing else there to identify with. Because a couple of weeks after Marc died they found people trying to dig his ashes up. And a German fan had taken the memorial his mum and dad had put there: 'He bopped his way through life.' His mum did get it back – she put a thing in the paper asking for it to be returned and it was, but then it got whipped again.

But with the tree you can pin messages on it, you can tie it up with ribbons, you can put whatever you want on it. And the fans leave messages for each other if they're not able to meet. So the tree is very symbolic actually. And instead of becoming a thing of hate which it should have done, it's become – well, it's a shrine.

And the funny thing is you never hear a fan knock Gloria. She killed him, there's no doubt about it, she killed him. But they'll never knock Gloria because she gave Marc so many years of love. And she gave him a son. People are more against June because she aborted two of Marc's kids she was carrying. Fancy killing two of Marc's children! But you never hear them knock Gloria.

And then in the daytime we go on to Golders Green. The flowers are always beautiful because all the fans bring flowers and just lay them there.

Maggie: Whole guitars of flowers.

Lorna: And we just sit and talk. It's a happy occasion. There's very few tears. You can't be sad when you're with Marc's fans because they're such a happy band to be with.

Q: You were telling me you have conventions.

Lorna: That's right. We've been to Swansea, Birming-

54

ham, Liverpool, London, Henley. We've been to the Isle of Wight, Leeds.

Anne: They have them every year, don't they?

Lorna: But the one at Henley was something else because before it started we went to the Town Hall where they were putting it on and we had a preview of the videos. They were spot on, brilliant.

Then comes the evening and his mum and dad arrived. Micky O'Halloran, Marc's roadie arrived, and his brother and all were there. And they put on the video and nothing happened. Nothing at all. They checked everything. But Harry, Marc's brother, he said: 'If Marc doesn't want it to be shown tonight, there's no way it's going to be shown.'

And there was no reason whatsoever because it had already run in the afternoon. They said: 'We just can't explain it.'

Q: Have any other things happened like that?

Anne and *Jan:* Yes!

Lorna: Oh! Have they! My other daughter-in-law's a Bolan fan and she was here with her son. How old was he then?

Anne: Well, he couldn't talk. And one of the first words he said was 'Marc'.

Lorna: He couldn't even walk.

We were having a séance and we were playing Marc's music and I don't know how but we had a tape on and it was all recorded, wasn't it? It was really freaky.

You can hear the glass going back and forward on the table and us asking questions and saying: 'Yeah, Marc,' and so on.

Then Ian [the baby] crawled to where Anne had an acoustic guitar standing up in a corner. And he pulled himself up on a chair and said: 'Marc!'

He was looking straight at something there. You can hear it all on the tape.

And he was jabbering away to Marc – well, presumably to Marc – we couldn't see anyone there. We couldn't understand what he was saying cos it was all baby talk. Then he started plucking the guitar: bm-bm-bm-bm-bm-bm, bm-bm-bm-bm-bm-bm.

We were amazed, weren't we? Because he was strumming it. It was really incredible. It wasn't a bang-bong sort of thing. It was just like a ripple.

Anne: It was the first day he walked then, as well.

Lorna: Yes. It was really weird.

And not long ago Ian was playing upstairs. He was kneeling down in his bedroom playing with his cars. I wanted to go to the toilet, and I was just going when he said: 'What did you do that for, Marc?' I thought: Who the hell's he talking to? I went back into the bedroom and there he was kneeling with this car. And I said: 'What did you say, Ian?' And he said: 'Our Marc,' he said, 'he's not playing this game right,' he said. 'I don't know what he done that for with the car.' And I went and asked his mum. I said: 'How often does he do that?' 'Oh,' she said, 'he often says: "Come on Marc, we've had enough of this. Let's go."' Really odd.

Anne: There was a time when he used to move things for us. If we had a séance. It was just after he'd gone.

Lorna: Oh yes, and he did automatic writing for me.

Anne: We had a party just after he'd gone and there was only about 20 of us, wasn't there? Three people came in when we were in the middle of a séance and they didn't like it.

Lorna: Oh, you mean up at the hall, at the Institute? Yes, that was his birthday party, wasn't it?

Anne: We said: 'Marc's here.' And they said: 'Don't be stupid.' So we said to him: 'If you're here open the door.' And it opened, didn't it?

Lorna: And I was sitting there selling Coke. And I had my finger on the Coke can like that, and I was watching the kids coming in and all of a sudden the can just moved off down the table. And I thought: My God! It literally just moved off.

So I thought: Well, perhaps I pushed it. So I put my finger back on it again and I said: 'Bolan, if you're here move it to the right.' And it moved to the right. And I said: 'Now to the left.'

So then I said: 'Get some letters.' And we got some letters. He was bombing around that table. It was incredible.

Lorna: Once Micky O'Halloran went to a séance with one of these famous mediums. And all of a sudden this guy went into a Bolan pose and Micky thought: What's happening? Nobody had said anything. But this guy just stood there in the sort of pose that Marc always used when he was listening to a playback. He always stood like that. And this guy stood there like that. But Micky never said a word to him and just came out and went home.

Well, I don't know how this man found out where Micky lived but he then phoned him one night and he said: 'Is that Mick O'Halloran, Marc Bolan's roadie?'

And he said: 'I wonder, could you come over to my place? Because I've got Marc Bolan here and he's going mad. He's throwing down guitars, he's walking around my living room. He's pouting, he's tossing his head and he wants to contact you.'

Micky went over there and the things this medium told Mick! Mick said: 'There's no way that anybody else could have known what he told me.'

Well, it *had* to be Marc. There was no way it couldn't have been Marc.

Pat: I don't want to hear any more!

Lorna: It's not nasty at all. You're just touching another world, aren't you?

Sheila: I don't know whether to believe it or not but there are so many things that have happened to prove it.

Anne: So you've got to believe, haven't you?

Jan: The scarf.

Anne: Yeah, the scarf. I was in Marc's room and a black scarf flew across the wall. My black scarf was hanging up with the posters in there. I was sat there playing records and this scarf, it swung right up the wall. I dived through the window.

Pat: The last time you had a séance you told him to follow me home.

Lorna: Yes and he did, didn't he? He pulled your hair and all.

Pat: I don't like séances. Oh, no way. I had come in and you were getting involved trying to get Marc so I said: 'I'm going home.' So I walked home. But, unknown to me, you told Marc to follow me home.

Lorna: No. You said, 'You poof,' or something to him, didn't you? And he said: 'I'll follow you.'

Pat: I went to bed that night, fell asleep. I know it was Marc because someone touched my face and I woke up. And you [*to husband*] were turned away from me, weren't you? He always sleeps with his back turned. 'Are you awake?' Snoring. I thought I'd had a dream. I came over the next day. Lorna said: 'Did Marc touch you last night?'

Anne: And we saw him once. Remember? There was Sharon, Maggie and me in Marc's room. The candle was in the corner, wasn't it? I looked and I saw Maggie looking and then Sharon was looking and we all looked at each other and I said: 'What can you see?'

And Maggie said: 'All silver bits by the candle.'

And Sharon said: 'That's what I can see too.'

And I said: 'That's what I can see as well.'

And there were all silver bits by the candle, sort of floating.

Lorna: But I haven't seen him for ages and ages and ages.

Q: Do those things tend to happen on special occasions or can they happen just out of the blue?

Anne: Out of the blue.

Lorna: Yes, mostly out of the blue. Marc was very into all that.

Pat: What about your automatic writing?

Lorna: Well, I got a pen and a piece of paper and I went into Marc's room and I said: 'Marc, if you want to get in touch just write to me.' And I just held the pen and just sat there. And I could feel myself breathing deeper and deeper and then my hand just went up like that, down like that and up again and it was half an 'M'. And I thought: I'm pulling out of this, you know, cos I thought if I go into a deep trance and someone comes in, opens the door, goodness knows what. . . .

[*The lights suddenly go out. Is this a sign from Marc? Hysterical laughter.*

Lorna: Has anyone got a 50p piece?]

Pat: [*laughing*] I find it hysterical!

[*Lorna asks again for 50p and Ewan finds one. The electricity goes back on.*]

Lorna: So I pulled out because it can be dangerous. So I

didn't do it. I left it. And another night I was sat down and I thought: I'll do it again. And I did it again and he just started writing, oh, just little things. And then he'd go on and write pages and pages and pages. It would go like the clappers.

Anne: Then you'd show us and we couldn't decipher it, could we?

Pat: Did it make sense?

Lorna: No dots on the 'i's', no crosses on the 't's'. It was just continuous. . . .

Pat: What did he used to say?

Lorna: Oh, he used to talk about everything. About the fans and about his music.

Anne: He used to draw and she can't draw for toffees.

Lorna: How he loved his mum and dad. Just trivial things. He didn't prophesy anything.

But you have to be careful. Because you might leave it wide open for evil spirits to come in. I've stopped doing it now. In fact, Micky O'Halloran asked us not to, didn't he? He said: 'Don't contact Marc any more.' He said: 'If Marc wants to make contact he'll do it but,' he said, 'don't disturb him. 'Cos,' he said, 'I don't think Marc wants that.' So we said: 'Fair enough.' And we haven't done it since.

Jane: I'd love to be famous

There was a programme on TV about what would happen if there was a nuclear war. And I think if a nuclear war did happen I'd be thinking: Is Boy George safe?

The first time I met him was at the Camden Palace. He wasn't famous or anything then – he was just dancing, and he kept looking over and winking. He came over and said goodbye and hello and all sorts of funny comments. I thought he was lovely. Love at first sight!

Later on when he was well known, I used to sneak out the back of theatres and wait by his car. And when I think of the times I could have talked to him longer than I did . . . All those times I could have had him to myself and taken more photos.

Now it's ridiculous trying to get near him.

I remember when 'Do You Really Want to Hurt Me?' first came out. I saw him leaving a club one night and I ran up to meet him.

I bent down in front of the car to talk to him and as he talked he held my hand for a little while.

Afterwards I kept dreaming about horrible things happening to hands. Weird things like being in bed and hands coming up from nowhere. And hands on their own, like in a horror movie.

If it's a working day I have to get up at half past six. Hopefully there's a Culture Club record on the alarm so it's not that bad.

But mostly I have the hump in the morning because I hate working in London in an office. It's the only thing I can get at the moment so I'm stuck with it.

On my way in on the train I listen on the little stereo headphones. Listening like that makes me feel better. Makes me feel he's singing it to me, that he's thinking of me.

We have a good laugh at work. The girls all like Culture Club so there's lots of talk – especially if he was on telly or something.

And there's lots of arguments with the fellows 'cos they *don't* like him. There's a lot of hitting going on in the canteen!

If he's been on telly they'll pick holes in everything he said and there's the usual 'poof' comments and that sort of thing. It annoys me because one of them doesn't even bother to listen to him. I think if he listened he'd probably like him.

I just laugh it off now. But it used to upset me. I used to think: How can they be so horrible to someone so nice? I used to get angry and feel I'd want to hit them. And I did hit someone once. He hit me back!

There's always such a lot of aggro going on in offices and I was thinking just today: Oh, if only I was doing what I really wanted to do. Which is to be famous, to be singing, to be touring around and meeting people.

'Cos I'd love to be famous as well. That's part of the

fascination, because he's like I'd be if I was famous. And I'd love to be like that.

On weekdays I usually get home about half six and my sister's not in till seven so I come straight up here and play my Culture Club records.

I picture George singing. And I think about the videos – the videos are in my mind as I listen to the songs.

It's always his eyes – I love his eyes, I always think about his eyes.

Sometimes I picture him in a park, running towards me in slow motion, and just the way he'd be singing it – as if we'd been making a video together.

If I'm happy, I picture him happy. If I'm sad, I picture him sad. It's always about how I feel.

Once when I was in the sitting room – I'd just lost my grandad and I was crying to myself – I kept picturing that George was on the settee next to me telling me to be brave.

And I couldn't really have dreamt it. I think I really saw him. I could see what he looked like, what he was wearing, and it was just like he was leaning over me telling me to be brave. It was only for a second, but I'll always remember.

He was all in white: white trousers, white top, white scarf, white face. He had a very sort of sad look, sympathetic. Just like I imagine he would be.

I think hc does help me.

Only a picture, but he helps me.

I've got a poster of George with his mum up by my bed. I kiss it every night before I go to bed. If I don't, I feel terrible and get terrible dreams.

I suddenly think: I can't go to sleep, I didn't kiss the picture.

So I sit up and say: 'Oh, sorry,' and I give him a kiss and it makes me feel better.

Sometimes my sister sees me and she tuts. But she's the same about Spandau Ballet as I am with Culture Club.

With my sister it's a sore subject. Like if one of my friends who likes George comes over and we're chatting about him, my sister gets a bit funny. She's really annoying!

Or if he's on the telly she switches it off, and we get into a row.

And George sent me a letter, thanking me for a letter I had sent him – this was when they first got famous. Usually I keep it in my bed in a plastic cover with one of my favourite pictures of him.

And every time my sister makes the bed it disappears.

I dream about him most of the time.

When I lie in bed at night maybe I think about a picture I've just seen or something. Or if there's a certain song I'll sing it in my head and that helps me to dream about him too.

One dream I've had a few times is that me and my sister meet him in a record shop where he's signing an album. George slips the album over to me with a time and a place written on it. I go there and it's a hotel and he's standing up against the bar. I start walking towards him and he opens his arms for me to walk into them.

That scene recurs quite a lot.

Sometimes I close my eyes and picture it. And then he looks all kind of blurry and dreamified, the sort of thing where you could get into his arms and melt. Really gorgeous.

I'd like to think that one day I will meet someone like him but so far I haven't. I'd like to meet someone just like him – just as down to earth and thoughtful as he appears to be.

Quite a few of my pen-friends are males and they like to dress up to look like him. But some of them are quite horrible actually!

If I could have a wish granted I think it would be to get to know him better, to spend a lot of time with him and really get to know him.

I imagine doing just the simple things with him: making tea or cooking, and what he'd eat. I think I'd like to know him as a husband really – whether he'd be caring, or angry and nasty.

What he's really like.

[Jane is 19]

Bernard: beamed through the air

From an early age I was interested in science fiction and spacy things like paranormal beings. And Bowie was a personification of that kind of thing.

So it was quite scary to see someone on stage who did look like an alien. He didn't look like a boy and he didn't look like a girl. But he did look very threatening and androgynous. For someone as young as I was, that was quite a frightening experience.

I think Bowie's got a strange face and a very fascinating face, and I don't think there could be another David Bowie – to have everything perfect in the way he has.

I remember I got really confused and at one point I really did think he was something alien. Seeing photographs of him I thought: He can't be real.

And when I saw him in '73 at the Hammersmith Odeon – my sister took me – in all that Ziggy get-up, he was such an awe-inspiring figure.

That impression was left with me.

The clamour for tickets for the '83 concerts was so immense because you are sharing two hours of your life with him – two hours in the life of someone you know won't be there one day. It's quite a marvellous experience to be able to at least say: 'I shared two hours with him.'

Maybe, you know, with 10,000 other people, but it's still a very solid thing in the eyes of the world.

For the Hammersmith show me and some of the other fans got together an arrangement of flowers in the shape of a red shoe. And we put a card on it with everyone's names who had donated. So that, you know, they were then a name to Bowie – which is nice.

It's nice for people to know Bowie's read their name.

At one point during the song 'Breaking Glass' he points to a member of the audience who then has a pointing match with him. And that was me at one of the gigs – we were pointing at each other.

And at another moment he whirled round again with his finger outstretched and I was there too. At the time it seemed quite incredible because it seemed telepathic. And you think: Well, was it just coincidence or . . .?

People were actually quite amazed that it was going on. They were turning to me and saying: 'I think he recognized you.'

But that wasn't the best one. The strongest feel of any kind of link I've had with Bowie is actually knowing that whatever I do in terms of writing the fanzine, that he is reading it and that he does actually own your work – which I think is the most amazing thing that could ever happen to any artist who does feel strongly about Bowie.

It is a bit odd really, having devoted so much time to him and never having actually met him. But then again it's quite nice in a way. I don't have any regrets about not meeting him. I think I will meet him one day, but it would be nice if there was an arrangement where I could actually sit down and talk to him at length.

I think that would mean much more as a first memory than just rushing up to him and saying: 'I'm Bernard from——fanzine.'

Those of us on the fanzine can sometimes work out what he's about to do next. That probably does amaze a lot of people – that there's some kind of mind link somewhere. Like when we read a story and we just know it's wrong.

I don't know whether that's telepathy or not. It's just *knowing* Bowie.

One time Sonia wanted to draw a clown. She dressed me up as this clown, a pierrot, and took pictures of me and started drawing. About two days later there was a picture of Bowie dressed up as a clown.

There are loads of little instances like that. It may just be coincidence but I would imagine if we do live and breathe somebody – because you have to, because you ought to – and you think about him hard enough, there must be something that will occasionally filter through. Beamed by something up in the air. . . .

[*Bernard is 22 and edits a successful Bowie fanzine from which he earns a living.*]

Lawrence: and that's not a fantasy (Cheryl Baker of Bucks Fizz)

When I masturbate I imagine her sort of stood there. Stood in the room.

I usually stare at a poster on the wall – especially one head and shoulders picture with her shoulders bare and a black scarf round her neck. And she sort of comes out of the picture and stands there in the room.

I see a full person in the room, stood there in black pants and a pink negligee. She stands there laughing – not laughing as such but smiling and giggling and teasing a bit – just laughing to herself.

She speaks, inviting me to come and get her, and when I get up she disappears.

She says things like: 'I'm here!' and, 'Over here!' – calling from wherever she's stood.

That goes on for quite a bit and eventually I come.

When I dream about her most is after a concert or after a meeting.

Every time I've met her it made me dead happy. It's like seeing a friend you haven't seen for a long time. It's just so exciting. It's so lucky. I can't really explain it. It's great. It takes you really high 'cos you've looked at the wall for ages and wanted to meet her and then you've met her.

And then there's still the concert to go through and I might meet her at the end again. So it's wonderful, especially when she stops and has the time to talk to you.

The annoying part is hanging about waiting for them, not knowing when they'll come. It would ruin a concert completely if I missed her, so you daren't go in case they come.

And you think: Is it worth waiting all this time? Especially when it's raining and you get soaking wet. But when they do come, there could be a thunderstorm and you wouldn't be bothered. Because here they are, and that's what you've come to see and that's what you want.

I was upset one time when she got off the coach and went in straight away and didn't even say hello. I shouted and Mike heard and went in and got her. It was just a mistake, she hadn't heard me. But it still upset me.

When I went to see her last time they pulled up in the coach and there she was sat with the drummer. I don't know why – because I've never felt jealous before – but I just wanted to hit him. I wanted to go up and hit him in the face. It just came over me. I was stood there thinking: She's sat there with *him!*

Then she got out of the coach and that was it. She was on her own then. So I pounced on her: 'Cheryl, come here. I want your autograph.' And we started chatting.

There's just so much mystery about her and happiness that I like a lot.

My bed's opposite my posters and I've got a skylight window so the light comes through and hits her picture. Even when there's not much light I can see it in my mind 'cos I know it so well. So she's always at the end of my bed. But it might as well be five miles away, because if I reach out she's out of reach. She just stands there smiling and laughing.

Some nights when I go to my room I take up all my scrap-books and have a good read. I compare pictures back and forth: here she's got the same dress on, here the same shoes on and I look at her hair – it's the same as in this picture . . . and so on.

By the time I get sleepy I've got her on my mind so much it just comes on. I masturbate and then I come. And when I come I always think: I wonder what Cheryl would say if she knew what I'd just done for her.

But there's no chance of finding out so there's no point in worrying about it.

At first my mum expected I'd pack it in. She said it would only last a couple of weeks, but it's still going strong. We used to have arguments. She said she didn't like certain records and I used to stick up for them. Or it was too loud, or look at the state of what she's wearing . . . I just ignore her now.

I often talk to Ginny, a girl-friend I've got, about what Cheryl would be like to go to bed with. She's a fan of Bucks Fizz too, only she fancies Mike Nolan. So we talk about what Cheryl would be like and whether she'd be serious or creased up and laughing and the sort of things she'd do. Together we build up this sort of Cheryl figure for me.

Then we do the same for her and Mike.

I like her hair. I run my hands through her hair. That's what I remember most about her in my dreams, running my hands through her hair.

And it being me and only her.

I like her hair and her ears and her eyes.

I bite her ears and that makes her laugh even more. She's a torment and a tease. She just laughs all the way through. She doesn't encourage you but she doesn't exactly put you off. She lets you get on with it. She doesn't put up any resistance at all.

She smells good – she smells of Cheryl.

And she's all hot and holding on tight. I lie on top of her. Sometimes I suck her and make her come that way.

In one dream I don't remember her getting undressed but suddenly she was in bed and I could feel her shoulders and naked body. Her arms felt rough and yet her arms were soft. They were all scabby at the top with flaky skin, like she'd got sunburn and she was peeling.

And then it changed as I went down her arm to her elbow and to her hand. Her hands were soft as well.

Oh yes, her hands were soft.

Ginny told me she often dreams about Mike.

She also dreams about me and Cheryl and Mike and her all together.

She might end up marrying Mike in her dream.

So then I say: 'Oh, you can marry him but I can't marry Cheryl! There's something wrong there!' She laughs at that.

But sometimes we have rows over it. It gets: 'What do you mean?' and, 'What do you mean by that?' And: 'I didn't say that.' And: 'Shut up!' or, 'Shut up or I'll put the phone down!'

Then one of us puts the phone down. The other one rings back: 'Don't you put the phone down on me!'

Once I was walking around with Ginny before a concert

and I was only messing about but I said: 'What makes you think Mike would take any notice of you?' And she said: 'What makes you think Cheryl would take any notice of *you*?' And she was very serious about it. We had a row and didn't speak until we were sat in the concert. After that it was all right.

At the end of a concert you don't really want to go. You stay there and hope they'll come on again. When they start doing encores you think: If I keep clapping for ever they'll come on again and again and again.

It's a bit of a let-down really. It's everything you expected and wanted but it's over now and it's past history.

Generally the day after a concert I spend two hours or more with Ginny discussing everything over and over.

When we get the photographs back from the chemist, we're saying: 'Oh, do you remember who took this one?' and talking about what they did and what they said. That also goes on for quite a bit.

And then I put them in my drawer with the rest of my stuff.

I look through my photos two or three times a week. I sit and compare things. Little things like ear-rings and details of what she's wearing or when she's got her hair this way and when she's got it another way.

Ginny's the same with Mike. If she gets a picture it'll be: 'Have you noticed he's wearing the same as he wore on December 14th 1981?'

My best possession is a signed birthday card from Bucks Fizz. I study it. Then it goes in my drawer which I lock up so I can never lose it.

In my dreams I'm aware of the feeling between the two of us and that it's just me and Cheryl and it's what I've always wanted. I'm also aware of thinking: This is Cheryl and I've got her, I'm holding her. Feeling she's there. And thinking: God, I'm in bed with Cheryl Baker! Can it be true or not? And I'm also aware of thinking: Oh, I can't wait to tell Ginny this. In my dream I can't wait to tell her I've been to bed with Cheryl and see what she says. And then it always stops. Before we even get started. That always gets me mad, that part.

She's lovely. I call her Chez and she calls me Laurie or Lawrence or darling. And she laughs her way through until, as I say, it always stops. We're making love and then it just disappears. I'd love to know why.

I'm left feeling I've been robbed of something. Why was it taken away? What did I do wrong? Where has she gone? Who took her? I just keep asking questions and there's no answer to them.

There was one dream I had where she'd done something wrong and she got put away in prison. I remember I cried for ages – this was in the dream – I just cried and cried. And the only way she could get free was if I took her place. So I took her place for the rest of my life.

In another dream we'd been together for ages and ages and we agreed to get married. I went to the church but she never turned up.

It was one of those small country churches, and inside was my mum and dad and Ginny. And the other members of the band: Mike, Bobby and Jay. Mike was our best man. Then someone came up and told me they'd got this message from her that she'd gone away.

And that one nearly put me off her. Because for the first time I was thinking: Here I am, I'd do anything for her, I buy all their stuff and look what she's done. For a couple of days I just refused to think about her any more.

I talked to Ginny about it, but she wasn't much help because she's in the same situation. She's gone on Mike and she's always going to like him.

But then I sat down and thought about it and I just couldn't work out why I was thinking like that. It was never going to happen anyway so why was I so bothered about it?

But I really was upset about it and that's when it nearly finished. But it didn't, and I just carried on being a fan.

Sometimes I feel I really want to know her and I just can't talk to her. Sometimes that makes me really angry. Ginny feels the same: she wants to talk to Mike a lot and gets angry because she can't.

I don't know what I'd do if I got Cheryl's address. It

depends. Some days I'm not bothered and other days I've got to know.

I have tracked it down to about five miles. Me and Ginny worked it out from the papers and what she said in interviews and we got a map. So we've got a rough idea of what area she lives in. We'll have to go knocking on every door: 'Does Cheryl Baker live here?'

If I found out I think I'd walk down the road where the house is and then I'd stand on the corner for about 10 minutes deciding whether to knock or not. I'd have to be in the right mood to go and knock. Then she'd either say: 'Come in', or 'Go away'.

It may take a bit of doing, but I think I would go and say hello and just have a chat and that would be it.

But what I really would like is that when Bucks Fizz eventually fizzles out I can become her friend. Just get to know her and become her friend. It's a very slim chance but it could be possible.

And that's not a fantasy.

[*Lawrence is a 16-year-old student. His parents are white collar workers. Ginny (16) is also a student.*]

A personal god – Bowie fans

Sheila: I first 'discovered' Bowie in November 1981.

Since that day, I have been addicted to him as though he were a drug. No, *the* drug.

My initial impression of Bowie was, I suppose, total confusion! He was *so* naive and innocent, yet so experienced and knowledgeable. He was so beautiful, yet so crude. He was so frank and open, yet bursting with secrets.

So weak and harmless, yet so very powerful.

He filled me with awe.

In 'The Man Who Fell to Earth' Bowie was Thomas Newton. I did think he actually *was* this character. Since then, he has *convinced* me that he is an alien, the very man who fell to Earth.

I don't want to be accused of blasphemy, but to me he

came to us a bit like Jesus. You could also call *him* an alien. They are both very wonderful, special people. Although I would never pray to Bowie or worship him as a god, he has the very same aura about him as Jesus. It's what I call beautiful, mysterious, and, above all, inspiring.

The most *obvious* change in my life since discovering Bowie is a distinct lack of money! I spend such an awful lot on his LPs, singles, posters, magazines, concerts, etc. In fact, I believe that liking Bowie has encouraged me to experiment more with the music world and try out *everything* I find! Though I'm frequently penniless, at least I can boast a good knowledge of everything from Buddy Holly to Brian Eno and Iggy Pop!!!!

Like any girl, I'd like to touch him – his hand or his face, and I'd like to kiss him. Not so I can boast 'I've kissed David Bowie', but so I can *believe* he's a real person.

I'd also like him to see himself from a fan's point of view and understand just how *intense* a fan's devotions can be. It may be embarrassing, but it's very real.

Rachel (17): My first impression of Bowie was, and still is, 'wow'! His lyrics and music are just amazing.

Whenever I think about Bowie I could just explode with admiration.

Marcel (18): To me Bowie was everything and is everything. I wanted to know him and love him – and who couldn't help loving such a wonderful man.

I wanted to have and be part of his life so I started to buy him: records, books, posters, etc – everything I could associate with him.

The impression he gives is of a personal God.

Sue: When I play his records I mostly just sit or lie and listen, and fantasize about *meeting him* (if only!) nothing more.

Sharon (16): I am not lonely but it is nice to be able to have a relationship which one can perfect for oneself.

I have adopted him as a friend, lover (in fantasy) and father-figure.

I feel more secure as he is always there to retreat to.

I have also gained in self-confidence because this security gives me the courage to assert myself.

Some of his music stirs an incredible amount of emotion in me which I never reach during other aspects of my daily life.

I love the darkness and desperation in his songs.

When I fantasize, it is about how I could reach the heights which he has reached, and become as influential as he is, and this can only be a fantasy!

Peter (23): Listening to a Bowie album seems to send me into a sort of trance. I seem to shut myself off from anything else.

I often meet David in my dreams.

Wherever I am David is near. When I'm not at home I carry a small picture of him in my wallet.

I can't really explain why I do all this.

It's just called devotion.

Melanie: I first became aware of Bowie whilst lying on the floor doing homework with the TV on.

He looked so weird that I abandoned my sums and watched him.

At first I was into the music, then I got into the man.

It became a religion, an all-consuming adulation. I lost the fact that he was an ordinary man with a life outside of his work.

Bowie has moulded the shape my life has taken.

He became my world and the escape I needed to realize myself.

Andrew: Those eyes of his mock me alarmingly, because he has fulfilled his dream I suppose.

Selina (18): When I listen to Bowie I feel as though I have a special friend.

I feel very close to him, as if I've known him for years.

When I'm angry or upset I just plug in and he seems to sort me out. It's funny how a voice can sort you out.

I have his photos and posters, wall to wall. I really like having him surrounding me.

I like to look at him when I listen to his music.

Michelle: In 1973, when I was six years old, in the space of three minutes I first became aware of Ziggy Stardust.

My parents were reading newspapers and I was sitting directly in front of the television as I always did then, watching. Suddenly this colourful man or perhaps it was a woman, I really couldn't tell, was in the centre of the TV.

I was amazed. I turned to my parents and demanded to know more about this thing.

'Oh . . . that's David Bowie,' replied mother, 'He's gay.'

Jenny (17): I first became aware of David Bowie when I was about six or seven years old.

I was a bit scared of him at the time – my parents didn't like him at all – and since they spoke about him as though he was some sort of monster I began to think of him as something really evil!

But I really got into Bowie after I was 13. I was obsessed by him.

I used to think about him constantly, dream about him.

Since then my feelings towards him have changed, basically because I've grown up and grown out of dreaming about when/how I'd get to marry David Bowie!!

But I'm still totally obsessed by the man – I totally adore him and feel as though I always will.

My walls are covered in his photos and posters. I like to look at them and be totally surrounded by him.

I admire most of all his ability to appear *almost* human but still retain something very special and different about his personality which no one I've ever met or seen anywhere else seems to have.

There's something untouchable about him.

Power

Jason: living in a film

I've just been through a couple of years of real utter confusion and mayhem, and Bowie was part of that. It was just me being a misfit, trying to find something. It got really messy. It became so I was living in a film.

It was just like an anarchistic cartoon film – you just see these crazy images rushing past you and then, in the end, you can't really make much sense out of it.

It annoyed me that the media had suddenly managed to penetrate people's lives so much that you couldn't escape from someone a million miles away, someone totally remote.

It was like someone haunting me all the time, a great big intrusion on my life.

He was always there. What scared me the most was a kind of godlike fear, the fact that his name was everywhere and you couldn't go anywhere without coming up against it. It was like everything leads you to Bowie in the end – whether you like it or not. A feeling that your whole life's just about you and Bowie. Both of you being in the world together and that's all there is to life.

I had all these difficulties and problems in life to overcome and Bowie's lyrics had all sorts of messages of what I was to do and I was decoding it all. It was making me act pretty strangely, obsessively. I had an illusion of going somewhere but I wasn't.

Through auto-suggestion I ended up thinking about being reincarnated as Bowie.

Which is pretty horrible I think. Because everyone knows about that symptom of being a fan of Bowie and ending up believing that you are Bowie and you're going to be reincarnated and everything. And so you do feel people are thinking: What kind of trip is this bloke really on?

I also had a sort of feeling that the world was run by zombies and that everyone was trying to find a way through and it was up to me to show the way.

I was taking drugs at the time. Hash and stuff.

But I think the real drugs involved were the power of the medium he was involved in, all that technology and everything. And the drugs, the actual drugs, just put a little bit more edge on everything.

I wouldn't like to be in the spotlight he's in. I'd try and do everything I could to avoid that. No one's ever really had so much power to get across to so many people – such bizarre imaginings and everything.

It's as if he can see everything that's going on. He appears to do everything better than everyone else somehow. And how does he have this extra magic that all the other groups somehow never manage to emulate?

There's one image of him sitting there quite reassuringly and smiling – as if he knows you. Everywhere I went I just saw him in that relaxed expression. As if, while I was fretting away having a terrible time, he was just calmly observing everything that was going on.

It was always the eeriness of the way he could get through to me through static, that was the eeriness of the whole thing – how you can be in touch with someone the whole time just through pictures and records.

Like the radio. You know they're miles away, sitting in a studio somewhere in London – but they get inside you. It's kind of a claustrophobic feeling where everything's brought together by the media.

So many people who don't know each other. Yet they all seem locked into one by the television and everything. Which is horrific really when you think about it.

That's why I don't have a telly at the moment, I'm totally sick of it all. I'm looking for some real people.

I was never outwardly a Bowie fanatic. But people started realizing I was without me really wanting them to. I think the way I was going about things looked as though I had read his whole script and was trying to act it myself.

Not many people get into a situation like that where life is a real crazy adventure.

I think I wanted to be very modern.

It was like I was living in the most advanced film there ever was. It had all the ingredients of films, but it was just that step further. It was just like being a super-being and everything you could do or be was a perfect art-form.

It was like some fantastic trip in my life, more real than real.

At the time I was totally oblivious of the rest of the world. It was just like being in a painting which had come to life. I was going to transform everything that Bowie had done into visual terms. Like going from one life form to another.

He was just pumping everything he'd got into what he wanted because he wanted it to be thrilling and exciting. It becomes obsessive, doesn't it? You go further and further.

But I think that now he doesn't want to be involved in all that heavy stuff. Probably it's just a matter of age. When you're young you're out to impress and you do everything to the extreme. Then you begin to realize that the dangers are real after all and you're not infallible and you could just be the guy that leads everything to destruction.

Maybe now he's got a sense of responsibility and while still keeping up appearances for young people to tell them that he's still a pop star and life is fun, I think he's scared of putting over any more art on them in case they go mad and, you know . . . like the things that led to John Lennon being shot.

I felt very sad when John Lennon and Bob Marley died so near to each other. It was like a good thing had been running very smoothly and then suddenly you had to think about death and people having to carry on without people who give you a lot of strength.

And so many things just seemed to lead to a meeting. I imagined David Bowie and Jimi Hendrix were me and my brother's alter egos and that eventually we were going to meet, all four of us. As gods, I suppose.

And I considered all the possibilities. Like whether we had to eat each other.

It was like in the secret service, you know, you get everything mixed round so you don't know who's who or what part you have to play.

But I've always felt I'd really hate to meet him. There's too much of the fictional character there. There'd be too much tension to talk to him just on a friendly, down-to-earth basis.

I think if I saw him in the street now I don't know how I'd cope. It's like some girls I thought about a lot but whom I didn't know that well. I think if I met him I'd have that kind of fear of coming close, of being close to someone without them knowing it.

[*Jason, 21, dropped out of university in his second year. He is now unemployed. His father is a Foreign Office official.*]

Sue's fantasy about Adam Ant

I'm at an Ants gig with a couple of my mates and I somehow wander away from them. I manage to get up front and Adam looks down at me as he's singing'. He's really turnin' me on and the bulge in his tight leather trousers is really straining.

I see a lot of other punkettes have noticed and are really randy for the sexy bastard, just like me! But he isn't eyeing them up. He's looking at me.

I jiggle my tits a bit and he flashes me a really gorgeous come-to-bed smile which makes my heartbeat sweat outta me and my fanny tingle!

So after a whole gig of him making me squirm with randiness, I'm just about to try to find my mates when a hand touches my shoulder.

I turn and it's this bouncer who sez I must go with him 'cos Adam wants to see me in his dressin' room. I flush all over with excitement and follow the bloke through the mobs of punks and punkettes to Adam's room.

The bloke knocks and a voice sez: 'Come in.' The

bouncer type gives me a tap on the arse and winks, then shoves me but doesn't come in with me.

The room is hot and stuffy and there's a kind of reddish glow from a lamp. there's a thick red carpet littered with fag ends, empty beer cans, etc, and in a dark corner is a low bed covered with black fur with smoked glass mirror on the walls round it.

A record player is playing one of his songs in the background, 'Press Darlings'. He's lying on the bed smoking a fag. The room is smoky and makes me feel dizzy. I feel hot and excited and I'm sweatin'.

Adam sits up and licks his gorgeous lips, then speaks. 'You look hot, darling,' he says, 'Why don'tcha take somethin' off?' I smile nervously and slip off my leather jacket. He gives a sexy laugh and beckons to me. I walk to him and sit on the bed.

'No, love,' he grins, 'Kneel on the floor. I'm your master, OK?, I nod but he wants a proper answer. 'OK?' he snaps. 'OK,' I say slavishly. By now I'm really, really turned on and aching for his vast cock to stab me and punish me, But I don't say much 'cos he's the master!

'You've nice juicy tits, girl,' he hisses. 'Get ya top off.' I obey and he smiles. 'Yes,' he mutters, 'very nice.' He stoops and kisses each one, an evil glint in his dark erotic eyes. He knows he's really teasin' me now.

Please . . . fuck me,' I stammer, not able to control it any longer. He laughs throatily and taps me lightly with the butt of a big black curled leather bullwhip he has by the bed.

'When I'm ready, baby,' he says. I can see he's more than ready but is loving to tease me with that bulge and everything. The sexy, sadistic bastard!

He tells me to stand. I do and he tells me to pull his boots off. I pull them off. 'Now get on all fours, punkie,' he growls, holding the whip menacingly.

I do and he rests his feet on my back. He then tells me to lick his boots clean. I do and he starts telling me how he's going to fuck me hard and fill with steaming punk spunk and make my fanny steam. I begin to moan at the ecstatic thought and to make it worse he wips that cock out of those skin-tight leathers and fondles it.

It's big and bulging. The knob glows in the red light all

wet and beautiful, the veins throbbing and thick on the long, delicious shaft.

'You know you've really got to earn this, fuck slave,' he laughs, seeing my eager eyes. 'So get lickin' those boots an' when you've finished get ya bondage strides off so I can inspect that pretty little cunt you have.'

'Yes . . . yes,' I gasp and lick then fuckin' boots clean. When he's eventually satisfied, I strip off my bondage and knickers, then lie on the bed as ordered. He smiles and nods and spreads my legs wider.

He gets more turned on as my cunt glistens with juice. 'Wait a minute,' he hisses, 'I think your reward is comin' soon baby.'

I gasp as he ties my hands to the bed and then hoists my legs over my head and ties my legs just below my hands so I'm in a very vulnerable position, completely at his mercy.

He skims his hot tongue lightly over my quim, making me wiggle and sigh with delight, then he begins to shove the butt of the whip in and out making squelchy noises in my well-juiced cunt!

'Please, master, I want your cock . . .' I plead. He pulls the whip out and laughs evilly. 'Right, if thats wot you want, randy bitch, it's wot you'll get.'

I give one helluva scream as his massive tool drives into me. He begins to pound at me like a great powered piston, gasping like a stud bull, Im sweating, so's he, and our damp, glowing bodies slap together.

Images of ourselves perform this gorgeous sex act in the dark, weird mirrors round the bed. It's like an orgy of two!

Panting, moaning and gasping fills the room and my head spins as I near my orgasm and his poundings and breathing become faster . . . faster . . . faster till we both suddenly give out the longest screams ever and his glistening body lurches violently filling me with so much cream some spills over the black fur and my pubes.

He pulls out tired but thoroughly satisfied. 'You're a good bitch,' he pants, flopping by me. He fondles my cunt and I smile and get my breath back.

My hairs are soaked with sweat and spunk. My spiked

blond hair is now limp, sticking to my forehead and cheeks. His black hair sticks in strands on his forehead.

We're both glistening with our own and each other's perspiration. His cock, now limp, glistening with some of his own overflowed juice and thick with come. His balls are soaked and even his belly has some on it.

He unties me lazily and flops on top of me, grinding his body into mine. He fondles me and kisses me, probing my throat with his slimy, warm tongue.

He then tells me to wash his balls and cock with my tongue and then promises to clean my cunt and lick the sweat from every part of my body as a reward.

Rosie: Barry and God

Me and my husband only live together now as brother and sister.

Because – and this may seem rather silly and stupid – but I just feel unclean with any other man apart from Barry. If I can't have sexual intercourse with Barry, I'll go without. I'll never be unfaithful to Barry.

My husband understands this. He realizes my interests are different to his and he does try to understand.

Sometimes he does say: 'You've got to make up your mind between me and Barry.'

But then he knows how much I love Barry and that if he got on to me too much I'd just go and live with one of my friends.

So I'm really fortunate. We've got a good relationship.

I've never felt this way for anyone else even though I've been married three times and I've had quite a number of boy-friends.

But I really feel for Barry and I think it's because he came when I needed love and friendship the most.

What he's done for me only I and dedicated fans can understand.

I never used to have any friends as such. Me and my mum had been very close. And then she died.

And about two weeks after she died the BBC repeated Barry's concerts from the previous January and April.

I put the television on and it was as if just at that moment Barry looked into the camera and was looking at me through the television. I know he wasn't of course, it's ridiculous, but he seemed to know. He said to me in a private sort of way: 'Rosie, don't worry. You've lost your mum but God will be good to you. He's sent me to help you and I will help you. If you love me and follow me, I'll help you as much as I can. I'll get you friends, I'll take you out of yourself and you can start a whole new way of life.'

Next day I went into town and bought *Pure Magic No.2*. And funnily enough there was a girl's address on a sticker on the record. She lived fairly locally, six miles away. I rang her up and she invited me to a get-together at her house the following Wednesday.

Joanne and I became good friends. She got me videos done, she got me photocopies of Barry which I'd missed.

Then I joined the official fan club. And about four weeks later I got a letter from Mandy saying she'd heard about me through the fan club and inviting me to a get-together at her place. I made more friends there and then I joined another local club where we all meet Friday evenings – we call Friday evenings 'Barry nights'. And without Barry and all these dear friends I've made through him I don't know how I could have coped with life. I mean no one can take my mum's place, but he's certainly done a very good job trying to.

And it's not just me. He's helped so many people. Like my friend Joyce Brightwell who lost her husband and through Barry she's been able to start a new life, make life mean something again.

Joyce and I have only met once, at the convention last year. But through what we call 'Manimail' we've become very, very close. If we're upset, if we're sad, if we're happy, we write and tell each other about it. We open our hearts to each other, tell each other all our problems. We understand each other. Because we've got the same love for Barry.

Barry is a lover, a husband and a very best friend. I tell

him everything. When I'm happy I tell him. And I cry to him.

But I must admit I do get very frustrated sexually.

When I have a sexual urge and I know he can't be there I often have to fight it. Joyce goes through the same thing. It can be very, very frustrating.

I love him. And I'd love to have his child. When he says he'd like a kid I pray to God – I know it just can't be but I hope.

Every night Barry's always here with me. Even if we don't make love he's lying here with me – he kisses me good-night and that.

And I think: Oh, if only I could wave a magic wand and make these posters come to life. And if a fairy godmother said you can have one wish I'd answer: 'Let Barry be here with me – as my husband, or my boy-friend or even a good friend.'

I kiss Barry's photograph every night and I say: 'Good-night and God bless. Have a good night. See you in the morning.'

I couldn't sleep without his posters on the wall.

Sometimes I imagine him in bed with me and we're making love. I close my eyes and we kiss and I touch myself and I imagine it's him. And I get sexually worked up...

When I wake up Barry's always the first thing on my mind. He's the first thing I see because my bedroom's full of posters.

I say: 'Good morning, Barry. Good morning, Biscuit. Good morning, Bagel [Barry's pet dogs].' I usually get up half-sevenish, something like that, and do a few jobs. Most days I have Manimail. I like to read it over a cup of coffee, to see who's written to me. I usually try and answer two or three letters a day.

My fantasy is that Barry's always here. The house never seems empty and if I feel like talking I talk to Barry. I ask him: 'Do you think I'm doing this right?' or, 'Where have I put this?' Or if I put a spoon down or a tea towel I say: 'Barry, have you seen this? Now, where have you put it?'

And I have a fantasy based on the fact that I know he

doesn't get up very early. So I always shout and say: 'Are you going to get out of bed? If you don't I'll pull your clothes off you.' So he starts running around the bedroom. And I say: 'Stop acting the fool. I've got my work to do. There's a time and place for everything.'

And I say: 'Shall we have a cup of coffee now?' I say: 'Now go and practise your piano. I've got some letters to write, and if you want anything, give me a shout.' He says: 'OK, honey, I will.'

And me and Barry usually do a few jobs together in the morning.

In the afternoon Barry always practises the piano while I do things for the club, answer letters, arrange sponsoring or just anything connected with Barry.

And then at night my husband comes in through the door.

He says it's like entering another world. He says: 'I never hear Barry's name mentioned all day, but first thing I hear in here is always Barry: what letters you've written, what you've been doing, what records you've been playing and all the nonsense you've been saying to Barry.'

And he says: 'I feel embarrassed to tell people at work what kind of wife I've got. I think you're round the twist.'

He knows a girl at his work who likes Barry. I've asked him to ask this girl to our house. But he says: 'I'll do no such thing. I don't want to be laughed at.' I say: 'Well, it's no laughing matter. It's real.' He says: 'I know it's real to you.'

And he says: 'The trouble with you, Rosie, is that you think everybody should be addicted to Barry like you are. When the neighbours come round,' he says, 'you're embarrassing. It's like you've got no other subject: Barry this, Barry the other. It gets a bit embarrassing.'

I say: 'Well, I understand your sister Hilary's got her interest in the Chapel.' He says: 'Yes, but she don't go on about it like you do.'

I say: 'Well, I don't think I do keep on about it,' you know, to me I think it's just normal.

And, as I say, we've got separate rooms now. And sometimes I say to my husband: 'Go and have a look in my room. See if Barry's in there.' And he accepts it.

But I know girls whose husbands won't let them have a picture of Barry in the house. They rip posters down.

Quite a number of my friends have had divorces through Barry. Like Elsie and Patricia who run the——fan club. Patricia's husband said: 'I think it's quite ridiculous you being so addicted to a man you're never going to meet. You're a married woman, you're grown up, you ought to have more sense.' And he says: 'You've got to choose between me and Barry.' She said: 'That's not very hard to do.' So they split up.

And, of course, I can understand men. I suppose in a way I'm very lucky.

It's as if your husband had pictures of Sophia Loren all over your flat and fantasized making love to her and kept saying: 'I love Sophia Loren. I wish she was here.' What would your reaction be?

So you've got to like try and see their point of view.

But me and a lot of my very dear friends have got understanding husbands.

They understand they can't do anything about it.

It's been like a jigsaw puzzle – I just can't understand it. I think actually it's Manilow magic.

Because I've only been an addicted fan for two years and I've got closer to him than some of the girls who've been fans of his since '78.

Like at the Royal Festival Hall I just couldn't believe my luck. I was in the fourth row, right by his piano and in line with his mike stand. And it was just like family – you forgot the people behind you.

After he'd finished singing his first ballad he put his arm out. I put mine out to him and he saw me.

And for a few moments our eyes met.

The person sitting next to me said: 'Hey, you two!' He heard her and he gave her one of his famous chuckles – which was fantastic. And all that night Barry knew I was there, you know, we kept looking at each other.

I cried for nearly a week after he'd looked into my eyes.

Every time I played a record I saw him and I would burst into tears. It took me a month before I could listen to a record or look at a video without tears rolling down my cheeks.

You have to go to one of his shows to realize the magic and the warmth and the love Barry creates among his fans. When they start singing 'We'll Meet Again' and all join hands you can almost feel the love. Something runs between us like an electric shock. It's just wonderful.

One day my friend, Hilary, said to me: 'Rosie, if Barry had lived 2,000 years ago who would you say he was?'

Me and Hilary didn't say anything. We just looked at each other and we knew what we both were thinking.

She said: 'Yes, precisely.'

I think he's the second coming.

He is a Jew, he comes from that race of people and I think Barry's a very special person. There's nobody else like him. There's other pop stars but they don't seem to do as much for the fans as Barry does. He's a different sort of singer, different sort of personality. He creates a lot of love and warmth. He helps people through a lot of things in different ways – which no other singer can do.

And I quite agree with Hilary. My husband thinks it's blasphemous, but I don't. He says: 'You're putting Barry before God.' I say: 'On the contrary, I don't put Barry before God, he's brought me closer to God.'

People who aren't fans of Barry, like my husband, think: Well, he's laughing all the way to the bank, getting richer and richer and you're getting poorer and poorer.

I say: 'No. Barry's getting richer financially, we're getting richer morally.'

[*Rosie is 43.*]

Marnie: I dream and double dream

Last Tuesday I was curled up in bed just thinking about Bowie and all of a sudden I felt this tingly thing inside me and I heard a quick squirting noise.

I wondered what the heck it was at first because I wasn't conscious enough to realize what on earth was happening inside me.

Then, when I turned the light on, I realized I'd had a ruddy orgasm – just by bleedin' thinking about him.

I'm so involved with Bowie in my dreams that it's hard to separate them from reality.

And when I had sex for the first time with my boyfriend I was thinking of my DB all the time, and I just couldn't erase him at all.

He was there and wouldn't leave my mind. I got very, very tense and my boyfriend said: 'What are you afraid of, Marnie?' I couldn't answer.

It does worry me at times, Bowie's too beautiful for his own good. Something tells me he was never meant for this world.

On some days of the week I don't like anyone else in the house. I just like to sit, you know, I just like to lie in my bedroom and go to sleep or something.

Or sometimes I feel unprotected, I don't feel safe. Like I've got my mum and my dad and things but I need somebody else.

And I don't want *anybody* else, you know, I just want *him*. Sometimes I'd like to get to see him. Quite a lot of times. I usually just cry or go to sleep then because there's no substitute, you know, no one can fill the loneliness when I get that low.

And sometimes I call him in my head. I shut my head and concentrate on his face and try to send him messages.

I did that today and it was as if his eyes were saying something special – to me and just me. It was like I felt something and noticed he was sending me a message back no one else could notice.

I wouldn't like to go through life and think he was never aware of who I was.

I want to explore him and really find the person behind the songs, films, plays and everything else he's ever done.

The real person inside there (I know there is one) is a shy and very sensitive man who hides his fears and hopes and dreams behind a calm and relaxed mood in public.

When I explore and find *that man* I'll be happy and content, but until then I'll just keep on wondering.

It's changed me quite a bit, you know. I don't go out all that much any more. I devote all my time to listening to records and things like that.

And it's like that every day, it's like a sort of responsibility, something like that.

I listen to his records every night. I lie on the floor and I put the speakers next to me ears, close.

I try to imagine seeing him and things like that.

I try so hard to dream about Bowie.

Sometimes I'll force myself into thinking about it so much that I don't just dream – I dream and double dream.

Q: Do you dream about him every night?

M: About every other night.

Q: What do you dream about other times?

M: Nothing.

Q: So whenever you dream and are aware about it, he's in there somewhere?

M: Yes.

[*Marnie was 14 when we first contacted her. She was interviewed and wrote to us for almost two years. She has since left school and now works on the production line of a factory making coats. Her father is a self-employed builder and her mother is a beautician.*]

Marnie's dreams 1: rag doll's legs

When I get really near to him it's always very dark. And it gets darker as I get closer to him. And then I can just feel like a knife in my stomach or something cutting into me, and I can feel sort of tingly feelings. That's when my arms seem to seize up. And then I put my knees up and that's when he gets angry. And he tries to push my knees down with his hand, and sort of grows sharper nails. Sometimes you can see his nails like bright lights or beams going at you. But mostly you can feel the pain.

I was sitting with my class in school and there was a huge noise like thunder and Bowie strode in the door and shouted my name over and over and then he was my eyes and he was singing something to me.

He swooped me up in his arms and kicked open a door and we were on a beautiful tropical beach.

He took me to a waterfall and we made love under the waterfall. I had this weird sensation all up my arms, all over my legs, inside my stomach and in my breasts of red hot liquids shooting up and down.

And then something unexpected happened.

He put his head against my sternum and drove his nose into it.

Then he scratched off my breasts with his nails and ate them and then I saw them just grow again.

Afterwards he tried to coax me into eating different parts of him saying how it was going to make us so much stronger than we were now.

When I wouldn't do it he clasped my back and pushed his head into my thighs and kept kissing me between the legs.

Then he ejaculated and smeared it all over me and I couldn't get it off no matter how I tried.

He sensed my discomfort and hurriedly scraped his tongue over my body trying to get the yellow goo off.

Then I wanted him to protect me again and he was very silent.

He kept kissing my body and was very gentle with me.

It was like he split personality. One minute he was loving and gentle and the next he was so violent and so angry.

Sometimes it's as if the music *is* him. Like when he hits me the music jumps into another part of the song. It's like he's the record, he's controlling it, and when he hits you or when he moves or walks about, it starts jumping. Then when he sits down it settles again.

Sometimes I can feel his tongue on my stomach, scraping, like something scratching me really hard. It's like a cat's tongue or something. Or a finger. Really hard. And it starts to bleed.

Then he pulls my navel cord out and I just sort of dissolve on the floor.

But there's no blood or anything. It's just like water. It's not thick like blood, it's just water.

And I can still feel myself when I've gone – when I've been pulled out.

I was trying to turn the telly off and he had the remote control in his hands and when I tried to get it away from him he had it in his other hand.

It was like when the telly flicks on and off – it was going in and out his hands like he had total control of it.

You couldn't get it if you tried – couldn't get through to him.

We were in a shower. And there was all this skin in the water and skin on the walls. And he kept squeezing my arms with his sharp nails painted red. But I couldn't scream – I kept trying to scream but nothing was coming out. And I had these vampire teeth and I kept trying to bite him on the neck.

I was on this operating table and there were doctors all around who wore different images of him. One had orange hair, one had blond hair, one had no hair – just the bald head and eyes. I could just see his eyes.

And watching us were people with no faces.

I was having a baby and they were telling me to push and this sort of light came out of my vagina and it was Bowie.

He had a microphone and he felt all hot and wet. He was tearing me apart and I tried to close my legs up but they wouldn't go together.

My legs were useless, like a rag doll's.

Sometimes there's white scarf things and he's trying to pull them round my neck and I'm trying to stop him cos it's getting tighter all the time.

This white scarf stuff is coming out of my mouth.

It's like a long ribbon of white silk and he ties it around my wrists and knots it so tight I can't breathe. It's as if he's trying to cut my breath off and cut my wrists off as well.

Then he flings me around like a rag doll and I can't do anything about it. It's like elastic bands against my skin, squeezing so tight that I'm all numb and lifeless.

And I've just got a sense of his power.

He can do anything and get away with it and I can't stop him.

Sometimes he says his song words. He doesn't sing then, he says them. And if you try to get through to him he won't let you. He just keeps on saying them louder and louder and you can't do anything about it.

Lilian: spanking Boy George

I always imagine pop stars in physical pain.

At the moment it's Boy George.

I think that's a very good choice because you can get all the stuff you need in the paper whereas before, with Blondie, it was difficult to get much to feed it with.

I didn't really buy many albums or anything until I was about 14 and then I got this Blondie album.

And I started getting interested in Jimmy Destri and I started having all these fantasies about him. Then it went on to Chris Stein and I started having fantasies about him.

The fantasies about Chris Stein mostly incorporated Debbie Harry because she was so involved with him. There was one fantasy where they both had this terrible disease. And it was a really mysterious disease. They went to this expert on black magic who said that to get rid of this disease they'd have to make love. But they were both very weak and in a lot of pain. And the only way they could get rid of it was to have sexual intercourse. So they'd have sexual intercourse – even though it was really painful. And I actually pictured this to an extent.

I imagine Boy George as a child has been naughty and his mother puts him over her knees, or sometimes over the edge of a settee. Then she takes down his trousers and smacks him with a slipper.

I imagine him crying.

Or sometimes I fantasize a friend of his has died.

He has this girl-friend he's very close to but it's a bit ambiguous to everyone else what their relationship is. And this woman dies.

I imagine he goes to see his parents. He goes into the kitchen to see his dad. His dad looks him in the eyes and they suddenly hug each other. Then their eyes go sort of watery. And Boy George is moving like he's sobbing but not crying out loud. Then his dad says something in Irish Gaelic to him.

And while they're hugging I imagine it by putting my arms round myself.

I often fantasize about hepatitis or migraine. They're two things I've come across in other people and I think: Oh, they're very painful.

And the other day I was even trying to find a medical dictionary to read how hepatitis works. Because I always want the fantasies to be realistic.

So I might imagine Boy George has hepatitis. He caught it a few years ago off this girl he slept with. He didn't know at the time she'd got it. And now he's sitting there sweating in a TV studio.

There are two DJs there: David Jensen and John Peel. And this hepatitis is getting worse and worse. So the DJs decide to give George a lift home. They drive off in a car with John Peel driving and David Jensen in the front seat. They're driving back to George's house and they get delayed so he slowly gets worse and worse.

Then Peter Powell gets in the back and says: 'Are you all right?' and George says: 'No.'

They eventually get him home and he goes up the steps and then nearly collapses on the second step. So Peter Powell gets out to help him.

Sometime I extend it so George goes into his house and lies on a settee and John Peel pops in for some reason and sort of half ignores him.

I act out the fantasies if I can.

I used to act them out in bed but it got to a stage where I'd sort of be talking to myself. And I think my parents heard me so I stopped it because I was really embarrassed.

But if everyone's out and the curtains are closed I'll act them out.

If I imagine someone in grief I act out crying. I don't actually cry, I just move my body like I'm sobbing and clasp my head as I picture them doing it.

Or sometimes I'll act out the fantasy of someone having a really bad migraine and maybe lie in bed.

And if I really get into the fantasy, if I really enjoy it, it's a bit awkward if someone comes in the room at that moment because my eyes will go all funny, my eyes will sort of look sorrowful.

I read in *Jackie* that Jon Moss says he's really frightened because George lets people do anything to touch him – and they'll do anything to get near him.

I think reading that I realized people do actually try to make things happen if they want them to happen.

And I thought: Oh, God, could I ever do that? That's awful! I hope I'd never try and do anything like that.

But I thought: What if I killed this woman called——?

I thought: What if I hounded out this——and killed her?

Of course, I wasn't actually planning to do it. But I thought: What if I did this? I could do it. I could be so desperate for this to happen that I would go and do it just so he'd feel the way I wanted him to.

This was all based on a newspaper story.

George and——were at this airport and they wrote this dramatic thing in the paper about how they kissed and then they bowed their heads and there were tears swelling in their eyes.

And Boy George turned round and said: 'Oh, I'll really miss her because she's very special to me.'

Then I started having fantasies about this person dying.

How he'd react and how his friends would react.

So I imagine she's been killed. And Boy George is really upset. Then they have this wake – I think wakes are really interesting.

Kate Garner from Hayzi Fantaysee is there. And Kirk

Brandon. Also, for some reason, John Peel and David Jensen.

And I imagine they all gather round this dead body.

Then they slit their hands at the wrist and press the slit hands onto the slit hands of the dead body.

Someone will make a joke during this ritual and say: 'I hope no one's got hepatitis!'

Then they all start crying.

When I masturbate I don't use my fingers. I lean over a table and rub myself up and down. I find it's easier like that. It just has to be the right height.

I've done that since I was about six.

But I don't always masturbate. Because sex is only one part of my fantasies. I think they may also be a fascination with pathos.

Because whatever I imagine has to be something really horrible – not just unpleasant.

I've had these fantasies over the years and it's sort of worried me. I've thought: What's wrong with me?

But recently it's coming to the stage where I think: Other people think like this. I'm not a disgusting person thinking things like this.

I've even wondered if Boy George has these sort of feelings. I've thought: Maybe Boy George has the same sort of fantasies I do.

Even so, I sometimes feel really guilty. I think it's awful to imagine all this and I wouldn't like any of it to happen to me.

How can I think this about people?

But then I think it's harmless in a way because it's better than wanting this to happen to someone I actually know.

I don't think I'd have this kind of fantasy about someone I admired or agreed with. Like Robert Wyatt for instance, or The Raincoats.

But with pop groups, you don't really take them seriously – or I don't – because the music is so sort of throwaway.

I also think it's to do with how pop stars are presented.

Because there's this unrealistic situation of them being famous.

And I've thought: How would I feel if people had fantasies and thought all these things about me? I mean what would it do to someone's brain? It would be awful. I couldn't stand it if *one* person was like that about me, never mind hundreds or more.

But then I suppose they are there for people to fantasize about.

Like that Mark Chapman killing John Lennon – it was the same sort of thing in a way. He idolized him and actually thought he was him, and he went through all these sorts of feelings.

In fact, I find the idea of murder quite exciting because it's a new feeling and because it's so dramatic. I can't really understand it or explain it.

They're really time-consuming, my fantasies, because once I get involved with them I'm just obsessed with that person for ages.

It's sort of like falling in love with someone – you spend so much time on them and get so absorbed by them.

And I think: I must be wasting a lot of time. But then you think: Well, everyone does this because everyone needs fantasies. And anyway I'm not wasting that much time.

I think perhaps that really my fantasies are a way of controlling my own life. Because I always feel people are trying to take control of my life all the time.

I feel sort of helpless in a way.

I often feel like when people have nightmares and they're walking down the street and they're really inappropriately dressed or walking down the street in the nude and everyone else is fully clothed, and it's that feeling of helplessness – that you can't stop people invading you.

It's as though people are taking bits of you and pulling bits off you and twisting them round and making them how they want you to be. Like a hole being cut in the top of your head and someone putting their hand inside and taking everything out.

They're taking your soul out.

[Lilian is 18 and preparing to go to university. She is the daughter of a government official.]

Love from the Sun King – Roger's letters to David Bowie

From the Beast

Dear David,

I hope this letter gets to you without the CIA or KGB getting a hold of it. I don't want you to get involved in this matter but you are already.

By the way, I don't wear a smile like the one I wear in the photo Mary and I sent you, and Mary isn't quite as haughty as she appears in the photo.

We are really quite sensitive people, David, as I gather you are, being an artist.

We have worshipped you from afar and appreciate what you are doing for us (Beauty and the Beast).

I haven't noticed any spies around here, though I imagine there were some in Detroit.

I'm not looking for fame or fortune. I'm Arthur. We need Camelot and we need it desperately.

I suppose the remaining Beatles wonder about me – (poor John) (what a way to go) I feel sad for Yoko – Mary and I wanted to meet them and even modelled ourselves after them.

Now you can tell the Beatles about me (the Sun King).

Maybe there is a way we can all get together – I'm glad you put us all on your Heroes album.

All Mary and I wanted to be is movie stars – she's so beautiful (and sweet).

We are really quiet, peaceful people who dropped out of college to become rock stars then movie stars.

I wanted to become President when I was a child but rock'n'roll took over and I haven't been the same since.

And then David Bowie came on the scene.

Who was this fantastic musical genius who was so prolific and prodigious?

I listened to his every word and musical note and liter-

ally fell in love with him. I wanted to do the same –
become a rock star or a movie star.

Maybe I'm crazy, maybe I'm just a frustrated actor.

But please write or phone.

Love on you,

Roger

Dear David,

I sent you a photograph of Mary and myself a few years
ago to which you wrote a song about us called 'Beauty
And The Beast'. I may have given you the wrong
impression that we are wealthy. We are not – we are
working class like most people. We appreciate the attention you gave us as a couple of 'rockers'.

To get to the point, you may see me as a beast but in
fact I am Kalki, the Indian Lord that Gore Vidal wrote a
book about.

He could not explain to you about Kalki and his wife
Kali (and I am in the process of trying to reach Mr Vidal
in Rome to thank him for writing the book about me).

You may wonder 'how does he know that he is Kalki?'

Well, I had a religious experience a few years back that
enlightened me as to who I am really.

I am dying to go to India to be with my people but can't
afford a plane ticket to get there.

Why I didn't tell you about this earlier is that I don't
want to frighten people.

Please inform Mr Vidal (since you are at 'the top') that
I am Kalki. I have studied your music since you first started
out and you are very special to me, David. I hope that we
may meet some day.

Mary (Kali) and I always dreamed of working in the
'movies' and then we could afford to go to India. We have
both been to Los Angeles to try to 'make it' but no one
there knew we were 'Beauty and the Beast'.

The reason I am telling you all this is because you are
the one person who put his address on an album, and
wrote a song about two of his fans.

Thank you for turning us from nobodies into somebodies, into 'stars'.

The trouble is, David, that nobody wants to know a
beast.

But please don't leave us in this limbo, because we have devoted ourselves to you and find you adorable.

If you want to write back or if Mr Vidal wants to know where I live, the address will be below.

Thank you

Kalki (Roger)

PS God bless you David Bowie

Dear David,

Hello again from the Suncoast!

I hope George, Paul and Ringo have gotten the message that I'm the Sun King they wrote about 11 years ago.

It sounds nuts, I know, but I found out through telepathy who I am – it finishes off the fairy tale you wrote about Mary and me very nicely I think.

I wonder what the American public will do when it hits the news?

I'm dying to meet Jackie & Andy Warhol – he's my favourite artist next to you and Dali of course (& I can't forget Picasso). I'm an artist myself – but much more interested in International Politics now.

I'm not really such a beast, David. It would be nice to receive a letter from you – does $ have to separate us? Sad if it does.

Mary is very beautiful and wants to be a movie star – I don't think she totally realizes that she'd be Queen if she married me. (By the way, I'm a Catholic and plan to remain so.) No one is greater than Christ. The West is Best! Mary has been very depressed. After all, she's stuck in New York, all by herself.

I miss her so. You'd love her – she's vivacious.

I'm really fed up with the crime in this country. I wanted to meet John Lennon – he was my idol in high school. But then you came along. I think the Seventies were great musically. But the '80s will probably be better yet.

I really appreciate what you are doing for Mary and me – I don't know how to repay you – just be my friend.

Love,

Roger Sun King

Love from the sunbelt!

Dear David,

Hi, Superstar! This is 'the beast' writing to you again – yes – David, another letter. You probably think I'm a nut – well isn't everybody today?

Mary and I understand power better now that you have made us into somebodies. You should put yourself up for Parliament, David – or better yet Prime Minister – I'm sure you could straighten out poor old Britain!

One thing I would really be thrilled to receive is a letter from you or a telephone call.

I know it is difficult – we (Mary, me and you) are all strangers, but I feel we are all family now.

I would love to be able to preserve Mary's beauty on film (another Garbo) but maybe she will go on coinage instead.

Thanks for turning us into celebrities, David – you are the sweetest rocker.

Love

Mary and Roger

PS Love to the Beatles

Julie: he's got a lot to answer for

The obsession started when I was 14. He used to play locally in Kingston and my brother would say: 'You must listen to David Bowie', and try to explain that he was a really good artist.

I was so young I didn't understand. But I eventually got the message and he opened up a whole new world for me.

I thought he was so extraordinary that he couldn't possibly be human. He was paranormal almost. And he wasn't actually like any other star of his time.

Or, indeed, before or after.

His silence was so loud. I mean he'd hardly say anything but he was so loud. He came over very clearly.

And when I day-dreamed about him, it was a question of glazing over and becoming almost incoherent when I spoke so that people had to prod me to get any response and I used to be away in this almost womb-like cocoon of protection.

At that time his music really drove home such powerful images. But my fantasies weren't very sexual at that stage because I was too naïve. I wasn't informed enough.

I had delusions of grandeur. I used to think: Oh, one day well go off together and he will understand that I am truly an individual. And he would marry me and we'd have this wonderful space age relationship.

At boarding school I used to think about him when I was in the class-room.

Him and The Osmonds – and at first I had a conflict there because I didn't know who to turn to.

The Osmonds were very immediate and easy to listen to, and very presentable. But they did nothing for my imagination at all. They were just packaged to please. Not packaged to prompt you into thinking all kinds of weird and wonderful things.

So from having looked at pictures and thought about it and written all sorts of peculiar essays about him – disguising the names because I didn't want people to understand what I was really saying – I guess from there it just grew into total admiration of a man who was so talented and so extremely diffident about everything.

I began to think he was a new kind of Messiah. I used to think he was the Coming of the Lord personified and all kinds of things. I really thought he had some kind of infinite power and wisdom.

Almost like Marc Bolan, I suppose, had a mystical quality that wasn't quite of this world or of this time.

Bowie was magic and he was supreme. He had the qualities of a type of ruler.

He was science fiction personified. To me he represented the most bizarre things which were evil and not of this world and completely beyond the imagination.

I really believed he was an alien of some kind. I didn't think he was at all normal, human.

I tried to masturbate for a long time over all this and I wasn't very successful because I didn't seem to be able to get a climax. And the actual act of masturbation was as much spiritual as sexual.

But when I fantasized I became very wet and I suppose I thought: If it's truly possible to walk through glass and reach him then it might be possible to touch him.

Because he really did convey to me the most peculiarly advanced stages of sexuality.

For a long time I used a hairbrush. But it didn't do much for me. Then I tried my finger because I thought that would be more tender and more like the real thing.

But that didn't work either.

I wasn't very good at it because I didn't really know how to excite myself. It took me about three years to find out where my clit was.

All that time I was thinking Bowie, all the time.

I had this thing where I'd stick myself in my room and switch off the lights and burn incense and play Bowie records on this old record player my brother gave me.

And I'd start to masturbate.

I used to think about us making love on top of a mountain. Because I always saw him in a very aesthetic sort of atmosphere with isolation around him: a cold, hard atmosphere with a lot of cloud – veering towards Major Tom or towards space.

Nothing of this world. Something which is beyond our understanding.

And I used to dream of layers and layers of clothes that we'd have of transparent plastic. And about ripping these pieces of plastic off to unveil something underneath.

And I had orgasms of a space kind. Something to do with hallucination really. I was actually hallucinating in orgasm.

I got very worried about it because at the time I thought I wasn't quite normal.

I tried to talk to people about it but I knew privately it would never do to talk about it. It was far too intimate and far too extreme. Therefore I tended to withdraw and become insular about it.

Then I just fantasized even more.

Eventually, when I saw him in *The Man Who Fell to Earth*, taking off his clothes and seeing him in the nude, I began to realize I fancied him even more.

And then it actually became a little more normal and channelled itself into something more erotic, because I was kinky about the fact he was so thin and he was like a woman. He seemed the perfect vehicle for my sexual needs and fulfilment.

To start with I was very clumsy about my masturbation. But then I learnt to lie back totally and relax and knock myself out on a feeling of pure ecstasy.

I would lie there – usually in some kind of underwear because I had a hang-up at the time about being totally nude. And I'd slowly take my bra off and then perhaps my pants and then very, very slowly I'd use a pillow – I used to kiss the pillow and then use it to get the feeling of a man's hand.

As Bowie was so thin I supposed he would be very fragile about it.

He would touch me with the merest of strokes and not actually grab my flesh in the way another man might.

Then I could allow myself the freedom of thought where I'd just lie there and I'd become extremely wet.

In fact I wasn't doing anything much to myself, but I was relaxing totally and playing his music and it used to drive me into a state of non-committed hysteria.

I just used to lie there and open my legs and I would feel absolutely dirty and then the whole feeling of wetness would come because I was being so naughty.

It used to amuse me that I felt shy. I'd laugh like I was being rather silly about it and worried that my mother might come in. But really I was dying for her to come in and see what I was getting up to.

I used to really get off on a particular record called 'Cracked Actor' which is terribly loud with the guitar instrumental. It was very overbearing and I used to actually reach a pinnacle where I would have to lie under the covers for fear of being overwhelmed.

I'd be very frightened of the loudness of the guitar and what I was feeling sexually.

When I saw *The Man Who Fell to Earth* I got influenced by the idea of skins peeling and the fact that skin can be taken away and produce juices of a kind that can reveal themselves at the height of sexuality.

So that when you make love you actually destroy certain layers of skin and form a liquid mass together.

It was incredibly sensuous and very wild at the same time.

I used to think that he would come to me late at night and we would go away together.

One time I actually believed him to be outside my door. But that was absolutely crazy. Obviously he wasn't.

It was my mother, in fact, knocking on the door.

I was drifting away and I was thinking perhaps he'd come one day to see me.

And I was terribly disappointed.

I remember my mother standing there and the shock-horror! She saw me in my nightdress – I was trying to undo my nightdress and I was making loud noises and my mother was wondering what the hell was wrong with me.

But I firmly believed – because I'd switched myself off – that he was there for me.

I was sort of humming. I was sort of buzzing as you do when you meditate, and I thought he was standing there.

I would look at him in his posters and try to understand the sexuality in his records.

I'd analyse them to death. I'd think that means this and this means that.

I thought the man was an absolute poet. I used to analyse his lyrics from here to kingdom come and try to get some meaning out of them.

It was being alone with Bowie that was so interesting because I had the privacy to fantasize and shut the door to everybody.

I looked at his photographs and I was in danger of being gog-eyed at the time because I had several on my wall. But the one I used to look at most was the one hanging over my bed with him in a hat and coat and looking through his glasses. And I used to think: Well, whatever he's thinking it must be one hell of a thing because his eyes seem so distant.

And I truly believed that nobody understood him and that I could, and whatever I did he'd understand because we were obviously meant to be.

And I thought of ESP. I read a great deal of books and most of them were flimsy paperbacks by unknown American authors of the £1.95 variety.

I managed to get it into my head that it was possible to communicate with him by thought transmission. So one day I communicated with him after a song and an interview on the radio.

And I had conversations with him in the posters. I used to walk around the room in a state of undress, but always protecting my small parts because I still had a hang-up about being totally exposed.

But I would always manage to excite him in some way.

He would see I was so intelligent that he would come to me and put his arms around me and then he'd say: 'Well, I have to leave you now but I'll be back.'

I actually used to have these conversations with him. I used to say: 'David, I want to go away.' Or: 'I would like to be in your show.' And I had ambitions at the time to be a pop star and I used to say things like: 'Oh, can I be in your film?' And also quite mundane conversations like: 'Would you like some tea?' And: 'I'll take you out,' and, 'There's a taxi outside,' and this type of thing. And we'd go out together.

Obviously we wouldn't make it to the front door but the idea was there and that was the important thing, just to have the reality in my own bedroom, within the four walls.

When I finished school I was unemployed for a while and I was really confused. And then I went on to drama school and then it got worse because I was confronted by all these Bowie look-alikes.

Then I finally had a sexual relationship in which I managed to bring all these fantasies into my sex life.

I went out with somebody who looked like David Bowie. It was a really silly thing. And of course it was a disappointment, because I found that obviously he didn't live up to the thing itself.

He was all of seven stone with glasses and knock-kneed.

Pimply as well. But I suppose I just wanted very much to have in bed anything that resembled Bowie. It didn't really matter who. Just the fact he could look like Bowie was an amazing achievement in my books and all my friends would be terribly impressed that I was going out with someone who'd gone to those lengths to look like Bowie. Therefore he must really be a little bit like Bowie, you see, because he looked so much like Bowie.

But it wasn't really any good at all.

I then went out with another chap who was much taller and was actually known for being a David Bowie look-alike.

Both those chaps were functional for me in the sense that they brought me a little closer to the idea of being way-out, and also because they wore the look well.

They looked good on my arm and they served their purpose.

But they disappointed me in other ways and they were very vain, the pair of them – and I don't really enjoy that sort of narcissism.

I also knew they were never going to be as intelligent as Bowie or as extraordinary.

But this was the next best thing so I might as well enjoy it.

When he killed off Ziggy Stardust at Hammersmith that really, really disturbed me because I really had a hang-up about these characters he had created and I really thought that he was responsible for creating them and he shouldn't put them to death, shouldn't bury them.

I was crying a lot and everyone was crying because he was killing off Ziggy Stardust and this was really a very sad thing.

The music was absolutely atrocious. It was so loud and I couldn't hear Bowie singing. And he was absolutely stoned, actually out of his head. And the amount of people that were stoned . . . I didn't know about being stoned then, but I caught on pretty quick.

I was watching them and I thought: Well, they're really on a different plane here. They're not feeling what I'm feeling.

I'm quite sure that Bowie was completely off his head

because his eyes would roll occasionally and the sweat was pouring. He was so excited. He was so pushed to the limit, to the very edge. And everyone around me was trying to see this and of course I got terribly squashed.

But the sweat and the smell was really horrible. Some people were sweating and others were wanking themselves off.

It wasn't very pleasant but I was absolutely stuck where I was and I couldn't move. I had to keep watching him.

I had a really good seat right at the front and I'd gone with another girl who was a Bowie fanatic and she was crying. Then she passed out and the St John Ambulance men had to take her away.

She was in a state of hypnotism almost, just gone.

There was hysteria, particularly on the left-hand aisle because people were going wild when he reached down to the audience. They were crying and screaming. They'd try and touch him.

And he'd tease them terribly. He was a right provocative little sod.

He'd tease people by holding out his hand to them and then run away, sort of get off on that and have a quick smile to himself. Then the jerk would run to the other side of the stage and do exactly the same thing.

And I suppose we were such gullible people we allowed him to do that. We gave him the licence to enjoy the thrill of it.

It's an incredibly mobile face he's got and it had so many weird and wonderful expressions.

When he sang 'Cracked Actor' and 'Panic in Detroit' it was just amazing.

Oh, those were the days!

And after I was just stunned, absolutely stunned. I went home sort of shocked. I remember going home as all fans do, in this kind of solitary confinement where you switch off on the train and everyone else who walks on the train you totally ignore them.

And you just sit there and you're just away.

And you think: Well, I'll never see Bowie again. It's over. Etc, etc.

That scene in *The Man Who Fell to Earth* where he uses the

gun was a perfectly accurate image of sucking the gun off and blowing it, quite frankly. And when he sucked the thing off I thought: Well, this guy, there's no end to what he would do.

And he showed his bollocks and everything on film. I didn't expect him to do that so it was absolutely shocking at the time.

He prompted something in me which I didn't know was actually there – he made it popular to sleep with men *and* women and he made it popular to be extreme – and what's more he made it possible to be like that every day.

I couldn't get that out of my mind.

It was rammed down my throat that I could dress like this now and I could go out like this and I could wear that amount of make-up because it was acceptable. To me, having that kind of opportunity was absolutely amazing. And I can only thank him.

But he was also a complete and utter enigma and the mystery that surrounded him made people fantasize.

A lot of what I read about him was fantasy reading made up for the immediate public to entertain the suckers. But then you do believe what you read. We people do believe the written word – it's all we have to go on. And kids of 16 or 18 they really take it all in because they really do worship these people.

And that's how I think it's dangerous. Because kids lose their own identity – which is so important.

The star expresses something up there that's very real to you and so you mistake that thing for yourself. And you get caught up in his life.

But you're another person with another story to tell.

You mistakenly think you can live his life and you get caught up in his success and think it's perfectly possible to achieve all those things.

They represent the success story up there and they're giving it out to the public, doling it out by the ton. Then they give out trite comments to the press and expect people to take it on the chin.

And you do, because you're so absolutely gullible.

It's almost pathetic that kind of idol thing.

But then he was extraordinary and he deserved all that idolatory, even though he's probably laughing now.

So I don't regret any of the money I spent or any of the things I used to do, the obsessions I had.

I think it was part and parcel of what I am now. I'd like to talk to him about it some time, I really would.

He was so stylish and so completely different from any other pop star of that time that he was lost in his own isolation. Because having created that complete balloon around him he mustn't let it burst. The pressure must have been enormous to keep all that fantasy going.

But he achieved it by sheer tactics, you know: Try this, let's see how the kids react to that. And then completely washing his hands of the whole business. Not actually accepting the responsibility for what he's done by becoming a besuited man with a blond hair-do and a lot of money and the ability to make his own films.

I just wonder if he doesn't think that everyone's a sucker. He's riding on the crest of a wave and he's a legend.

But I sometimes wonder who kicked it all off, whether it was some massive publicity stunt or whether it was actually David Bowie who had the initiative.

Because I'm sure he's extraordinary, but I don't think that he's so extraordinary that he didn't have a lot of help from the right people to create all that and to bring out those records.

I think he should be made aware of how he's influenced people's dress, their manners, their behaviour.

Because I now have the kind of wisdom to know how pop stars can damage people by their life-styles and by the kind of money they throw around and the kind of images they present on television.

People can get so taken away with it that they're actually in danger of believing that they are that person.

Well, I never believed I was David Bowie – I mean, I couldn't have been further from it, being rather fat and frumpy and very much a virgin – but I actually believed that I could have a relationship with him.

This was *his* influence and it was rather damaging. And

I think he's so detached now from what he's done to people that he doesn't realize in all his wealth how he's influenced them.

Because he's actually walked away from them and has lived a life of cream because we've allowed him to.

It's a terrible thing he did really.

He's got a lot to answer for.

[Julie is 25. She's an actress and worked with David Bowie on The Hunger.]

Possession

Diary of a groupie: we came together

Tuesday 9 November

This evening I arranged to go to the Camden Palace with Karen and Paula.

On entering, the first people we saw were three of The Belle Stars who always seemed to be there lately. We went straight to the bar and bought lagers, then went for a dance.

As usual, being Tuesday evening, they had a sleazy act in store which turned out to be a really fat woman aged about 60 wearing a tu-tu, accompanied by an equally aged man in a lurex jacket. Halfway through the act the woman proceeded to strip and it turned out to be quite funny.

After that was over we went upstairs to the Cocktail Bar and as usual Steve Strange was there. Karen decided she fancied him and grabbed his bum. We all fell about laughing and he turned around not knowing which one of us had done it.

Paula did the same to a man I recognized as a dancer from Top of the Pops. He also turned around but said in a really camp voice: 'She's cheeky!'

Somehow I got talking to what I thought was a girl but turned out to be a gay Welshman in full drag who spent all his time making pornographic films.

Karen dropped a glass of wine and it happened to soak Steve Strange's trouser leg. Having not said sorry, she had ruined her chances by the looks of things as he looked like he wanted to kill her.

This seemed like a good moment to go so we got a taxi, made him stop off at the Kentucky Fried Chicken, then made our way home.

I had had a really good time and we promised to do it again very soon.

Saturday *13 November*

Today Suzie and Kate came to stay as we're going to see Classix Nouveaux at Slough College. They arrived at about 6.00pm (four hours late due to Suzie oversleeping) and as I was expecting them earlier I had plenty of time to get ready.

When we got there I was quite annoyed to find we weren't on the guest list and had to pay £3 but I suppose you shouldn't take these things for granted.

Thursday *18 November*

Tonight we went to the Camden Palace again and I really think it was the best time I ever spent there.

There was really a lot of well-known people there including the gorgeous Steve Strange and Tok, two of the Flock of Seagulls and Martin Kemp from Spandau Ballet.

We gathered something was going on, and there were rumours flying about that 'The Anvil' was going to be filmed – a documentary about Visage and Steve Strange.

We were standing on the stairs when I felt a bright light on me. I turned briefly to the side and Jackie and I were being filmed – and for such a long time too. I just hope they don't edit it and cut us out.

Wednesday *24 November*

A package came for me today. I had won a competition in a magazine and the prize was the new Ultravox album 'Quartet', which, unfortunately, I already had. I think I could sell it or something but it was still a pleasant surprise.

Saturday *4 December*

Today I had a much needed lie in. When Jackie rang me at 5.30 I had not even got dressed.

We were going to see Ultravox tomorrow but we didn't have anything to do tonight so we decided to go tonight instead.

I had never been so near the front in the Hammersmith Odeon before. I really enjoyed myself, they played really well and I thought they were the best band I've seen for ages.

The only thing was that from where I was standing

I couldn't see the drummer Warren Cann who I really fancied.

I didn't see his face once.

Thursday 23 December

Today I went to the Camden Palace with Jackie, Linda and Sarah to celebrate Christmas.

On our way in we were searched so I felt extremely glad that I was not doing my usual trick of bringing in my own drink with me.

As we passed through the foyer Jackie spotted Boy George who was leaving.

But my eyes turned to X of——who was talking nearby. I knew I had to talk to him as I'd fancied him for ages.

Jackie bounded over to Boy George thanking him for getting us in at Sheffield and, much to her delight, he kissed her. He chatted briefly then left just in time for me to see X disappearing, closely followed by three Japanese girls.

I followed him for quite a way and on impulse I suddenly grabbed his hand. He turned to look at me in a way that said: Do I know you or not? I said to him: 'Can I have a kiss, please?' He said: 'Yes,' and putting his other hand over mine he gave me a wonderful kiss.

Not wanting to make too much of a nuisance of myself, I just said 'Merry Christmas' to which he returned the greeting. Then I went.

Jackie and I ran to tell Linda and Sarah who we had kissed. All the time I was thinking of going to find him again and ask for another one.

I bumped into Linda who agreed to help me find X again.

I looked all around and didn't see him so I presumed that he had gone and then there he was, large as life, talking to two men in the cocktail bar.

I watched his reflection in the mirror so he could not see me waiting for him to leave and then I saw my cue and walked over to him.

I asked him for another kiss and he agreed. I saw Linda hovering in the background. I went to walk away again, not knowing what to say or do now, but he pulled me back.

I couldn't believe it, here I was talking to the gorgeous X and he was asking me my name.

Linda discreetly left me with him and we talked for ages with me so dazed I could hardly take any of it in.

It was difficult to keep a flowing conversation going so I thought it would be best to leave while I was making a good impression rather than to stop and bore him. So I told him I was going and he asked me why. I said: 'I don't really know what to say and I don't want to bore you.' He said that I was not boring him to which I replied: 'You wouldn't tell me if I was.' He objected that he would.

Then he said: 'Do you want to know the truth? Well, I thought it was extremely courageous for you to approach me as you did. I think you've got a lovely smile and I like the way you kiss!'

I was even more stuck for things to say after that so I returned the compliment saying that I loved his smile on his last video.

This, of course, gave us something more to talk about and he told me all sorts of amusing things about the making of their videos.

After this we didn't seem stuck for conversation any more.

He asked me about my job [in an insurance company] which I tried to make sound as interesting as possible – extremely difficult!

We talked about places we had been and of course my minimal amount of travel didn't sound the least bit impressive compared to his but he politely listened.

He told me he was going away to spend Christmas with his mum.

He then asked me to wait for him while he went up to the Restaurant. This is it, I thought, he's not coming back, but in no time at all he returned, saying would I go downstairs with him?

I leaned over the railing to tell Jackie, who was sitting below, that I would see her in the foyer. She looked *so* surprised to see who I was with.

He was such a gentleman – on the way downstairs he was opening doors for me.

We talked for a while near the cloakrooms and then, after looking thoughtful for a while, X said: 'Can you remember phone numbers? Try to remember this one – it's mine. You can ring me any time. And have you got a number where I can phone *you*?'

We couldn't find any paper so I tore the back off my cheque book. I couldn't let a chance like that escape.

I saw Jackie come downstairs and she began to queue for our coats. I wondered what would happen now so, taking my courage in both hands, I asked: 'Shall I come home with you to help you pack?'

With a look that made me want to melt he said he would like me to. I told Jackie I would see her later and ring her on Christmas day. We set off to get a taxi and X insisted on carrying my bag for me.

In the taxi X told me about tricks he had played on Midge Ure the previous day, and while he was talking he took my hand and held it until we arrived at his house which was the top half of a maisonette in Highgate.

When we arrived we had a reception from three girls who had apparently waited to wish him a Merry Christmas. One of the girls kissed us all, starting with me and ending with X – it was so obvious that he was the only one she wanted to kiss.

X made polite conversation with them for a few minutes, then we went into his flat.

He showed me to the front room where I sat down on the settee. I was gazing around me at his unusually furnished living room. He switched the video on and we watched Top of the Pops, which I had already seen earlier that evening.

X asked me if I would like a drink. Thinking he meant tea or coffee I declined. He said: 'No? – but you must, it's my last day of the year in London.' I asked him what drink he had in mind and he said: 'Champagne – not your average Möet but Bollinger.' Champagne is all the same to me but it tasted lovely. Then X played a tape while we ate American candy and drank champagne.

When the tape finished, X busied himself putting his suitcases together, then sat down beside me and wrote a Christmas card and presented it to me.

It was the simplest message: 'To Mandy, Merry Christmas!, X' but to me it meant such a lot.

I thanked him and as I set next to him, my leg touching his, it was like electricity.

I felt excited by his nearness. He put his hand over and caressed my neck. By this time it was quite late. X suddenly said: 'You're not bored are you?' Nothing could have been further from the truth.

X then kissed me, at first just a peck on the lips like before. Then he pulled me to him, kissing my neck.

He kissed me passionately, yet tenderly. I had never before experienced the feeling I was now experiencing.

We kissed and hugged for a while until he took my hand and said: 'Come on.'

He led me to his bedroom which, like every other room, was painted white.

I didn't notice a lot about this room for obvious reasons, except for the framed photos of Greta Garbo. There were also several pictures of X, one of which was particularly stunning with X wearing some kind of uniform and jackboots.

The bed had no sheets on it as, he explained, he had not been home for some time. I helped him to make the bed and then we kissed some more while undressing each other – a somewhat hurried moment as the room was so cold due to lack of central heating.

He got into bed first and held the covers open for me to follow. The bed was warmer than anywhere else as he had an electric blanket. I cuddled up to him – I could have said 'no' but it seemed so pretentious somehow.

I thought so much of him – a feeling as much physical as it was mental. We kissed and clung to each other while he whispered to me, as if to say some guarded secret.

He whispered that my skin was so soft while we kissed and caressed each other.

I couldn't wait until he entered me and when he finally did it was everything I expected.

We made love slowly. It was the most sensuous feeling I have ever known. He asked me how long had I wanted to make love to him. I replied: 'A long time.' He said that he hoped he wouldn't disappoint me. He didn't.

He apologized for being bristly. I didn't mind – there was nothing about him I disliked.

Between kisses he told me that the moment he saw me he had wanted me and was so glad I came back to him, and that when he'd said that he liked my smile he also wanted to take me and squeeze my breasts – which he was doing now.

He told me to close my legs while he was still inside me and it felt wonderful because although he couldn't enter me as much as he could with them open I could feel *him* even more.

We rolled over until I was on top while he complimented me on my love-making. We rolled over again until I was under his wonderful body.

We came together – something I had always wanted to do.

He said: 'You're so beautiful you're making me come.'

I clung to him desperately and he gazed at me and kissed me more.

I lay under him for about an hour and we drifted into a sleep.

I couldn't sleep properly as I was so aware of him. We both awoke and he was now lying beside me. He pulled me close.

I laid my head on his chest and we went to sleep again.

I awoke once more while X was sleeping like a baby. I gazed at his beautiful face while he clung to me as if never to let go. I wished he wouldn't and then I knew no more until suddenly it was 11 o'clock – which was terrible as his train left Euston at 12.15.

X dived out of bed and into his clothes. I wished I wasn't there and wondered what he now thought of me, after making love to me and falling asleep and getting up too late to catch his train.

I asked him to pass my clothes – which he did, kissing me as he leaned over.

I felt relieved he didn't hate me.

I got out of bed and looked in the mirror, trying to get rid of the remains of last night's make-up and struggled with my hair to look presentable. There was no time for a wash as the cab was arriving in 10 minutes.

X flung a second suitcase on the bed and started frantically filling it. I kept getting in his way and that made me feel terribly self-conscious, but X put his hands on my hips and said: 'Could you just move a minute, sweetheart?'

It was then that I knew he still felt as much for me as he had the previous night – nothing had changed.

It came to the moment when we had to say goodbye.

He took me in his arms and kissed me. Then he pulled me to him and kissed my face and said to me: 'I would like to see you again when I get back, but it won't be for a long time.'

'When?' I asked. 'Not till the end of February. But I promise I will contact you – I'll send you a postcard.'

We kissed again. I've never known a goodbye last so long. He hugged me until I felt I would lose my balance.

He whispered again in his own special way: 'Sweetheart, I want you to have a very Merry Christmas and a Happy New Year and I will contact you – I promise.'

I turned around with tears in my eyes. I was really in love with him and hoped with all my heart that he had meant all he said.

I went home clutching my lovely Christmas card (my only souvenir) and feeling sort of sick at the thought that he might not mean it after all.

When I got home I told my mum most of the story to which she said: 'Don't depend on it.' At this I immediately burst into tears – I suppose all I can really do is wait and see.

I've got a feeling that time will go slowly now.

It seems like a dream now as I'm writing.

I can't identify the X I know with the one in the videos and photographs – the unshaven X I fell in love with.

Now when I see X in magazines or on television he seems so far away and out of reach. I've never felt so much for anyone before and that's what I'm afraid of – when you feel so strongly things tend to go wrong. I'm not a fool – I realize what men in bands are like but somehow that doesn't matter to me.

All I know is that I desperately want him again.

When I took my clothes off that night I could still smell X, his own special body smell, especially on my chest, where he had leaned on me all through the night.

Saturday 25 December
Christmas day. I awoke late, immediately thinking of yesterday – only it seems so distant now, like it didn't really happen.

I try to go through it in my head, things we said and did but it seems a million years away.

I wonder what he is doing now.

Friday 31 December
I met him now a week ago and was with him for one night only, yet he made such an impression on me.

When I think about it I can see him just using me but at the time it was so different.

I wonder if his views have changed about me now. He has not seen me for over a week. Perhaps he's forgotten I even exist.

I just pray to God just to let me be lucky this time.

Monday 10 January
Today, after not having heard from him, I decided to ring.

I rang the first time at about seven o'clock and only got the Ansafone – I was relieved in a way as I was nervous of talking to him.

When I rang again at 8.20 someone picked the phone up and I asked: 'Is X there, please?' A voice said: 'Speaking.' I was completely taken aback and I just said: 'It's Mandy!' X sounded really surprised and my first thought was that he didn't remember me. So I asked him if he did to which he replied: 'Of course I do!' That reassured me and I carried on the conversation.

I asked him about his holiday which he said he'd enjoyed.

Then I didn't know what else to say to him so I said I would go, and then he said: 'I'm really glad you rang me today, Mandy. Another day and I would have been gone again – I'm so glad to hear from you.'

So it didn't seem that he wanted me to go yet and he started to talk about the tour.

He said to me: 'I won't be back until February. I came home two days ago and I've got to pack enough things for a month and I've had to find somewhere to park my car. I wish I had longer at home because I would have liked to have seen you before I went off again.'

I was obviously glad to hear him say this and also a bit embarrassed. I didn't know what to say. In the end he said: 'Anyway, I'll see you soon – it's been lovely speaking to you.'

I didn't know what to think. Things sounded really promising but he hadn't written or phoned and he didn't make any definite plans.

I'll just have to wait and hope again.

Wednesday 26 January

Today I took a half day flexi-time from work so I could have a lie in.

I had stayed the night at Jackie's flat and left her in bed while I went to Leicester Square to buy *1984* by George Orwell. This was the only place I had seen it since I lent my copy to someone who had neglected to return it and had now mislaid it altogether.

Once in the shop, I also bought *Animal Farm* (which I half-read at school and never completed) and a book entitled *Coming Up for Air* which I liked the sound of.

From there I progressed to work, buying a salmon and cucumber roll on the way for lunch.

Thursday 10 February

Today, after trying twice yesterday, I managed to ring X and actually find him in. He came to the phone and as usual he was really nice. He told me he had been to France, Germany and Scandinavia and he had brought the weather back with him.

He told me he was glad I rang at this time and caught him as he had to go out later – but he would ring me tomorrow afternoon or evening. I put the phone down feeling not too confident.

Friday 11 February

Today I had a flexi-day off work and I stayed in hoping X would ring, although I had a funny feeling deep down he wouldn't.

My feelings proved true – he didn't ring, and although

I half expected this I couldn't understand why he led me on.

I may be wrong but I still believe he meant what he said when I was with him.

But that was now two months ago and a lot must happen to someone like him. I must also accept he probably knows a lot of people just like me.

The old cliché sums it up: 'That's life.'

I suppose it was all a dream really. I was hoping for too much and when you feel so strongly about things they always seem to go wrong.

Tuesday 24 May

It is now 12.30 at night and I have just arrived home from the Marquee. Normally after having been out I'm too tired to write my diary, but tonight I must capture my thoughts.

I had arranged to see a band at the Marquee for the second week running – this time with Debbie – and was looking forward to it very much.

Not only do I like the band a lot but I had a suspicion that X might be there.

I had a funny feeling of anticipation in my stomach on the journey down but thought it unfounded when after searching high and low there was no sign of him.

They did quite a long set, and as I'd missed the end last week, we decided to stay for the encore.

When they came back on stage the singer said: 'Introducing our special guest: from——, Mr X.'

I couldn't believe my ears and felt sick and happy amongst a hundred different emotions.

When the set was finished, I felt determined not to let him get away – I'd come too close.

I hung around for a while and walked into the hall and saw X surrounded by girls.

He started moving towards the exit where I was standing. He saw me and his face lit up. He kissed me on the cheek and held my hand and asked how I was. He remembered my name like I knew he would – other people seemed to think he would forget me after sleeping with me but now I can prove them wrong.

I just had to say something so I said: 'What happened

to that phone call?' To which he answered he had been very busy. I told him I thought he was bullshitting, and he said that he really meant to ring but people ring him all the time and he never gets round to doing anything.

I felt myself getting nowhere so I came straight out with what I was thinking and said: 'I know you will think I'm being silly but after all those things you said to me I really wanted to see you again.'

He said: 'I don't think you're being silly.' Then he said again he would ring me.

I said: 'But you said that before and didn't.'

But he persisted and promised that he would.

I told him to be truthful to me and not to say things if he didn't mean them because if he didn't want to see me I would understand.

Yet again he promised he would.

'Tomorrow,' he said.

Wednesday 25 May

A miracle happened – X rang me!

I was so surprised I didn't know quite what to say. I really didn't think that he'd keep his word.

He told me about his trips abroad and I listened, taking in every word carefully. He spoke of the band he'd guested with and said he was sorry he didn't speak to me for too long last night as he thought it was the wrong time and place. I understood what he meant because when I saw him he was surrounded by girls.

He told me people were making too many claims on him and he was not free to please himself.

I felt a bit guilty then because that was what I'd been doing.

He also said he needed time to himself because, being hardly ever at home, he can't get much privacy.

For the first time I began to understand how he must feel.

He said: 'I've got your number,' meaning he will call when he's ready, which I hope he does.

From there we left it. When I came off the phone I cried and cried.

I was not really upset but very happy because although

I know that my X has no thoughts of lasting relationships (I knew that anyway), I felt he cared enough to ring me.

For all I knew he might not even have kept my number, but he had and he used it for the first time.

I felt as if we had a special friendship, as I also thought last night from the way he greeted me and looked into my eyes while holding my hand.

I don't know what will happen now but I still feel the same as I did five months ago.

Please, God, let me see him again.

Tuesday 31 May

Today was the final day of the band's residency at the Marquee. This time I went with Val.

I knew X would be appearing again. I was still not sure exactly where I stood but had the feeling things were looking up after his phone call last week.

I waited until the end and saw him surrounded by people and knew this was certainly not the time to talk to him.

Later he came out into the bar and stood fairly near me.

I didn't think he had seen me yet and I didn't know what to do so I walked to the other side of the room near the doorway.

I guessed he would have to go back past me so I waited there talking to Val.

I could tell he was in a hurry as he was dashing every-where and he almost walked through the door without seeing me.

I called him but he didn't hear me so I pulled his arm.

He turned around and I said: 'Hello, all right?' and he said: 'Yes thanks, I'm fine.'

And that was it. He walked away again.

It hit home hard that he didn't care for me at all and I wondered if his phone call to me last week was to politely get rid of me.

I thought about the situation carefully and decided that I must never contact him or try to see him again.

I suppose I always really knew that nothing could ever come of our meeting, but I had to keep hoping.

I felt that seeing him again would perhaps change things

but nothing has changed. I don't think he wants anyone regular hanging around.

Perhaps I had a chance once but now it's too late. It was too long before I saw him again and everything is over now. I must try to forget him even though I still love him.

I feel sad but in a strange way relieved as now I know for sure that I can start planning things without him.

I wanted to grab him – close encounters

Barry Manilow fan: Our seats were in the fifth row and I couldn't believe how close to the stage our seats were.

I remember walking down to my seat and my legs were shaking so much, I felt a tremendous relief when I sat down.

Then the concert started, and after all those months of waiting he was here. I knew Barry was standing there, but my mind wouldn't accept it. It was like a mirror image of the TV screen.

Kajagoogoo fan: I stood still, just staring at them all on stage. It felt like I could not move – I was absolutely stiff for a few minutes.

Marc Bolan fan: It was like a dream. My eyes were fixed on him from beginning to end.

Who fan: During the concert I can remember feeling: This is The Who – the legendary Who. I was so amazed because the ticket didn't seem important but when I saw The Who in the flesh I was speechless.

Jay Aston (Bucks Fizz) fan: When I have seen her, every time I have thought how beautiful and sexy she is. I would feel funny inside when she started singing and after that I would concentrate on watching her every move.

Barry Manilow fan: As he walked into the hotel all the guests stood up and applauded.

I was holding onto the back of his fox-fur jacket and he turned and saw me and said: 'Hi'.

I was so stunned I opened my mouth to speak but I couldn't say anything.

I couldn't move. My legs just wouldn't take me any further.

When he spoke I was in a daze and I remember hearing his voice in slow motion.

Julie (14) [won a competition to meet the band]: The night before we met Kajagoogoo I could hardly sleep. I sort of hurt inside. I felt sick every time I thought about them. I felt like crying because I knew it wouldn't last. I'd see them and I would be there for what would seem like a second and then we would be leaving London.

We went backstage. I walked in. They were strangers we had never met before but they treated us really nice.

I was in a daze. It was absolute paradise. We had made it.

I just felt stunned and I couldn't believe it. It just wouldn't sink in.

Hollies fan: As we walked through the door I saw Allan Clarke. He was sitting round a table with his wife and some friends, together with their children. I couldn't believe it, I nearly shouted out loud – here was this great star sitting drinking tea in an ordinary café, and being ignored by everyone. We sat down nearby. I felt ill, I thought I was going to be sick my stomach churned so much. I wanted desperately to talk to him but didn't know how to. In the end my wife could stand it no longer and we got up together and went over. I said: 'Mr Clarke, sorry to bother you but may I have your autograph?' He looked up and said: 'Of course.' I told him I had all his albums and he seemed surprised. He wrote: 'Thanks, Allan Clarke' on the back of my wife's chequebook (the only paper we had) and shook both our hands. Then we thanked him and sat down, and he carried on as if nothing had happened!

Debbie, Bay City Rollers fan: We walked round and round

this building and I didn't really believe he could be in there, this was stupid.

Then we sneaked up the stairs and knocked on his door. No answer. But we knew he had to be in so we thought: We'll hang around. And every time someone came by we'd walk along the corridor all innocent.

Then, just as I was looking through his letter box, all of a sudden the door opened and there was Eric standing there. I just looked up and he said: 'How did you get in?' and I said: 'Oh, we walked.' And then my friend who had a camera, she just went hysterical. So I snatched the camera off her and started clicking. She was crying her eyes out. And I really felt like hitting her at the time because I felt: Here he is, standing here normal, and she's just going hysterical and he'll probably rush off. But he didn't. And he laughed and joked with us and we all had our photos taken with him.

I went home on the bus. I was crying all the way with tears running down my face.

That was the 3rd of December and it was my birthday the next day. And my mother put my cake on the table with – as usual – a tartan ribbon and one of the Rollers on it. And she put my dinner on the table with my birthday cards. And I just sat there crying. She looked at me and said: 'What's wrong? Don't you like it?' I said: 'I met him.' 'Who?' 'Eric.' And then it hit her what I'd just said. And I couldn't eat my dinner and there were tears rolling down my face.

Police fan: It's a really weird feeling seeing your hero whether it be acting, singing or talking.

Even now, although I've seen them for a quarter of my life, my stomach still turns over and my eyes just don't want to move away from them.

Then when it's all finished you feel stunned, sad and happy all in one.

Kajagoogoo fan: I was packed tight in a screaming queue. I felt sick and faint. I almost did faint but the thought of not seeing them stopped that.

To actually see your 'idols' in the flesh gives you an

exhilarating feeling. I feel I want to scream with happiness. But after a few hours, or the next day, I feel depressed.

Bay City Rollers fan: At the concert I remember thinking: Right, if I can get hold of one leg, maybe my friend can grab his other one and together we'll be able to get him. But I couldn't find her.

And I'm not quite sure what I'd have done if I'd got him. I've often wondered about that.

Boy George fan: When I do get to see him close up I just want to grab him and cuddle him. I love being near him. I think he's lovely.

When you're near him it just hits you all of a sudden that you're happy.

He fascinates me.

Eileen: stuffing Barry Manilow

The dolls started in Christmas 1982. I made a prototype doll having seen Barry on television.

I hand-made the entire jacket. I got some silver lurex and all the sequins and stuff. I couldn't call it Barry Manilow 'cos you're not allowed to – I just called it a Barry doll.

Then I went to the Albert Hall concert in January '83 and I took the prototype doll with me. Some girls caught sight of it inside my coat and they said: 'Oh, God, look at that, look at the eyes – it's got to be Barry.' I said: 'Well, correct.' 'Oh, has he seen it?' they said. I said: 'No, how could he possibly see it?' And they said they reckoned people would be very impressed by it.

Well, with that in mind I made four more prototypes and I took one of the dolls along to Arista Records. I remember it was a Wednesday afternoon, pouring with rain. I went in there and I spoke to the Press Officer. She took one look at it and said: 'My God, it's Barry. It's brilliant!' Why didn't I go and take it to Paul Pike who was handling all merchandise at that time?

When I'm making the dolls I think all the time about Barry. I play his tapes on my little tape recorder. It just gives me inspiration to do it.

I don't enjoy sewing the bodies. But I tell you what I do like: I like having a load of bodies just left as bodies – I like bodies everywhere. There were bodies at one time all over the living room table – just the basic callico. I used to hang them up on a line sometimes across the room. It was like a body shop. There were bodies everywhere. There were bodies on the settee, bodies on the table. Friends used to phone me up: 'What are you doing?' 'Stuffing Barry Manilow.' 'Charming!'

When somebody picks one up like this [one arm under doll's knees, the other under its shoulders], they start to nurse it. It's stupid really. Whether it's because people think Barry is vulnerable – I suppose he is. They seem to treat it like a baby, as if it were fragile. It's pathetic, but I can understand it.

They talk to them as well. Sometimes it's as if they're talking to a child. I do it too. And I make my dolls talk back to me in an American accent. My friend comes round and we have a bit of a muck-about with them. It's stupid and I'm thoroughly ashamed of this sort of behaviour. But, I don't know, you just talk to them. I talk to them like I talk to my animals. I suppose it's loneliness, isn't it? Got nobody else to talk to. It's like talking to yourself. Like I apologize to him if I drop him on the floor when I'm putting his feet on.

But I tell you one thing I wouldn't do. When I'm sewing him up, if I've stuck a needle in his back, I certainly wouldn't think I'm using him as an effigy or anything like that. It's not as if the thing is alive.

I guess I basically talk to my work. I think artists have done that for years gone by.

But some people kiss him. And my friends up from Yorkshire were behaving oddly enough with him when I showed one to them. They started making him dance – they kicked the legs up. 'Cos these dolls have got very long legs, you see, just like Barry.

And they do other unmentionables which is so stupid. It actually annoys me what else they do to him. I shan't even mention it. That *is* idiotic. That I don't approve of at all. I don't have to tell you what they do with him . . . I mean, they come here and they sit and watch a video and they're fiddling about with him.

[*Eileen is a professional soft toy maker. She is in her late twenties and single.*]

A piece of them – objects

Jake: I think of The Hollies every day and get moody if more than a day goes by without hearing their music.

I now own 90 different albums by the group or by Allan Clarke, plus picture singles and rarities. We paid £55 for an interview album from US radio with Terry Sylvester (who has now left the group), and £33 for a flexi-single given away free with a Swedish magazine with a message from the group in 1966. My records are secure in cases but the signed one and copies of photos of me with the band are in frames on the walls.

My other pictures, the pens they used and one drumstick are in a cabinet by the hi-fi. I also have albums of tickets, articles and photos I have gathered from different sources.

I look at my collection every day I am at home and remember each time I had seen and met them. I *most* enjoy the fact that some of the things The Hollies themselves have touched or handled.

Lesley (18): The Police fan club is very good indeed. I always write to Paul [the organizer] and I feel like I know him well although we've never met.

He always writes back and last year he got me my most prized possession. He asked Sting to sign a photograph for my 18th birthday.

I didn't know anything about it until it arrived at my house with the words 'HAPPY BIRTHDAY LESLEY – STING'. I couldn't believe it. I nearly wept in front of everybody at college. I couldn't and still can't believe that 'HE' actually wrote it just for me. It still gives me goose pimples.

Mortimer

I'm 22 Yrs Old on 22/8/83, I Have Long Black Hair, Same Style As Suzi's Parted Down The Middle. And I Work In The Furnaces In Front Of Fires All Day 7·00 To 4·30 And It,s A Roasting Job In This Weather And I'm A Singe Man, Who,s Never Had A Girlfriend, As I Don,t Think I Could Afford One With Suzi About, I Have Spent Over £5,000 On Suzi Since 1973, This Tour I,ve Just Been On Cost Me £500 Alone, With B+B Etc!

Henry (16): I don't own anything of Cheryl's but I wish I did. I know this may sound perverted, but I'd like a pair of her pants to hang on my wall! Mind you I wouldn't mind any other article of clothing or such.

The smaller items of my Bucks Fizz collection I put in drawers. The records go into cases and the larger items go under my bed. Occasionally I like to look at the things but usually I leave them until night and then 'check' to see none of the souvenirs have been jolted out of their position.

I really enjoy my collection because it feels like I have a piece of them in my possession.

I screamed your name – concerts

Debbie: The atmosphere kind of frightened me. Because, you know, you can't turn round and say: 'Keep your hands off, he's mine.' Because you've got thousands who like that same Roller.

Then we went in, and that was a mad push – put your programme down your sock so you won't lose it.

I wasn't interested in the first group. And then the interval came and your stomach's turning and turning and the lights went down low, and the MC came out and all the fans were standing up on their seats to dive over, and when they actually came on with the rush of all the fans we got splattered onto the stage.

It was really good.

This bouncer, I remember him grabbing me round the throat and my friend bit him and then it was just going great.

I was trying to grab Eric's trousers. I got them the third time and the bouncer hit our hands and pulled him away.

After about half an hour of that my back was aching so I thought: Right, I'm going to get right up to the front. But just as I got there this bouncer came up and grabbed me and picked me up.

I said: 'Leave me alone,' and he said: 'You're going out.' I said: 'I'm not. I'm staying here.' So he goes: 'Right, you are out.' And then I started crying because I thought: After all these years to be thrown outside. You might chuck me right out of the building and I'll never see them again. And there's me crying.

So I grabbed onto a railing and then another bouncer came up and by the time they finally got me out I had four bouncers and a policeman on me.

I remember them dropping me on my head. I just banged to the floor. But that didn't worry me. A St John Ambulance woman came up and said: 'You can go back in if you stop crying.' So I stopped crying. 'Can I go in now?' 'No.' So I started crying again. I could hear the music going on and the girls screaming. And in your head is going: What do they look like? What are they doing? And what are you missing when all the screams go up?

In the end she said: 'OK, you can go in now,' and I wanted to hug her but I thought: It takes too much time, you know, that very second I could be in there.

So I got in again but all the bouncers were in the aisle so there was no way I could get back down to the front.

I stood on a chair and I can remember I just went hysterical. I can remember thinking: This is stupid. But I couldn't stop screaming and pulling my hair.

The girl next to me just stared at me.

I had butterflies in my stomach and my mouth kept going white all around and I'd wipe it off.

And I'd think: What on earth's this? I was actually sort of foaming at the mouth.

And I felt sort of sick thinking: Maybe another fan will get to them and I won't.

I just wanted to get them.

And then you just climb on anyone's shoulders, people you don't even know.

And when they finally ran off stage I ran down to the front. But it was too late, they were gone. I found my friend and we both cried.

I went home and I thought it was the happiest day in my life.

But when I woke up next day I felt I wanted to die.

They'd gone, you know, and I'd probably never see them again. So I spent about a week crying. I just couldn't stop crying. I couldn't eat, I couldn't play my Rollers records. I was just mad.

Derek (18), Nena fan: It's important to get as close as you can. It is for everybody and that's why there's always a crush at the front.

You want her to notice you, to say hello, to touch your hand. And then if she touches you it's electrifying.

Afterwards you feel you could go and sit down at the back of the auditorium in the last row and just be happy because she's noticed you – you've got what you wanted.

Helen (22), Barry Manilow fan: The first thing that hits you is the piano. It's there on stage and it's all covered over.

Then the tense excitement, almost verging on hysteria. I feel I've got to cry or I've got to laugh or I've got to do *something* or I'm just going to stand there and scream and scream and scream. I'm very, very tense.

Then when he comes on we all go bananas. We all leap up and down and shout and yell.

It's not just him and his music, it's the way he involves his audience. And how the audience responds back to him and how people in the audience respond to each other.

If someone cries during a particular song, someone, maybe a complete stranger, will put a reassuring hand on their shoulder.

Everyone understands what everyone else is feeling.

So it doesn't just come from him, it comes from the fans too – it's a combined effort.

When I come out of a Barry concert I've clapped so much my hands are swollen. And I've got no voice for days afterwards. But I've had the best of times. I feel pure, ecstatic joy while I'm there. I know I'm having the best of times. And it's the only way you can show him how much you love him – by leaping up and down and shouting.

So we sing, we clap, we dance, we shout things out to him – we have a good time and we're on a permanent high during the whole concert.

Afterwards it's numbness again. It's horrible.

After Blenheim we got back home at five the following morning. And I just sat there from five o'clock in the morning until about six in the evening and I just cried all day. I don't know why. I just did it. I couldn't pull myself together at all.

Sally (17), Kajagoogoo fan: You get this knot in your stomach and with the beat of the music your chest starts to pound. It's just amazing. A great feeling.

You're on such a high, you really are, just the atmosphere around you. Then you come out into the cold night air and then it's finished. You just feel empty, like you've used all your energy up. You just feel weak. Then you come home. You get into bed and your ears are ringing. They hurt sometimes, your ears, from the noise.

Marnie: Then at 8.30 Harvey Goldsmith announced: 'Ladies and gentlemen, for the first time in five years: David Bowie!'

Suddenly I could feel a presence like nothing I've ever experienced before and these bright lights were shining and this man waltzed in casually but a bit afraid (understandable with about a thousand people gawking at him).

He began singing and I felt a big lump welling up inside me.

I was almost certain I was going to throw up but instead I just choked up and tears were streaming down my cheeks. If I'd carried on I'm sure I would have filled the arena. Mum said to me: 'Calm down,' but I just replied unashamed and astonished: 'I can't help it.'

I had a mixture of changing feelings inside me. I felt shock, happiness, fright, hysteria and a sort of perpetual dream state feeling – all at the same time. It seemed unreal. It still hasn't really sunk in.

These new feelings made me realize just how much I

care and really love that man. I know if I met him one day and he was just one of life's business men I'd still love him – as plain David Jones.

He wriggled and twisted his slender body round the stage and it was fantastic and marvellous. He sang 'China Girl' and I thought it was so beautiful the way he made his eyes, voice and body all speak at the same time.

He glanced for a moment in our direction. I caught his glance and it seemed like there wasn't a soul there at that moment in time. There was just me in my seat and he was crooning and pouring that beautiful love song out to me and just me.

It was so unreal. The sounds were strange. I could hear Bowie's breath on the microphone.

After it was over I felt awful but I thought: I'll get to meet him one day.

Dear Nick,

There you were right in front of us. I just couldn't stop screaming and calling your name. I went all hot and cold and I felt completely drained. The moment I had been waiting for for two years had finally arrived.

I screamed your name. You looked at me and smiled. (I know you smiled at me because you looked straight at me.)

Well, at that point I went crazy.

It was like a dream.

Chains – telephoned fantasies

Woman: I have a fantasy about David Bowie. I dreamt I took the female lead in *The Man Who Fell to Earth*. As we lay intertwined, naked on the bed, he proposed to me and proceeded to taunt me with a pistol by licking the barrel and pointing it up my crutch. There you are. Thank you.

Man: Wendy from the Plasmatics. My fantasy is to bite off both her nipples at the same time. And then taking the gun she carries and exciting her with it. And giving her an orgasm at the same time as having sex with the guy in the group. It may sound silly but it's what I fancy.

Young girl: My sexual fantasy with a star would be with David Bowie. I would make mad, passionate love to him all day and evening. He would whip me with chains till I was bleeding but I would love it.

Derek: dreaming in German

I've never felt any sexual attraction towards Kim Wilde although I do find her good looking and I've got pictures of her up on my wall. I find her body good looking but it doesn't arouse me sexually. It's just that her image is a good image which I like to look at. I like to look at the way she does her make-up, her features, her eyes, the shape of her lips, her shoulders, her hair.

With Nena it was a more sexual experience. I found Nena a very attractive woman, a very sexually attractive woman, and I managed to satisfy myself through looking at her.

I had listened to a song by Nena which was her first hit in Germany and I thought: Oh, that's a German sounding Kim.

And I switched from Kim to Nena.

At first I hadn't even seen a picture of her so it was purely her music I enjoyed. In fact I enjoyed thinking: Well, I'm liking this person for their music rather than their image.

Then when I saw the image I liked that a lot too. I thought it complemented the songs and I've been a devoted fan ever since.

It usually happens in a half-asleep situation. I'll be asleep and drift out of sleep and have a fantasy and masturbate.

I masturbate using my hand and rubbing myself against the bed. It happens perhaps once a week.

Sometimes I'm asleep and I wake up just as the orgasm is coming.

The image of her in the fantasies is usually a picture

from a magazine or record cover. I imagine her with me in the room.

What will turn me on will be her face, her mouth and the way she laughs. And her eyes, her teeth, the way she walks. Like she is on stage and on television – the way she laughs with her mouth open, the way her eyes move, the way she opens her eyes, the way she frowns, the way she giggles, how she smiles in a sort of teasing and provocative way.

That's what turns me on rather than thinking about her breasts or her thighs.

But I do imagine her vagina. How it feels rather than how it looks. Because I don't really know about her body.

I started having the fantasies before I met her. Then when I met her it reinforced what I'd thought before and they were stronger because I could imagine more. It was a 3–D person instead of 2–D.

The way she laughs and the way she speaks is cute. So they come into the fantasies. But while we're making love she is completely serious. And then afterwards she laughs and jokes and giggles – she does giggle an awful lot.

When we make love she teases and provokes. She tickles me and passes snide comments. I call her Nena or the German for darling. I speak German to her – German is my second language and I can dream in German.

She's a passionate, close, warm lover, caressing me all over and I do the same for her. Sometimes we have oral sex as well – mostly fellatio. Or I see her showering and go into the shower and she feels my erection and lets me inside her.

Afterwards she says I was great and I was the best and things like that – always complimentary things, because they're my dreams so it has to be OK for me.

It will be a whole evening session, a whole night from say 10 o'clock in the evening until the morning, or until we just fall asleep from sheer exhaustion.

Sometimes it gets to a stage where it doesn't matter whether it's Nena or not. It could be any woman. Because I suppose about two or three minutes into the fantasy it's just the normal fantasy of 'a woman' – you can't really see or really recognize or smell of anything.

Just all the womanly things detached from any sort of person.

When Nena first touched me it felt like a current passed through my arm. My body had come into contact with the star.

That star and you, you've both had a point in your lives where you've been together. That's how it felt like for me. You've had that one moment.

Then maybe you look for another experience. Like talking – where she will hear you and she will answer you – you will exchange words.

I suppose then it would go on to – it will start off with eye contact, then tactile contact, then speaking and then physical contact and then kiss and then more . . . like, say, sharing a day with her.

With Nena I've had eye contact, shaking hands, talk and a kiss.

I kissed her and she giggled and I thought it was cute, like she was thinking: Oh, I'm being kissed by this guy.

I felt: She is being shy towards me whereas I should be shy towards her.

I kissed her on the lips. She was taken aback, taken by surprise. I just felt good, just happy at that moment.

But it wasn't as good as when she touched my hand because that was more like my hand was actually chosen. I think there's a lot more contact from one person to another through the hand rather than through the lips.

[*Derek is a 19–year-old clerk and the son of a customs official.*]

Suzy: he rides me like a stallion

I have so many fantasies. It's gone back ever since I knew about him [Nick Heyward], first saw him on TV. Used to be innocent and then, well, more of an age now so . . . I suppose I got a bit bored with all the same dreams and there being no sex in it and they just began.

Looking at his photos I imagine he has a big cock. About a good nine and a half to ten inches. A nice size. So there's more to suck, lick, hold and generally excite in a sexual way . . . A bit like eating a sausage . . . with a tiny eye right at the end.

Maybe I'll go under, lick his scrotum, hold it, tickle him.

And with me it will be: legs open, tongue wide as anything, and as far as he can reach into the vagina.

And then just licking all round.

'Cos when I had it like that with a fellow I liked it so much I didn't want him to stop.

Then he'll stroke the pubic hair and outline of my vagina and maybe feel inside and it hurts so then he says: 'Oh, I'm sorry, love,' and he pulls his finger out and licks me again to heal it, kiss it better.

I left school six years ago and I had two jobs – in a canning factory and a clothing factory. I was made redundant from each one and then I went on a two-week training course. But I'm still unemployed after two years. There's nothing much going out here in the country though I may find work in the fields, even though it can give you backache.

To pass the time of day I think about Nick when I'm walking down the street, shopping, hoovering, washing up, watching TV.

I read a lot about him, collect his pictures, send them to other fans of his. And I've written him quite a few letters – but he's so busy and that. He does his best though and I like him very much.

I keep all my pictures of him under my bed. Sometimes I'll come in here and look at his photos and feel in a sexy mood, or just kiss his picture.

Or I'll play his records. That makes me happy and I imagine he's singing to me and I'm travelling around with him to Scotland or Malta or Antigua or wherever he's going.

Or he sets off to America and I follow him, pretending I'm a stewardess or something.

There's always plenty of dreams to think about.

There's a nice picture of him from *Smash Hits*. He's in a wicker chair, and his eyes are saying: 'Come on.' So you're standing in a newsagents thinking: Oh yeah?!

He's in a white shirt with his nice grey pegs on. Really

smart. But it's the eyes and how he looks that makes you want to touch his hair and what have you.

When he looks at you like that for six to eight minutes it makes you feel weak at the knees.

I've got another photo of him actually on a bed. It's a real turn on. He looks like the kind who says: 'Come on now.'

You can actually see his scrotum in that one. So I touch the picture and try to take off his belt and trousers, undo the zip.

And I kiss his lips and touch his hair. I actually look at the picture and pretend he's looking at me and I run my tongue over my lips like he's kissing me.

Sometimes I put my arms round myself and imagine it's him.

I like his eyes. I like his height. I like his hair and his lips. I like the way he smiles and the way he talks and laughs. And I like his figure. I think he's got a nice little bottom. Sometimes I just give him a pinch or smack his bottom and that helps. Say if he comes around and we're married and he gets in your way when you're cooking and that, I'll just pinch him or smack him to keep him under control.

I was about 12 when I had my first orgasm. A nurse at school told me about sex and how you can reach an orgasm. So I moved about like she said, rubbing against the bed. I sort of got a reaction and found a little bit of wet and it was an orgasm.

And one lunchtime at school I was sitting at a table and a boy got his hand and went up my skirt and tickled around and that felt nice. He just stroked and I liked that – I felt excited.

Sometimes I might just be watching Nick on telly and I just come – just like that.

It's a tingling feeling, maybe a very fast beat of the heart and butterflies in the stomach. Like when I first saw him – that was the feeling. And it was nice.

I'm easily excited and I orgasm easily. I'm a sensitive person, nervous, so that helps.

Mostly I orgasm at night when I'm thinking about him. Sometimes in the morning. Not much during the day.

I don't like to use my hand 'cos I've heard you can damage yourself like that. So I get into a comfortable position in bed or I move around in a chair.

When I'm in bed I lie either on my back or to one side. And I lift my legs up to my stomach because that's how I can get most comfortable. And while I'm lying on my side I'm thinking about him but when I'm going to have an orgasm I'll lay on my back. And then I just push and rub on the bed.

To reach a climax it's like groaning. A lot of groaning and then going 'aaah!' afterwards. Not like you go 'ah' to a baby but in a Donna Summer way.

Then I imagine he's to one side of me and I'm still on my back and I fall asleep with him in bed with me till morning.

Sometimes I orgasm but I don't feel satisfied. You get frustrated but you think: Well, I'll try again tomorrow night, dreaming about him.

Making love is very nice. He rides me like a stallion. It's like rocking, sitting in a rocking chair. Like I'm the horse and he's got the rein.

He's tender and gentle and rides me like a stallion. He'll start off slow and then he'll go galloping away.

Say it's a winter evening and it's getting cold. We put the fire on and he lays down and he's got his head on my lap and he looks up to me and says: 'How about it?'

I lay down with him by the fire and we just begin.

When he looks up at me like that he has the expression he has on that *Smash Hits* picture: staring, with a 'come on then' sexy look.

Sometimes he undresses himself and sometimes I'll undress him.

I start with his shirt and then his trousers. As I do it I kiss his body and then, when I get to his penis, I kiss and rub him off.

Then he'll be all naked.

When he undresses me all my clothes have to come off. 'Cos I like to imagine myself naked.

He undresses me very slowly. He touches my hair and then he touches my cheek and then he kisses my nose and then my lips and then my chin.

He kisses down till he gets to the first blouse button and slowly undoes it.

Then he kisses all over my body.

Like 'I Want to Kiss You All Over' by Exile.

He kisses and fondles my breasts. And then he touches my pubic hair and rubs underneath.

When he's got my legs open he goes inside me and rubs my legs as he's doing it. I like that too.

First of all inside me, he's all soft. Then, as he gets right inside the hole, he starts to get hard and as he keeps pushing he gets harder and harder. Then he's reached me where it's really satisfying. And then I'm holding onto his back and I'm clawing him. And making a sound like Donna Summer in 'Love To Love You Baby'.

Sometimes he licks me out first and then sometimes I suck him. Sometimes I come just from licking, sometimes from making love as well.

When we have oral sex he stays there for a long time – because that's something that really turns me on.

And then I do the same to satisfy him. And it could last up to two to four hours.

I've never tasted sperm but I imagine it's either very salty or it's like eating ice cream. Licking ice cream and tasting and then swallowing it. Just like swallowing saliva only it's like swallowing ice cream or yoghurt – and that's nice!

And then he'll go to sleep. We fall asleep together.

And when I go to sleep I dream about him with a smile on my face.

He's got a flat at Kew. I often imagine what it looks like inside.

It's a nice flat. Cosy. The wallpaper's blue and he's got quite a lot of yellow things in his flat: yellow socks, underwear, pillows, sou'westers, yellow vinyl discs, yellow book covers, yellow cups and saucers and cooking utensils.

The furniture's nice – Schreiber. And Hygena for the kitchen. He's got a nice washing machine and a tumble drier.

And Flotex 21 carpets – so if you spill tea it won't stain.

And a nice double bed. Slumberland bed.

And he puts different coloured sheets on the bed: pink or white. Or he says: 'Just go and get the pillowcases, whatever colour you like.' Or maybe he'd like to be made love to all in yellow. So we make love in yellow or we make love on the white and pink rug which is in the living room by the fire.

Or on the sofa.

Or we're in the kitchen and Nick says: 'Right, I want to make love to you.' And you could be washing up or something like that, at the stove. You're just standing there kissing each other and then he sort of lifts you up and he gets himself onto the table – careful it won't collapse! Then we just begin to make love.

Sometimes I dream about what it would be like to have his baby. 'Cos I read in a German magazine that his ambition is to have a son. We make love and decide to get engaged and then we get married. It's a nice white wedding with a three-tier cake. And about two years later we decide to have a baby – well planned for and wanted. The baby is a little boy and he's delighted. Then we go in for another one and it's a little girl. So we're a complete family.

Once I cried over him. 'Cos I saw him on television and it just made me very upset. I thought: I wish I could have him and I can't.

He was on television with two girls. I thought to myself: Oh, I wish I was as lucky as those two girls. And I could have pulled him right through the TV screen.

[*Suzy is 22 and single, the daughter of a farm labourer.*]

Obsession

Debbie: everything was Rollers

At school we used to scratch their names on our arms
with pins. Then when the scabs came off you had a great
big scar with the name on.

And if they were coming on telly I'd make sure everyone
in the family took the wrappers off their sweets before –
so as not to interfere.

Then after they'd been on, I'd feel lost. Empty.

I'd sit there like I'd lost someone.

I wore my Roller gear practically every hour I wasn't in
school uniform. I went hiking in it, I went horse riding in
it, ice skating and everything in my Roller gear.

I'd wear a V-neck jumper like some of them used to
wear, or tartan shirts and the braces and trousers and
stripey socks and badges and ties and hats . . . Everything
was tartan and I used to have my hair up with tartan
ribbons and I wore tartan shoe-laces.

And I covered my school books with pictures of them.
And my school bag had their names written all over it.

I gave up my school work. I wasn't interested in all that.
All I wanted to do was listen to the Rollers and collect
Roller things and spend most of my time dreaming about
the Rollers.

After school me and my friend Susan used to get our
tartan scarves out and we talked about the Rollers. Everything was just Rollers. We even gave up boy-friends. And
the headmaster wrote on my report that I thought too
much about them and he wished I could get on with my
school work.

I was always having rows at home. Like my mother
thought it was a waste of money. In fact, I tried running

away to Edinburgh with my friend. We didn't get very far – about 12 miles up the motorway.

Then when I was 16 I decided I wouldn't take my 'O' levels. I'd leave school and get a job and as soon as I could afford to I'd go up to Scotland and find the Rollers. And that's what I did.

My happiest times were when I lived in Edinburgh knowing that if I wanted I could just get on a bus and pop up and meet them. Zoom off, a nice day, talk to them, and you'd come back and you'd be happy.

If I could go back I'd like to live in Edinburgh and do it all over again.

We were all Roller fans then and we'd wait and sit and talk for hours outside their homes, waiting for them to come out, and when they finally came out run over and speak to them. I was never at home – I was always at a Roller's place. All the time it was Rollers, because you knew where they lived.

We used to go up to where Woody lived with his mother and father. We used to go round the back to where his father had planted lots of trees and little bushes. And we pulled them all up so we could sit of an afternoon and watch Woody playing football with his brothers and things like that.

I'll never forget one time one of my friends went up there with us. Woody didn't know we were there and he was in his bedroom and he came to the window with nothing on and stretched in front of the window . . . and she fainted.

With Stuart, we got to know where his nan lived. And then we waited and we followed her, and she went into this house so we guessed that was his place.

You'd sit outside waiting for them to arrive. You got to know the pubs they used. You might be able to learn from magazines that one of them had moved from so and so, and we'd work out where they'd gone. Or we'd bump into one of them in the fish shop, or find another fan who knew.

I was living with a Roller friend at first but we had an argument. Because after she met Woody one time in Perth she decided she didn't like him any more because his bum was too small. Which I thought was stupid. How do you like someone for six years and suddenly go off them because their bum is too small? I just couldn't get over it. And she started liking Eric who was my favourite, so that caused arguments, and then we had a huge one one day and she moved out.

Once when I was in Edinburgh and I had already met them a few times, I was working in a department store. I was in a little glass booth where you give out change for the tills. They lock you in because you've got about £2,000. So I was sitting there one day and one of the girls ran up and said: 'Guess who's just come in the shop!' It was Eric. I phoned the supervisor and I said: 'Look, Rhona, Eric's just come in. Could you let me out just to meet him for five minutes?' 'No, we're too busy.' So I said to one of the girls: 'Go and get him for me and bring him up here.' She looked at me like I was stupid and went: 'I'm not going to get him.' 'Will you come in here and take my place then?' 'No, I'll get into trouble.' Then I saw him walking up and I just went hysterical. It's something that snaps inside you. You don't say I'm going to cry over you – it just snaps. And I cried my eyes out. Because I knew he was there and I couldn't touch him.

When my Canadian pen-pal came over, I forget whose idea it was to have a séance, but we got a round table and some cards and cut them out and put them in the middle. I don't think any of us thought it was going to work. But then the glass started moving. It went round and round and all of a sudden we got through to my pen-pal's brother who'd died when he was two – which none of the rest of us knew about. And my pen-pal actually started crying so I thought it must be real.

So we started asking could we meet the Rollers again soon and would it give us their phone numbers. But although the glass was moving, none of the phone numbers made any sense. It also said we wouldn't meet the Rollers and we had to grow up. But all the time it was like whoever it was was trying to keep off the subject. And we tried to get through to one of the Rollers' mothers who was dead. But the glass just kept on saying: 'No, keep off.' Then we tried getting in touch with Elvis Presley but that was no good. So then I tried getting in touch with my great-grandfather to ask him questions about the Rollers. And all of a sudden my father's father – who I'd never known or thought about – came through. But the phone numbers he gave us didn't make sense either.

I had so many pen-pals then and we'd all swop our news and send each other stories. And you could write a book of the sex stories. Everything was in them. What each fan thought of her favourite Roller. They used to go from one person to another. I remember the first one quite shocked me but then I thought: Well, if someone else can write like that, I'll have a go. So I would day-dream and put it all in a story. Like if I day-dreamed I married one of them and had a child.

But there was this one Roller fan who really annoyed me. We hated each other because we both liked Eric. And in the stories I used to write, when I married Eric we always had a little girl and I called her Lisa. And one day I saw this fan and she said to me: 'Oh, I've written a story and it's going to happen, it's really going to happen: Me and Eric are going to have a baby called Lisa.' That really got me because that was my name and she couldn't touch it.

Once I went on a drinking spree and people kept giving me double vodkas and at the time I was too polite to say no thank you. I remember conking out and that's all. And it was embarrassing because I tried to strangle my best friend because she said something nasty about Eric. She joked: 'Oh, he's bent', and, 'Look at him, he's right ugly'. And she kept on and on and on until I just started strangling her. When I woke up next day I thought they were making it up until I saw the marks on her neck. Normally I would never do a thing like that.

Another time I was in the pub and I got tipsy and I was sitting there and there was this guy who looked like Eric. There was a girl with him and the more I looked at him the more I kept thinking: Is it Eric? I started getting really mad, thinking: Right, what's *she* doing with him? And that's when I have to stop drinking, because I don't know what I'll do.

I suppose I did day-dream sometimes about sleeping with the Rollers but then I always figured it would be like a groupie and I wouldn't want to be one of those. 'Cos when we met Eric once at his London flat he said to us, you know, 'Come in.' We all said no. He might have been quite innocent but we weren't going to take that chance. Because I'd met Woody's mother quite a few times when I lived in Edinburgh and she used to say: 'You can sleep with them any time but they won't think much of you after that.'

I knew quite a few groupies. One of them went with Eric and I think she slept with other people as well because she always had money to go to Japan and things like that. Every few weeks she was off somewhere. Sometimes I got jealous of fans like that. But I'd rather work for the money.

Once I got a letter from my pen-pal in Edinburgh saying Eric had got engaged. It was as if someone had hit me with a brick wall. I just stood there until my legs went. I can't even remember what was going through my mind – a million thoughts. I felt as though a chunk of my life had been taken out and was missing. Because, you know, you dream so much about marrying someone like that and then he goes and gets married. Thankfully it wasn't true and he's never got married. But even now I think: What would happen if he got married? How would I take it? And every year I pray he won't get married.

You take whatever you can get. One of my friends nicked the number plates off Woody's car. And I've got Alan's identity bracelet. My friend got it, she nicked it, and when she went off him she said: 'Do you want it?'

I collected their dog ends too. You see them smoking and after they've gone you go round with your plastic bag. I think I've got about six. All kept in a plastic bag which is in a tin so the smell doesn't get out. Your parents are cleaning up and they say: 'What on earth are these?' So you grab them quick before they go in the bin.

And I've got spark plugs I've pinched out of their cars.

If you know where they live and the car is parked outside you just pinch the spark plugs. I did have about four but I gave most of them away to friends.

One day we went up to Derek's and Derek had left his milk bottles out. So we pinched his milk bottles and put labels on them: 'Derek's Milk Bottle'.

I'll never sell any of it. I'd rather give it away.

But my photos are the most precious things.

I had stuff actually printed onto table mats. Boots had an offer – they were doing enlargements on table mats, so I had some done and I gave them to Eric's mother for the New Year. I thought he might see them and remember me.

When I went to see Alan at the airport one time I got a furry toy which I called Alan. And I got teddy bears and snakes in Edinburgh and toy ducks that make noises – and I gave them each a Roller name.

And you start repeating the names.

Everything was Rollers. Even when me and my friend were making chips we would cut out E's and F's for their initials so we could have Roller chips.

You just couldn't believe how anyone could talk about the Rollers from the time they got up till the time they went to bed. Me and my friends must have covered the same topics again and again: What you would like to do if you married them, what you'd have and what kind of house . . .

It was just like living in a dream. You would talk about it until someone brought you back to reality. Even now people say to me: 'When are you going to grow up?' And I just say: 'Oh, I'm not.'

When I go home now, because they've had the house changed and all the walls knocked down, my parents have had to stick all my Roller stuff in the attic. So every time I go there my dad has to go up and get it all down. I'm sitting there with all this Roller stuff 'cos I haven't seen it for so long and I still like to look through the pictures and see what I've got. And my mother goes: 'Why don't you throw it away now?' But they know if they threw it away they would never hear the end of it.

There's too much money to throw away . . . and nothing

to show for it. Including going up to Edinburgh and travelling to their houses and seeing where they were born, it all cost well over £1,000. At least. Because after a while you get fed up with totting it up and once it reached about £600 I just gave up – it was too frightening.

It's his voice – it just makes me go kind of funny inside.

But when I listen to him it really gets me down sometimes because I know he's just a dream. So a lot of times I put on a record and take it off immediately. I do still play Rollers records now and again but mostly I won't because it does bring back the memories that I'd like to meet them and I feel too old now. And Eric, like I said, is hard to find. So if you ever do a biography on Eric, you come and get me!

But I do get really depressed sometimes. I just get sort of down, don't care about anything. Like when my Japanese pen-pal lent me a tape of a Rollers concert and I must have listened to about two songs with all the fans singing along with the Rollers . . . and I just had to turn it off and I sat there and cried my eyes out.

My mother would say: 'Look, all your friends are engaged now.' Well, even now, you know, I'm not really interested. I know I'll never go out with Eric, that's just a dream, but if people won't accept me liking the Rollers then they can just get lost. Like my boy-friend I was going out with a few weeks back, we split up. He said to me: 'Why don't you stop liking the Rollers?' And I thought: Well, you like football so why can't I like the Rollers? And another boy said to me: 'It's the Rollers or me.' So I said: 'It's the Rollers.'

I always put the Rollers first. I wish I didn't. I was sitting here thinking about that the other night, thinking it's not right, you've got a life to live.

I'll be sitting talking and doodling and I'll write something like 'Rollers' or 'Eric'. I did that the other day at work. You just don't think about it in the end, it's automatic.

It's stupid really because all he is is a picture on a wall. It's just something you do. I mean I know he's real but like where I might fancy some boy in the street and know

I could go out with him, I don't think there's any chance I could go out with a Roller. Go up and talk to them maybe, and maybe sit in a café and see them around. But never go out with them. For a start I can't see them going out with a Roller fan. And I don't think I could keep quiet about being a Roller fan.

Probably if I got to know Eric I might not like him. In a way I wish I could meet him and then say: 'Oh, get lost,' and be really nasty and then I might go off him. That's what I need. But it's an impossibility because he's really hard to find.

But I don't dream so much now.

Like before I dreamt of marrying him, but now I think, well, you know, he lives in one world and I live in another. I go to work and come back and he's in America. You just never run into him. He probably goes to clubs I couldn't even afford to get in. And I mean I wouldn't even want to be with all those people.

So I've given up dreaming.

But I'm quite happy following the Rollers. I don't think I could ever get married until they're out of my system. Maybe if they completely disappeared I'd forget about them. But at the moment I've been able to follow them in Germany, through pen-pals, and now they've announced they're going to make a come-back in Britain.

[Debbie is 23. Her father is a postman. She works as a secretary for a major record company.]

Obsessed

Dear Police fan club,

I've got a question: When Sting was in London recently, was it possible that he travelled on the tube at about four pm? I was also in London at the time and had to travel by tube and I saw someone who I felt certain was Sting! He was dressed 'normally' – cords and jacket, with a rucksack (blue) on his back and was reading a book on either sociology or psychology. I wanted to ask but I was very nervous and wary in case it was the wrong person! He was only on for about four stops and he got off at Holborn. I was sitting next to him! If it wasn't him it was his spitting image!

Marc Bolan fan: At junior school my desk top was carved in song lyrics, titles and corkscrew-haired doodles! I had 'Marc Bolan' or 'T. Rex' on everything.

The whole village used to save any pictures of Marc they'd find in their papers and pop mags for me so that every inch of my walls was covered in smiling, grinning, frowning and sulking pictures of Marc.

Bolan seemed to mean more and more to me every day. But living in Wales I didn't know any other Bolan fans to share my growing interest and there certainly weren't any clubs that played Bolan music. So the lure of a big city was very strong.

I travelled to Leeds by train with a small suitcase of clothes, make-up(!) and nicknacks, and a huge case full of my Marc Bolan and T.Rex records, pictures and scrap-books.

There was no way I could leave home without them!

When I moved to Leeds I got in touch with a Bolanite pen-friend I'd had called Steve who knew of a London Bolanite who wanted to move to Leeds.

The three of us managed to rent a house together.

The house rocked with Bolan: every sound and every picture was Bolan. A nearby heavy metal club played Bolan, so we made it our regular haunt.

The year and a half I lived there holds some of my happiest memories.

Lene Lovich fan: I am 23 and single. I am working as a storeman for International Stores but recently I've been put on short-time due to a large co-op opening down the road and taking half our business. But I like being on short time – it gives me more time to write letters to other fans etc.

Dear Nick [Heyward],

I've missed nights of sleep trying to draw a map of the area you live in.

I've written 165 or more letters to people asking to meet you as well as 32 poems.

I've made hundreds of phone calls trying to get people to tell me your address or phone number.

So please, don't you think I'm a true fan of yours and that I deserve an answer to the 42 foot letter I wrote you?

Nichola: I have to shout

Soon as I wake up I never stop thinking about them the whole day. Never ever. Because in the morning I see them all round my walls. So first thing I think about is Duran Duran.

I get up and wash and I'm thinking about them the whole time. Then I go to school and I never stop talking about them to my friends.

My school books are covered with their faces so I can look at them all the time. In every space there is I write 'Duran Duran' and 'Nick Rhodes'. Often when I'm thinking about them I just write 'Nick Rhodes' on my hand or in a book. I don't realize I'm doing it, it just comes out. I can't help it.

And when it's time for bed again I dream about them before I go to bed. And I go to bed dreaming about them. I turn off the light but I can still see 'cos the light of the moon comes in and you can see all the pictures by my bed.

So I look at the posters and I drop off to sleep thinking about them.

Usually I take one of my magazines to school with me with a picture of Nick Rhodes and I leave it out during the lesson so that he's there and he's looking at you.

Because in these pictures it's like he's looking at you. And that's how I imagine it usually – that he's there and he's looking at me and he can see me and hear me through the magazine.

When I stare at one picture for a long time, especially where he's sitting on his own and staring at you, and then

I look away quickly, I can see from the corner of my eye that his lips are moving and he's smiling and everything.

He's come alive and he's watching me, and he can see and he can move. So I imagine he's here with me all the time and he's watching me all the time.

So if I do something I'm careful, because Nick Rhodes is watching me.

Like when people say he's ugly I'm careful not to get angry and swear at them. I'm careful to speak nice. Because if Nick Rhodes was in this position he'd speak nicely. He wouldn't shout and everything. So I think: Oh, he's watching me so I've got to be good.

That's not all the time because I'm not always good!

Usually what I think about is that they're human beings and they've got to be doing something this very moment and I wonder what it is.

'Cos I know Duran Duran exists. I know Nick Rhodes exists and I like him and I'm spending money buying things on him and everything.

But he doesn't know I exist.

When I first saw them in concert I went mad! I kept thinking: I've seen them in real life, in their skin!

As soon as they came on I couldn't stand up because my knees were shaking.

They were just brilliant. Oh, God, I just couldn't control myself. I was only a few steps away and I could have gone nearer.

I couldn't believe it! I couldn't believe they were there. I thought I was dreaming. I kept saying to my sister: 'I'm going to wake up and it's going to be a dream.'

I can't write down my feelings for Duran Duran. I always speak them. Because it's such a strong feeling. You can't write it down because you can't find the words. You have to shout it out. When you really get talking about them it makes you happy and you just feel like shouting out how brilliant they are.

And at their concerts you can scream and it makes no difference because everyone else is screaming.

But you can't really do that outside because everyone will hear you.

Sometimes I can't wait for school to finish and the nights when I can go back and think about him. So that I can go to sleep and get rid of this horrible feeling.

Because sometimes this feeling is really horrible. It makes me feel so depressed that I can't wait to get to sleep. When I'm asleep is the only time I don't have this horrible feeling.

Sometimes it's all right. Sometimes I feel closer to them when I've just seen them on TV. But when I haven't seen them on TV and I haven't seen them for ages, that's when I have to go to sleep to get this feeling out of my stomach.

As soon as I wake up in the morning it's there again, in the bottom of your stomach.

Sometimes it's really strong – that you love them and everything. It's an emptiness in the stomach which just makes you feel depressed. It's a heavy, horrible feeling – kind of a sad feeling.

And I never had this feeling before I heard about flipping Nick Rhodes, before I knew he existed.

I imagined we went to America in a plane and we were in a really nice, luxurious flat and we were eating strawberries.

Just a really lovely house, and me and Nick.

There's all nice, pure white walls and white furniture and a furry pink carpet. And a glass table with glass cups full of strawberries. And one of those mirrors with the kind of rimming round the edge that lights up.

The lounge goes into the bedroom. A green furry carpet, with green walls.

And the kitchen is green as well, with all this very modern plastic stuff – like they've got at Pearce's in Enfield Town – hanging on the wall.

When we're in a restaurant together it's always a nice place with Duran Duran playing in the background and those low lamps you get in Chinese restaurants. And all five of us sitting there. We're all talking – we never get round to eating. You can't really hear what we're saying, you can just hear the murmur of everything.

But at the cottage it's just me and Nick Rhodes. It's always snowing and we never go outside.

The fireplace is bricks and there's a mantlepiece above it with pictures of Duran Duran in frames leaning against the wall.

And it's all warm with no spiders coming through the bricks or anything.

And a brown woolly carpet.

In front of the fire there's a great big white sheepskin rug. And a brown puffy couch. And behind that a table with drinks. And a television in the corner. And usually we're sitting in front of the fire having sparkly lemonade.

In that cottage we're mainly silent, we just say a few little words. Kind of a quiet mood.

Our first kiss was in that cottage.

It just happened out of the blue. We were in that cottage and we kissed.

And the next thing I knew we were in bed.

He's soft and he's gentle and he's sweet. And then he asks me to marry him.

I've never actually imagined marrying him. I only imagine him asking me to marry him and that's as far as I go.

'Cos when you're married there's nothing much more to think about. You've got there.

So I just think of him asking me to marry him and then I go back to the beginning and start all over again.

Whenever I see them on television it gets a lot, lot stronger. And I realize how much I do like them. Because it kind of fades away when you haven't seen them on TV. When they go away it fades away. And you don't feel as much. But when they come back you realize how strong you like them. And I realize how much I love Nick Rhodes and how much I like Duran Duran.

When I found out Nick Rhodes was getting married to this Julie Anne I went really mad and started punching the walls.

I didn't scream or anything because if my mum found out I was punching the walls she'd go bonkers.

And I had a picture of Julie Anne and Nick, so I scribbled all over her face.

After that I couldn't stop crying. I just couldn't stop. My God!

I remember it was a Sunday evening and I was in my sister's room and I read it in *The News of the World*. And I felt tears coming so I went out of my sister's room and ran upstairs. I couldn't stop crying the whole day.

Now if I think about it I just break down. Like if my mum has a go at me or something, I just come in here, see all his pictures, and I remember he's getting married and I just can't stop crying.

I cried at school too. That was so embarrassing but I just couldn't help it.

And I was angry as well.

Just stupid things came into my head. I thought: How could he do it? And then I thought: Well, it's his life, isn't it? He's got to lead a life. Just 'cos he's famous . . .

I thought: Would I still love him if he was a dustbinman or something? And I know I would. Even if Nick Rhodes was just my next door neighbour I'd still like him.

But I wonder whether his girl-friend would. And I doubt that very much.

I hate her! She's so lucky. She's just lucky. She doesn't know how lucky she is. I just don't like to think about her because I get angrier. Hate her.

There's nothing exceptionally pretty about her anyway. Nick Rhodes could have done better.

So I wrote to him: 'I suppose it's your life – but why do you have to get married?'

I'm really going to try and stop him. Anything I can do. I don't want to hurt him but I'm going to try and stop it.

So I'll write him another letter.

My friends are writing to the paper – I don't know what they're writing but I'm going to write something as well.

Then I'm going to find out where he's staying and just go down there and . . . I don't know how, but I *will* stop them!

If it's the last thing I do I'm going to meet them all. What's the point of sitting at home with flipping posters staring at you and listening to their records? I like them so much I want to meet them.

It's so important. Not just, you know: 'Hello, you're Duran Duran. Can I have your autograph?' – and then go. I want to meet them and talk to them.

And then go out to eat or something.

Q: Do you want to add anything?
N: Yeah. Nick Rhodes, if you're reading this, come to my house!

[*Nichola is 14. Her father is an architect.*]

The wiggles in your mind – letters to David Bowie

Like a phoenix I emerge from flame
Bowie by nature – self-extension my game.
The Devil incarnate? – A mind with no name.

David,

You may recall me from a crowd outside the Blackstone Theatre in Chicago last July. I gave you a blue cigarette and my coral necklace. There was a note saying I would send photos of my sculptures to an address in London.

Things went rather badly for me when I returned to Philadelphia. I was unable to have my sculptures poured to bronze and in fact at the present I still can't even get a camera to take photos of the waxes.

I have no idea of where you are or what you are doing. I look for news as best I can and feel rather desperate.

When I awoke this morning I was possessed by a feeling of loneliness, almost fear. As is my habit I quickly pinned the moment back and traced it to the source inside me. It was an image of you clutching something to yourself. I was shocked that it was you. I am not quite certain whether it was my own loneliness projected in that way or whether it was yours that I received. Since I am always lonely for you and it felt quite sudden and mildly foreign I think it was yours.

You need never be alone. My heart is always open to

your heart and I am very careful to keep that channel clean and agile. It is the only path I have to you and I prize it above all things but loneliness for you can never be a real threat. I hear you. Even if I didn't want to I would.

I am your friend, David. Feel free to push unmanageable emotions in my direction. It may help you and can bring me no harm. Feel free to draw new source from me. It may carry a flavour of me but the content will ring as pure as gold.

Your friend
Melanie

Dear David,

I hope you believe I'm Ziggy. You have no choice anyway.

I haven't had a girlfriend for five years except the rave one-night stand or the beautiful passionate prostitutes.

Matter of fact I'm going to see one this weekend. My last girlfriend five years ago put me in the nut house (the cunt!). Shit, they were the worst nights of this rotten lifetime.

Julian

Dear David Bozo,

What are you, some kind of devil/deva mind reader thief baron of coincidence – you make me crazy. Why are you dressed like my tarot card fool with the xerox inside and scary monster song – ain't you got no ethics?

About that would-be dream-incubus I wrote you about last Spring, I thought it was out to chop me to bits and I thought I'd blown up for good. Seems I was wrong about that, but I forgot about it until a situation on my night train brought it back to mind.

I kept getting pictures of the crucifixion and I was sending back pictures of a picture from Heavy Metal magazine of Prometheus chained to a rock with a star of David around him and the quiet eyes of a woman overhead.

Man, you do blow me away. Real life might be something else.

Love from your enemy

Bernard

Dear David,

I am just writing to say that it was nice to see you at the BBC Pop Awards looking so amazingly well. In fact, I was quite shocked because I have this psychic power, gift really. I saw your new hairstyle! Some time in 1986 your life-style and career will change. Does the place Dorking mean anything to you? Zowie was there too. This happened the day before John Lennon's death. Well, what more can I say.

Love Melanie

Dear David Bowie,

Hold on a second, David, this fan letter thing really intrigues me!

Here I am, a little speck on earth, sitting alone imagining that I could actually be communicating with David Bowie.

I don't think there is anyone that can compare with you for being handsome. But my admiration for you and trying to figure out whether I am handsome or not has lurked somewhere in my subconscious.

Then when that terrible John Lennon tragedy occurred the whole thing was very eerie and I felt guilty and scared of the way I was thinking although it was never really an obsession, but it might have been.

I mean, the small wiggles in your mind might just become an obsession with time.

Alan

Chloe's fantasy about The Police

My main fantasies are about Stewart Copeland and Sting from the Police. I often fantasize, as much about Stewart as Sting because whenever I am 'with' Stewart, Sting is watching me.

This is probably because as Sting gets all the attention, I deliberately go with Stewart because it's as if I know that Sting wants me too, but I won't go with him.

I'm usually at a disco or concert where I'm such a fabulous dancer that Stewart joins me and we dance and chat. Then he takes me home. In the car he sits in such a way that I can see his groin. He's wearing tight trousers and so I can see the outline of his balls. I look at it and make some witty remark. Stewart relaxes and unzips his fly so I can masturbate him. At my home we make arrangements about our next meeting. We arrange a weekend during October, then he kisses me – he thrusts his tongue in my mouth and gives me a long French kiss. Then he goes and I wallow in the memory of that night.

Sting visits my school. He's brought his son, Joe. I get on well with Joe, and as Sting had seen me with Stewart and we'd chatted before, he asks me if I want to work for him as a 'nanny' for Joe whilst the family are on tour, so he can have some evenings with his wife. I say I'll think about it.

The time has arrived for my holiday with Stewart. But I get cold and say that he should be thinking about Sonja – his girlfriend. He tells me not to worry as she's gone away and won't be back until the end of the week. So I agree to stay with him. Once in his home, he shows me his room and helps me to unpack.

I notice that he runs his fingers though my underwear. I feel my nipples tingle, and I want to touch them because they hurt so much. Now Stewart is lying on the bed, so I go over to him and undo his shirt and take it off. I let my fingers circle his right nipple. I feel it harden and Stewart groans. I slip my hands down his body and stroke the hard bulge that's growing in his pants. I unzip his trousers and pull them off. I am just about to take off his underpants and stroke his hard penis when the doorbell rings.

Alarmed, I go and answer it. It's Sting. He tells me he's left some tapes of his here and asks if he can go and get them. I'm so wound up that I let him, and quickly go back to Stewart.

I lick his thighs, slowly moving up to his balls. They are large and hot. I squeeze them. Spunk squirts up and falls on his pubic hair. I gently continue to lick the shaft of his hard purple cock, resting on the head before I slide the whole head and shaft into my mouth and sucking him until he comes. I greedily drink his hot spunk. Stewart's balls are now so hot that I gently blow on them to 'cool them down'. He's been lying down and groaning until now. Suddenly he pulls me down, pulls off my top and bra and sucks my left breast. I close my eyes, tingling sensations move up my spine, and I relax. However, I am conscious of someone else in the room. I open my eyes and see Sting in the doorway. Our eyes meet. His presence makes the ache in my groin subside. I'm angry with him for making me feel afraid – and guilty. Stewart meanwhile has got the rest of my clothes off. He nuzzles my tits and I love it, and I flatter him. He gets excited and I'm pleased.

I glance at Sting. His hands are squeezing his balls. He looks embarrassed and I laugh. Stewart turns and sees Sting, so he quickly goes.

Stewart is a good lover. I come first. We spend the weekend in bed, making love, eating foreign food and talking.

Time has passed. I walk around in a daze, reliving the weekend. Then, one day, I am sick. I sit in the kitchen with a mug of tea. I am conscious of the human life moving within me. After my visit to the doctor who has told me

I am pregnant, I feel anger. I feel used because Stewart hasn't phoned me since the weekend and when I phone to tell him about the baby he is always 'out'. I decide to keep the child. I also get a court order to prevent Stewart ever seeing the child. The baby is born on 4th July. I name him Armstrong (after Stewart's middle name). He is just like Stewart in every possible way.

Months pass. I get a job at A&M studios, so I often see The Police – and Stewart. But he does not recognize me. But Sting does and he chats to me when he has time. He asks me if his offer still stands. But I say no – he must not know of my young son. He is disappointed, but takes my address, just in case I 'change my mind'.

A week passes, and I have no regrets about refusing Sting. Besides, I tell myself one night whilst feeding Armstrong, how could I take a toddler around the world?

A Police record is on the radio. Before I can switch it off, Armstrong gets up and dances. I am so surprised that I do not hear the doorbell ring. The door opens and I turn round to see Sting applauding. 'He's Stewart's boy, all right,' he laughs – then stops when he sees the shocked look on my face.

He realizes that I haven't told Stewart and is angry, but stays and plays with the baby. He refuses to listen to me hinting, saying that it's late and he should be going home. In the end, I take Armstrong away from him and get him ready for bed.

Once I've got him to go to sleep, I start to get ready for my bath. Sting is still in the living room, so I shrug and go in the bedroom. Suddenly I feel strong arms around me, and hands cup my breasts. Sting nuzzles my ear. 'You've got lovely tits,' he croons. He squeezes me. I feel his hardness against my bum. I turn round and look into his eyes. Slowly, never taking my eyes off his face, I unzip his fly and pull down his pants.

I ease out his hard swollen prick from his small, black underpants. They are too small to contain his large balls, and I can see the swollen flesh straining against the material. I lick my fingers of my right hand and touch the swollen head. Sting groans. I ease out the entire shaft of his penis and run my hand down the shaft. He stops me and quickly takes off my clothes and lays me on the bed.

He takes off his clothes and sucks my tits before asking me if I'm ready because he certainly can't wait any longer. I grasp his penis. It is moving in my hand like a frustrated animal. I smile, nod and push his prick inside me, whilst he mounts me, and we spend the rest of the night making love.

I wake the next morning to the swish of sheets. Sting wants to make love again. But I stop him and quickly go and see if Armstrong is still asleep. I have a cup of tea, and leave some of the warm fluid in my mouth. I enter the bedroom and slide his prick into my mouth. The tepid fluid makes him groan and come in my mouth. He turns me onto my back and we make love again. However, just after he comes, he gets up saying: 'I'm sorry. This never should've happened,' and dresses and leaves the flat.

I am not surprised to find out that I'm pregnant again. I go and ask A&M if I can have maternity leave, but Sting is in the office so I run out before he can catch me. I hide in a café but he finds me and tries to talk to me. I realize that he wants to adopt the baby. But I won't let him. He tells me not to worry about money – he'll pay for everything. So I let him. The baby, Phillip, is born on October 22nd. A few days later, I leave the hospital. I quit my job and move to another part of London where Sting and Stewart cannot find me.

Here the fantasy has different endings, the most favourable being that somehow, somewhere we all meet again and are on 'good terms'. But usually my fantasy never has an ending.

[*Chloe was interviewed three years after she wrote this fantasy.*]

Chloe: and then I met them

It was the shock of seeing them. I was 14 when I first saw them on stage. I suppose there's a kind of sexual current at concerts because I thought: God! This is it!

And it all started from there.

I kept staring at Sting. And I felt my knees go weak – I know it sounds a cliché but they do! I felt myself swaying and I had to grab the chair in front of me. And I couldn't look at him again so I looked at Stewart and Andy. Then I turned back to Sting and he was playing a slow song and it seemed his voice was very soft and I seemed to be dragging towards it in some sort of way.

I was on cloud nine after the concert for about three weeks. I couldn't come down. All the time I felt very hot and flushed. I was so hot I kept thinking the central heating was on full blast, but in fact it was just me.

That night after the concert I lay in bed shivering and shuddering. I kept thinking: God, it was brilliant! I was still on a high from seeing them and I was shuddering and then I started squeezing myself, thinking: God, they were brilliant.

And I came.

It was a strange sensation at the time because I didn't really understand what it was. It was like a shudder and after I felt exhaustion and a sense of well-being.

And it happened every time I thought of the concert, every night for a few weeks after. Then when they left the country it abated. But when I read something or saw them on television it happened again.

When they came on the radio it would make me jump because I wasn't ready for it. I couldn't have any control and it unnerved me. It was so unexpected it made me jump and I didn't know what to think. So I often turned it off because it reminded me too much of the concert and I thought: Oh, God, how long will it be before I see them again?

But with the records I was more in control. I could put them on when I wanted and take them off when I wanted.

I played their two albums non-stop. And every time I played 'Bring On the Night' my stomach dropped, I felt really sick.

I was frightened sometimes because I thought: What's happening? I can't really do anything about this.

There was nothing I could do. I couldn't stop thinking about The Police. How can you? It just got to be an obsession.

When I went to see them in Tooting Bec, Sting was

wearing these tight white trousers and all I could see was his bum – nice, small, tight bum.

And when I went to see *Quadrophenia* a warm flush came over me. I suddenly wanted to go to the loo! I thought: I want to go and wee.

Sometimes if I looked at posters of him in his swimming trunks or white trousers I used to think: How big is he? And I'd look at those tight white trousers of his.

This would be last thing at night and I'd drop off, semi-conscious, and start thinking about those tight white trousers and about undressing him.

Every single day the first thing I did was go into the newsagents and buy every single magazine that had The Police in them. I used to take them to school. And my friend would bring hers too to see if she had anything different. We would read them and swop notes and all the rest of it. And I covered my school books with pictures of The Police from magazines like *Jackie*.

I used to fantasize at school whilst I was writing out questions or colouring graphs or doing a sum – so that it looked as though I was working. And people never knew. They thought I was busy working. Especially with boring lessons like Maths. I'd be staring hard at this logarithm and all the time I was thinking: This is boring, I'd rather be with Sting.

Sometimes during Biology or Sex Education the lab smelt of chemicals and ether so you'd just whisk off on it, in a dream situation.

In fact, during Maths and Biology I could get high just by thinking about it, depending on what I'd read recently. Because Sting would talk blatantly about his sex life. For instance, I read a thing in *Ritz* magazine saying he did it on the dining room table. So obviously I would be thinking about that. And about trying out various different ways and positions.

I didn't really need to masturbate when I was thinking like that because I could actually get an all-time high just fantasizing.

I would be sitting in the lesson, staring hard at a logarithm, and I would actually orgasm!

I would actually come, right there in the class-room.

But I learnt to cover it up. I felt guilty and I learnt to shut myself off.

The most intensely pleasurable thing about the fantasies was that they were secret. No one else knew them. Also I felt in some way they could become true if I made the effort. Because I had their addresses, I knew where they lived and I knew people who had travelled all the way down from Scotland to meet them. So I thought: Well, I live in London and any time I want to I can meet them.

Only I didn't really want to. Because in some ways I was afraid the reality wouldn't be like the fantasy. And that was confirmed in the end.

I was a virgin then. But I didn't have any idea to sleep with anyone because I was so het up because I wasn't sleeping with Sting.

I had met a guy on holiday and we swam together in the nude. I'd seen his penis – I'd seen it erect and I'd seen him come.

But I preferred my fantasies to reality because they were safer. I also had my reputation to think of because being at an all girls school if they found you were sleeping with anyone it was murder. You were branded.

Anyway I just wanted Sting and no one else.

And then I read that Sting was married.

There was this magazine. You know these fact sheets they have. And Sting said: 'Married with one child.'

I suddenly felt ill when I read that. I immediately phoned my friend who confirmed it. I couldn't believe it. I slammed down the phone on her. I didn't cry but I felt such a deep sense of shock. It took me about a week to get over it. I couldn't believe it.

Around then I had a dream that I was late for a concert. I was running to get to the concert but for some reason I was running on the spot. When I got there the concert had just finished and all the usherettes were sweeping up. And there was this feeling of frustration. So I just rushed home and found they'd come to my house and I'd just missed them.

Another time I dreamt I went backstage and Sting was asking me history questions and I was answering them correct straight off. And he kissed me and said: 'Brilliant.' Then I woke up. And the whole day I could feel the kiss on my cheek. Because when I woke up it felt wet.

In my dreams I felt warm. Like when I watched them on television I felt warm.

When they talked on television I could hardly concentrate. I couldn't really hear what they were saying, because I was staring so hard at them. And when I saw the videos round at my friend's we used to press 'pause' loads of times. Like when he sings 'Don't Stand So Close to Me' and takes his shirt off – we'd play that bit again and again and again.

But there was anger in it too. Because *they* had no idea I had these feelings for them. It was very frustrating really because I didn't really want to like them, you know. Because they were unobtainable – they were married and they had kids; they were feeling perfectly happy in life. But at the same time you couldn't go off them. It was like stuck in the middle.

And I suppose what made my anger more frustrating was that I couldn't direct it to any person. I had to direct it to the band but the band weren't there. They were just like a picture on the wall.

All this continued for two years, from when I was 14 to 16.

Then, as I changed to sixth form college, I was changing as a person and my attitudes changed as well.

Also at that time *Ghost In The Machine* came out which wasn't half as good as the first three albums. It was quite political as well and I don't like political songs. And then Sting was going through his millionaire stage: 'I'm so rich but I'm so depressed I want to die.'

When I went to see them at Wembley Arena I was looking forward to it but this time it wasn't half as good.

Sting was sort of playing *at* us, not *with* us as he had before. And I resented that.

Because the reason I'd liked them was because they were so naïve and so fresh, but now they weren't. Suddenly they were great big rock stars in Wembley Arena.

So it faded. And then I met them. And that crushed it for me. I thought: Oh, God, that's it.

It was Sting and Stewart, in a pub. And they were being so pretentious and they were being really nasty.

I just couldn't believe it because they were so different from their interviews.

It was a Saturday and my friend and me had been wandering aimlessly round the back streets of London. I suddenly thought: Oh, I'm thirsty, I want a drink. And we were sitting in this pub having a drink and my friend said: 'Oh, my God! Look, look!' 'Oh, no, it's Sting!' 'Go and talk to him.' Because she knew how much I ranted and raved over them.

I said: 'No, no, I can't. You go,' that sort of thing.

And while I was plucking up courage they started talking and having an argument.

I was really shocked at the time, really shaken. They were having a generally bitchy time: I'm so depressed, I'm so harassed – all that business. It really shook me up. I remember going weak at the knees. I was staring at him. It must have been so obvious, this schoolgirl with her mouth agape. First I was thinking: Is that him? Isn't that him? And then I was plucking up courage. I wanted to latch onto the conversation so perhaps I could join in. But there was something about them which my instincts told me: I don't want to go over there.

I suppose it just shook me because I'd built up this picture of him and he didn't fit this picture at all.

We went out of the pub. We decided we'd go out before they did. As we walked out we turned round and said: 'Goodbye.' And Sting said: 'Oh, yeah, goodbye.'

I felt a lurch in my heart but I managed to walk out.

I felt sad, disappointed. It hadn't been like I thought it would be. All my fantasies about meeting him, slipping over and chatting to him, they totally collapsed.

And later that day I was telling my friends: 'Hey, guess who I met – Sting.' And they said: 'Wow, what happened?' 'Well, nothing.'

Even so, I've got fond memories. And I've still got the posters up at home because I never had the heart to take them down. Felt like a traitor.

Because obviously they were my obsession for two years

and you can't really cut two years out of your life. Whatever kind of relationship it was I can't forget them. They'll always be there.

[*Chloe is 18 and a university student. Her father is a solicitor.*]

Nancy: it took a lot of courage

I first became aware of David Essex when his first single, 'Rock On', was released.

I felt very drawn to him. He had something special about him. I don't mean only his good looks and good voice, but something else.

Anyway at that time I was about 20, so probably thought to myself that the feeling I had towards him would pass, but in fact, as I got older, it became stronger.

Then I read an article in *The Sun* newspaper about David, saying he was lonely, etc. I don't know why, but after that I had a very strong urge to meet him. It was terrible, it just took me over. I couldn't think of anything else.

I was depressed, desperate. It was weird, but I knew no matter what I did, I couldn't shake this feeling.

I mean, I like to think of myself as quite an intelligent person. I'm now 29 years old, married with three children and I work for the Social Services as a Community Care Visitor visiting the elderly and disabled in their homes.

I just didn't know why, but I was just desperate to meet him. It was the worst feeling I have ever had.

I decided to phone the reporter who had interviewed him, to see if she could help. It took me a few days to pluck up enough courage. I would just sit there staring at the phone. (By the way, I hadn't told anyone else how I felt, which seemed worse, having to bottle it.) Eventually I dialled the number and asked to be put through to her desk. First I got the wrong reporter, which made me more nervous. Eventually I was put through. I was very nervous but took a deep breath and explained to her that I wanted to meet him and could she suggest any way I might try.

At first she laughed, which made me feel terribly embarrassed and hurt, as I knew she was mocking me. I think she must have realized this because then her tone changed and she asked me if I felt like writing to him.

At first I said no because he too would think I was being silly. But then she said what a nice man he was and she would send the letter to him if I wrote it.

Again it took a lot of courage but I did. I explained how much I needed (not wanted) to meet him and that I wasn't a teeny-bopper or anything like that. Just wanted to say hello, how are you, etc.

I think, by this time, it had become a sort of obsession. It was a bit scary, but it was like when you see somebody in a room or at a party and you know you have to meet them.

I tried to put it out of my mind but couldn't.

Anyway I got a reply, about three weeks later, from his secretary. It was just a note saying David asked me to thank you for your letter *BUT* unfortunately etc, *NO*.

A photo was with it signed 'To Nancy – David Essex', which I don't believe he signed. Probably she did.

I felt even worse than before. The feeling lasted for quite a while.

I tried writing twice more.

I felt pretty stupid but this feeling wouldn't go. It was so frustrating. I mean, just to have said hello, goodbye would have been enough. I thought about other people who met the person they want to but with me, no one wanted to know. They wouldn't take me seriously.

Then last summer I went to see him on tour, at Margate.

I know it seems strange, but I was disappointed. I sat there watching him but felt numb. All I could think of was everything I had been through this last year because of you up there.

I only wanted to say hello to you, that's all, but you couldn't spare me that.

I felt a bit resentful, I must admit.

Near the end of the show, we were allowed up near the stage. At first I hesitated because it was nearly all teenage girls, but then I thought, what the heck, so I went closer.

I suppose I was about five feet away from him and again

I thought so near and yet so far. At one point he looked straight at me, right into my eyes.

I know it sounds daft, but at that moment I felt as if he knew what I was feeling.

Later, my friend and I went to the stage door.

But I realized I wasn't the same as all the other girls there. I felt awkward and uncomfortable. They just wanted a glimpse of their 'idol' so they could scream and swoon at him because he's a pop star.

I wanted to meet him as a person, just that.

Then his bodyguard came out and pushed everyone out of the way, was very rude and moved the Landrover further towards the stage door. Some girls behind me said that David usually signed autographs but made you line up to be fair.

At that point I felt great, thinking well, at least I might get to say hello to him, even if I would just be a face in the crowd.

I was wrong.

He came out with a bodyguard either side, his head down, and got straight into the back of the Landrover. He didn't look up at all.

Some of the girls banged on the window and called him but still he didn't look up. They weren't shouting, screaming or anything, just calling him, but he didn't even bother to look at them.

I know he must get sick of girls screaming at him, but I couldn't help feeling how rude. A smile doesn't cost much. Or a wave. Just something instead of complete ignorance.

And then they nearly ran people down with the Landrover. It sped off and some of the girls had to move out of the way really fast.

I think that if, one day, I discovered why I want to meet him so much, the feeling will go away, but I suppose only time will tell.

Two groupies: Lynne and Kelly

[*Lynne, 19, and Kelly, 20, have been following bands since the mid-seventies. Lynne is single and works as a clerical assistant, Kelly is married and unemployed.*]

Kelly: The first rock star I ever went with was Richard Jobson from The Skids. I was really young and I was sat in this bar and he was really flattering me. I thought: Oh, well, this guy's in love with me. I was 16 and I was just so flattered he was paying me some attention. He was sat at the next table and I was with a friend and then he came over and he had this bag of grapes – kept offering me grapes.

Lynne: You didn't tell me that bit!

K: I don't tell you *everything!* So he kept offering me these grapes. And then my friend went to the toilet and he was saying: 'Come back to the hotel.' And I thought: Oh, he just wants a drink. I went back to the hotel and went into the hotel bar and then he said: 'Come up with me.'

And I sort of went upstairs.

Up to that point I didn't really know what I was in for. But he was really nice. He didn't abuse me or throw me out of the room afterwards. And I stayed there all night – I got my friend to phone my mother.

We had sex and that was that.

Afterwards I was a bit sort of doubtful, insecure, you know. He probably thinks I'm a right old slag, everything like that.

L: That's always there, that feeling, because they get other girls so easy and you think: Do they think of me the same way?

Its probably impossible that he's ever going to recognize me again, but whenever I see him in a club or something I'm hiding because it's like embarrassing.

K: I suppose all music portrays sex. I mean, the first time I saw Classix Nouveaux on stage I was just captivated. I couldn't believe it. I mean Sal, he's gay, but he's got this real – I don't know what it is about him but honestly, you can't believe what you see. And when I'd seen them a few times I just couldn't stop going.

L: It's also something to do with admiring what they do. If you really like it and they're successful . . . It's difficult to explain.

K: We started going to every concert we could go to. We used to go abroad, all round England.

L: Kelly used to come and stay with me, didn't you? And we used to go to clubs and things. We went to three countries with one band. We went to Italy, Holland and Paris.

K: Sometimes we used to get lifts and that with them but most of the time we'd travel separately.

L: Trans Alpino!

K: Sometimes we'd fly. But only when we could afford it.

L: 'Cos when we go abroad, although we know they'll probably put us up, we like to have our own room and everything. Because, of course, if they pick somebody else up then we don't get the chance anyway. So we like them to know that we're not relying on them to do us any favours. We've got our own money to get a room and buy our own food and that.

K: We always manage to arrive in style but they don't realize how we struggle to do it.

L: Go without food. You didn't even have your rent, did you, when we went to Paris?

K: God, it must have cost us thousands, really thousands.

L: Must have done. When they've done a tour we've been to all the dates. And paying the fare and staying at hotels. And all the time we do it on a real shoestring.

L: Sometimes it's really hard. Like that hotel in Holland. There was six of us in a double room and we'd all walked in through the door with our sleeping bags. And they knew something was wrong. So every time we ordered food and the waiter came in, four of us hid in the bathroom.

K: Another time I was at a hotel in Norfolk. This was early on when this particular band were so poor they used to stay in grotty hotels and share a room. And I didn't have anywhere to stay so they said I could stay with them. In the morning they said to me: 'Well, you go out first and meet us outside.'

Just as I came out of the room I came face to face with this chambermaid. And I thought: Oh, Jesus, oh, no, this is it – because it was such a small hotel and she was the owner's daughter so she knew who had booked in. And she went: 'Excuse me, but can you get their autographs for me?'

L: And then there is the other chambermaid story.

K: There was a chambermaid in a lift . . .

L: With BP. They were staying in this hotel in Nottingham and BP got in the lift and this chambermaid followed him.

K: And they stayed in the lift for about an hour. He came out rather dishevelled.

L: Some girls, if they live in a remote town or something, they wait all year for them to come back again, don't they? They sort of hang around expecting to be remembered.

K: It's a bit sad sometimes. Some of the girls go up and they go: 'Oh, hi,' and they get: 'Am I supposed to know you?'

And I really sort of feel for these girls.

L: If that happened to me I'd probably start crying.

K: I'd probably just shrivel up and die. 'Cos it must be so awful. They probably think: Oh, they'll remember me, I'm the only one. Mainly because they're so young.

But I really feel a bit sorry for girls who get left in the hotels. Sometimes the band will go to the bother of taking them back to the hotel – and sometimes the hotel's miles out of town – and they'll just leave the girls in reception or whatever and run off and leave them. I've seen girls get so upset then. Sometimes it's quite young girls who obviously can't afford to get a cab back to town. And I do feel a bit sorry for them.

Sometimes I think if I had a room of my own I'd let them sleep on the floor because I do feel for them. 'Cos I know what I'd feel like in that situation, I'd just be totally wretched.

I've sat and talked to them for hours and hours and then I go to bed and they're still there. I don't know whether they stay in reception all night or whether they try and get home or what. Sometimes it makes me wonder though, 'cos some of them are so young I wonder what their parents think.

L: I think a lot of girls like that end up with the roadies. More out of desperation for somewhere to stay.

K: The roadies don't come in till hours after the band . . .

L: But it must be an awful feeling to think: I've got this far, and all of a sudden be dropped.

K: I've had a go at the band sometimes, saying: 'God, you're so cruel. How can you do that?'

L: They like to lead people on sometimes because they know how much they really like them. But I think that taking them as far as the hotel is going a bit far.

K: I remember one time being in a bar and there was these two girls that Gary and Mick had picked up. We were all sat together in this bar but these two girls sat separately. And the boys were all buying rounds of drinks and they never once included these girls. They were going: 'Oh, silly cows. Look at them sat over there. Old slags.' Then Gary goes: 'I'm going to bed now.' And he got up and he goes to this girl: 'Coming?' And she just trotted out behind him. And I just thought: What can she be thinking of to do that?

L: And Mick left his one there, didn't he?

K: Sometimes when they're really awful to the girls I think: Oh, I wish you'd catch the clap off them or I wish they'd get pregnant and come after you. They've been so lucky and I really wish somebody sometimes would bring them back to earth.

L: But if they did get pregnant I don't suppose they'd do anything about it. They'd probably deny all knowledge. 'Cos it's expected to be up to the girl really, these days, contraception. They don't even ask, do they?

K: No. They just take it for granted. Even if you told them you weren't protected, they'd say: 'That's OK, I'll be careful.' They wouldn't care.

L: You think: I'm glad that's not me.

K: Yeah, because they really are so rotten to them. And we hear them saying really rotten things . . .

L: And they're always going: 'Oh,' you know, 'I can't understand these girls,' and everything like that.

K: They pass them round as well, don't they?

L: Yeah, they do. They pass them from person to person. They could at least be a bit discreet about it.

K: A lot of the time they sleep with these girls and then

throw them out as soon as it's happened. We've always managed to stay in the room all night.

L: Dig our claws in! We shall not be moved!

K: But I think that's probably because we were known as friends before.

L: It's better to get to know them first, 'cos then they know that you're friends rather than just there for them and nothing else.

K: When we first met Classix I was with the bass player. At first I used to sleep in his room but I never used to do anything with him. The morning after the first time I ever really slept with him I came running into Lynne's room – he was still asleep because we'd got really pissed on vodka – and I was really worried and saying: 'Oh, God, he'll probably never talk to me again.' It was playing on my mind and everything. But soon as he woke up he came into our room and he was telling us what he was going to do and where he was going and everything. So I felt better.

But then that night we went to a club where they were playing and he ignored me quite a bit. He started chatting up this other girl and I was really upset. I was thinking: 'Oh, no, he thinks I'm a real slag. He really hates me.' And he took this other girl back to the hotel that night.

So I was really upset about that.

And then he chucked this girl out after about an hour and he came in to see us and he was talking to us and I was thinking: He's got a bit of a cheek!

But he was being really nice and I thought: Well, it's only to be expected. He's been doing it for so long you can't expect him to stop just 'cos he's slept with me.

That was the only time when I was really jealous. But I got over it.

K: Sometimes we used to sit there going: 'Err-err-err.' [*Crying sound.*] You know. 'They've gone off with other girls,' weep, weep.

L: But we always got over it. 'Cos next night they'd be back.

K: I don't really care about them going off with other girls as long as they always come back to me.

L: And sometimes they used to use us to scare other girls off.

K: Once we'd got to know them, if they didn't like any of the girls there they used to say: 'Oh, this is my fiancée', or 'my wife' – to chase them away.

L: I think they thought of us more as friends. The drummer once said to me: 'You're not like fans, you're more like friends.'

K: That really sort of pleased us. We liked that. After all our efforts and money spent.

K: I don't really know what I expected to start with. You always have these big ideals like they're going to sweep you off your feet ...

L: They're going to marry you afterwards!

K: But I suppose deep down you know that there's no chance whatsoever because you've just gone about it the whole wrong way.

L: And even though you like them you think: Would I like being married to them anway? 'Cos I mean I'm quite jealous and I know Kelly is too. I mean, going to gigs and seeing what goes on, you wouldn't want to let him out of your sight, would you?

K: No.

L: And I'd hate to feel I couldn't be at ease ever.

K: 'Cos we know exactly what does go on. But I suppose you do have certain dreams and fantasies. Like you put them on a pedestal and you've got all these ideals about them. It's so difficult to know what to expect. Some people can look so nice outwardly, and inwardly they're really vicious.

Mick used to have a really evil temper. He didn't often get annoyed but when he did that was it. He used to go really mad. And yet even though I know him now, I still tend to think things of him that he isn't really.

I've still got him on a sort of pedestal.

L: You choose to forget the bad things really, don't you?

K: You think of them as being wonderful people, you know, everything that everybody ordinary isn't. You think of them as different people, not human, untouchable or something.

L: I think, too, if they're quite successful and they've got a lot of money – it's not necessarily that you feel attracted to the money but they might have cars, flash motorbikes and things like that and you think it's really good to go in the car or whatever. You don't think: Oh he's got a real lot of money, I must get to know him. But it's an added attraction.

K: We used to love to be seen with them, didn't we?

L: Especially when we knew they'd be horrible to other people. We used to think: They're not horrible to us.

K: I always used to like being seen with them in the bar of a gig. Or walking out at the end with them. Like I remember once in Manchester when I was getting a lift to the hotel with the band and all these girls were surrounding the band and going: 'Ooohh, ooohh, ooohh.'

And I was sat there and I felt so proud. You just sort of feel important somehow. Sort of the 'chosen one'. And it's a really nice feeling.

L: But that's not the main thing really. Though I suppose it is at first, when you first want to get to know them.

K: At first it was. But now it doesn't really bother me. I like to be seen with them but I don't like to go up to people and say I've been with so and so or I know so and so, because I'm not really out to impress like that.

L: I get quite bored when people talk to me like that.

K: Yeah, so do I. And I always think people are going to talk behind your back, saying she thinks she's really good because she knows so and so.

I mean, you could get a real reputation. Someone would tell someone else and they'd spice it up a little bit and so on. And you don't know, it could always get back to the band.

L: And if it gets back to them they're going to think: Oh, she's really showing off because she knows us. That's the last thing you want them to think.

You don't want them to think you're just there to see *them*. Even if you are. Usually we are! But you can't let *them* know that.

K: So you tend to act differently with them. You try to be more distant because you don't want to seem so pushy. When I go to a club and there's an ordinary everyday bloke I fancy, I'll chat him up. But you daren't do that with a band. In fact, I find I clam up if they come over.

L: You're always conscious of what they'll think.

K: They say: 'What have you been doing lately?' And I just go: 'Oh, nothing really.' But there's so much that's happened I could sit down and talk to them for hours. Only I always feel well, you know, I might bore them.

L: They do all these really great things, go everywhere in the world . . . And I've only been to about five countries, and not for very long.

K: Or you wonder if they're just asking out of politeness or whether they really want to know.

L: You always think it's going to seem so humdrum to the lives they lead. Like one guy was telling me about all the things he does with photography, and he's got a car and he's got two motorbikes and he likes going shooting. And when he rang me up I was saying: 'I'm going to start learning to drive.' So he said: 'Oh, I've just started flying lessons at Biggin Hill.' I went: 'Oh, really?' And I thought: What do you say to that? You just feel what you do is so boring compared to them.

K: The only really exciting thing I ever do is to go and see them. But you can't really say: 'Oh, I went to see you.'

K: There was these two girls called Connie and Alex. They went to Holland with us.

L: 'Fraid so.

K: Unfortunately. The band really hated them. I've never seen them quite so horrible to anybody. We were all sat in a bar at night and they were going: 'Shut up! Go away!'

Connie had slept with Mick, hadn't she? And he then threw her out of his room.

Then Mick said I could sleep in his room.

They saw me go in and about five minutes later they knocked on the door.

He goes: 'Who is it?' They didn't say anything. So he opened the door and they were going: 'We don't want to go to bed yet. Do you want to have a party?'

He's going: 'Fuck off!'

And they were sort of peering round the room and having a look at me and going: nudge, nudge, you know.

And they were going: 'Don't you want a party? Don't you want to stay up?' They were really terrible.

Then Connie went and slept in BP's room. And she

came on. So she was asking him if she could borrow a pair of his knickers and everything.

L: And then she said: 'Have you got the clap or anything?' So he chucked her out.

K: He just told her where to get off. They were just pathetic.

L: We couldn't believe why they kept going back. I think it was pretty obvious nobody liked them. And they were a pain in the neck, weren't they?

K: It was really funny because the younger one used to boss the older one around. She made her do all the dirty work. She would say to the older one: 'Go and tell them to come in our room,' and things like that.

L: Then there were the two blubber whales. Well, that's how they were thought of. On this particular tour the main band *and* the support band all had these girls.

They called them 'the two blubber whales' and I never even knew their names.

K: Nor did I. But they had a right reputation. The band used to say: 'Who's going to have them tonight?' And that was only if they were really desperate – if they couldn't find anybody new.

They were quite funny those girls. They were from Newcastle and they were just really pushy and they just pushed their way in. They'd just go up and throw their arms around them.

L: That's something I couldn't do. We try to be subtle.

K: But they seem to be getting so young now. I mean I know I was only 16, but they seem to be 14, 15-year-olds.

K: Like that girl in Cambridge who was after Mick – she was about 13.

K: Yeah. And she was so brazen about it, wasn't she? Low cut top, down to here. She was just flaunting it. I don't think she cared who she had really. They seem to be getting so young. Makes us feel like old veterans!

L: When you go to bed with them you feel you've really got to live up to expectations. You think they've obviously gone with a lot of other people and you think: Oh, what are they going to think of me?

I don't know if they give you marks out of ten or whatever, but you feel you're under really great pressure against the other people.

K: When I was with Mick I used to do things like when I got nervous I'd put him down.

L: I do things like that too.

K: And then after I'd said it I used to really regret it.

But often when I was alone with him he'd say something to me and I'd make some quip or some remark. And he'd get really offended by it and be really upset. I think why I put him down was because I didn't want him to think I liked him just because he was in a group. So anything he did I tried to put down. It's stupid really but I just had to do it. And he used to get really nervous with me as well.

I had a go at him once because once he chatted up this girl and she left before the end of the gig. He'd had his eye on her and she'd been talking to him and everything, and he'd asked her back to the hotel and she'd said yes. And she didn't come.

In the dressing room he was going: 'Where's that girl gone?' Somebody said: 'Oh, she's gone home.' He goes: 'Well, are you coming back with me then, Kelly?' And I just blew up.

I went: 'Who do you think I am? I'm not a substitute!' I felt really hurt because he'd said it like that, sort of like: Oh, that girl's gone, I may as well have Kelly. And it just really upset me. That made me feel really cheap and used and everything.

Still went back though. But at least I had a go first! Felt better.

I've often had dreams about Mick and in nearly all of them I've rejected him. I suppose subconsciously I'm afraid of him rejecting me so in my dreams I get back at him. It's strange because in dreams things happen that you know you'd never do. Like rejecting him for other people, or just being really nasty to him.

Like I had a dream that I went to bed with him and then just walked out on him.

Or I try to humiliate him.

And I have dreams about whipping him.

There was one time in Glasgow when Mick had said that I could stay in his room and so I didn't book into a hotel.

And then he picked up this girl.

And after he'd done with her he went back up to his room but I didn't know what his room number was.

So I thought: I'll sit in the bar all night. But then Jimmy, who was the newest member and didn't really know anybody and came from Finland and couldn't speak much English, was trying to talk to me because I was about the only person he knew. He said to me: 'You can sleep in my room,' and I said OK. I started sleeping on the floor and then he said: 'You can share the bed.' And I didn't think anything of it because I thought: He won't try anything.

Then I went to sleep and I don't know whether I was dreaming or not but I woke up and I thought: Jesus! What's happening?

I thought: Well, I'm sure I didn't say yes.

I was really worried because at the time I really, really did like Mick. And I thought: What if Jimmy goes and tells him, I won't stand a chance any more 'cos he'll just think I'm an old slag.

But I don't think he could speak enough English to tell him. Thank God!

One time we were in Paris with this band and they had a new keyboard player and I don't think he really knew what we were about, did he?

And we were talking to him in this club and he was really out of his head – I don't know what he'd been on.

L: He'd been taking coke.

K: And we were just talking to him and generally being nice and saying what a nice bloke he was.

L: Yeah, he was. He was being ever so nice.

K: So we got back to the hotel and we were in our room and I heard him calling to me: 'Kelly, Kelly, come here.'

L: He wanted you to take his shoes off, didn't he?

K: Yeah. He was going: 'I can't get my shoes off.' And I genuinely believed him. So I went into his room and took his shoes off and I was just about to go out the door when he run round me, slung the door shut, pinned me up against the wall. He was going: 'Give me a kiss,' and I goes: 'No.' He goes: 'Go on.' And I said: 'No, fuck off. I want to go now 'cos I want to get some sleep.' And he was going: 'Please.' And I goes: 'No.' And he started getting really violent and he was really hurting me.

L: He really did mean it, didn't he?

K: Yeah. He was really grabbing my arm hard. And I said: 'Get off me.' I said, 'you're hurting me. Just leave me alone.' And he just picked me up – I mean, he was really strong – just picked me up and threw me onto the bed and sort of dived on top of me. I was really frightened. I was fighting him and trying to get him off me. In the end he was pulling my skirt off and trying to rip my tights and everything. And then Sal knocked on the door and said: 'Oh, we've got to go now.' So he sat up slightly and I caught him off guard and just threw him off me and ran out the door. I was so scared.

L: And he said something about: 'Come on, it will only take five minutes.'

K: Yeah, he goes: 'It will only take five minutes.' So I thought: Well you must be pretty lousy at it then!

But I was really scared.

L: You was all bedraggled, your hair everywhere.

Q: Is he still with the band?

K: No, they threw him out. They realized how dodgy he was.

K: When I was in Grimsby with the——s they came over to me and my friend and they wanted to take us back to the hotel. We said: 'Oh, no. No.' At the end of the night they chased us down the road. They were trying to drag us there forcefully. We just ran down the road and hailed the first cab. We were really terrified because we'd heard about them.

L: You never really know what they'll do, do you?

K: No.

L: If you don't know them.

K: You tend to sort of stick to the more refined looking people.

L: Never know what they're like underneath!

K: I mean, you've got to be choosy. So for one thing I'd steer clear of anyone like the——s. I mean, they're all king ugly for a start. But they've got such a reputation.

Like once, two of my friends had gone in their dressing room and they was naked and there was a bit of a come on and everything. Three of them went through one of the girls in the dressing room. Then they took them back to the hotel and apparently everybody had them, right from the group to the roadies, the manager, everybody. In succession.

But they hadn't known this was going to happen, you see.

And then that——turned up and he was the one who started all the abuse and everything. He started beating this girl around, hitting her about the face.

Then they got this toothpaste and squirted it up inside one of the girls. And then apparently——turned and pissed all over her and, you know, they were being really disgusting.

I don't know what I'd do in that situation. I don't know how I'd cope. You don't know whether to tell the police 'cos you'd be afraid it gets in the papers and things like that.

L: You'd have to admit what you'd done, wouldn't you?
K: Yeah.
L: And they know that. That's why they do it, 'cos they don't think you'll say anything.

L: I sometimes think that it's all just a lot of money with nothing to show at the end of it all. But then I think it's money well spent because we've had a good time.
K: We've got memories, yeah . . . I never regret a penny of the money I've spent.
L: Sometimes I come home and I think: Why did I spend that extra £50? And then I think: What the hell, I enjoyed myself.

And I don't regret any of it. No. No regrets.

Love From Ziggy

Julie (25): I was at the Hammersmith Odeon when Bowie killed off Ziggy in '73. I got trampled to death! A lot of men were throwing off their underwear and showing their cocks all over the place. A lot of fluid was flying about. One girl was actually sucking someone off at the same time as trying to listen to what was going on. I thought it was so extraordinary because nobody had any inhibitions. I remember that around me nobody gave a shit really about doing these things because it was rumoured that maybe this was the last time Bowie would perform. Maybe this was the last time Ziggy would be here. And everyone's got to get in on this because otherwise you're just a square. So everyone just took their clothes off. And wanking was nothing. There was a guy next to me was wanking in time to one track and I thought: My God! What does he do when he's alone? Then I suddenly realized that all the things I'd been doing were perfectly OK. Because here were people doing it with each other and sharing it. How wonderful, you know. So get off on that. And I thought I'd never seen so many cocks in my life.

Dear David Bowie,

I am very nurotic forgive me I can't even spell, write properly or even string fucking sentences together. My mind, body, soul are exhausted. And I'm very violent within my mind anyway. I'm fucking rooted!!!

What can I say to you seriously, well I'm all right, and I will be ok, thanks to you and everybody else in Hollywood you keep me and a rare few of us integrated.

I'm just a spider from Mars looking for a lady Stardust all I want to do is be happy and live in peace gee its hard isn't it.

What concerns me is some other crank will think he is Major Tom. Please believe me you have no choice anyway. I don't say it because he was murdered. Jesus Christ is fucking DEAD it is me who knows its all a dream.

Not much more to say other than crap. I'm ok, hope you are too, please drop me a line so I know you received this letter.

Lots of love to you and everybody else

Steve (*Ziggy*)

Ecstasy

Laura's fantasy about Pete Townshend

I ~~fkn~~ reckon my fantasy
is perfectly ordinary + must be shared
by every other heterosexual 14 year old girl.
I'm in this pub, right, + this geezer
comes over + starts chatting me up. I
suddenly see through the thin disguise
+ realise its my all time hero + idol, Pete
~~Feckst~~ Townshend (this is _not_ a piss-
take, I swear on my own deathbed). I
start responding favourably + after buying
me a Tequila Sunrise (well, its sounds
good), he utters those magical words:
"How about it, then?"
I nod enthusiastically, and after I've
swilled down me Tequila Sunrise (well, I couldn't

waste it, could I) he takes my arm, & + leads me out to his Mercedes.

Back at his flat (the one his wife doesn't know about) he takes me straight to his bedroom + I flop down on the 12 foot diameter circular bed while he locks the door. He reappears, minus jacket and (thin) tie + I'm by now minus jacket.

He takes me by the shoulders + kisses me, at first gently, then more and more passionately, his arms holding me closer and tighter. I put one hand on the back of his neck, running it gently round on to his cheek, then back, ruffling his hair at the nape of his neck. With the other hand I reach for the zip on his jeans; this acts like a signal + he pushes me down onto the bed, unbuttoning and removing my blouse. I relieve him of his shirt + start on his jeans whilst he tries to work out how the fasteners on my bra works He gives up, but quickly gets rid of my jeans. By this time I've reached his prick. He kicks off his jeans, and lies back in ecstacy ecstacy as I start to wank him off. I enclose his prick in my mouth + caress it with my tongue. + then I start to suck hard, raking it with my teeth. He then decides that it's his turn, and rips off the rest of my clothes (not much to rip off anyway) (He has been rude for the last 5 minutes). He runs his hand up between my thighs + finds my cunt, softly parting the folds of skin + pressing his finger into the damp passage. After a quite, long pause while he ~~left~~ leaves his finger inside my cunt and kisses my tits and whole body softly but passionately, he extracts his finger + then starts to insert his tongue, licking + teasing, pushing his nose (well, its big enough)(sorry, Pete) up between the flaps of skin.

I reach for his prick again, + he realises its time. Straightening up, he runs his palms down my front, feeling the curves + contours against his hands. Suddenly he is on top off me; I feel his weight, pressing down on me, and, ~~instead~~ of his finger reaching for my cunt, its his prick, hard, long and hairy. My whole body reaches upwards + my nails dig deep into the flesh of his back. I feel his tongue licking my

teeth; I meet and touch it with my own. I work my way down his cheek, onto ~~to~~ his neck, pulling and sucking. I bite deep into his neck + think: "This sure beats the hell out of dominos"

———

Alison: a reason to dream

I was sitting watching TV with the family when an advertisement for Barry's 'TV Disc' came on. I found myself spellbound. The music and that face were beautiful.

When he looks straight into the camera it's hard not to believe he's looking right at you and not only singing but also communicating with you.

Barry won me over, heart, mind and soul within minutes and it's been that way ever since.

Not having shown any signs of being interested in 'other men' I felt quite shocked by the effect Barry had on me.

Some long lost feelings had been awakened, and how!

It seems ironic now, but my husband phoned in the order for me.

He's a beautiful man who with his music has enriched my life. He has shown me that I can feel love again. It really is just like first love all over again.

All the joy, happiness, passion, pain – the whole experience which I thought I would never feel again. Now I'm alive inside, and it can hurt sometimes, but I'm glad – because I'm not emotionally dead any more.

Comfortable complacency is no longer enough. For this I will always be grateful to Barry.

He inspires me in so many ways – beautiful feelings become beautiful words. So I've started keeping a journal of poems, lines, quotes, etc.

And I know it sounds 'mushy' but I've also become aware of the beauty of nature. Everything has come to mean more – sunsets, sunrises, bird song, the scent of lilacs, bluebells, roses, the chill in the autumn air, the nostalgia of April evenings. It's hard to explain, but because I love Barry all these things become special, almost tangible.

He's the love in my heart, the music in my soul, my looking glass to the world about me.

Knowing about Barry has *most* definitely changed my life. I really feel that my former mundane existence has gone for good.

I feel more confident, more my own person.

I think the best way to explain it is to say that I now feel the same as I did at 16 to 17, full of inner confidence, excitement, lively, emotional.

Once again I have a reason to dream, and I feel that something good could happen.

My social life has changed completely. I have made a lot of friends through our common love of Barry. The friends who come regularly to my Barry nights number between 12 to 15, and I write to a further 14 both here and abroad. Apart from fortnightly get-togethers most weeks we usually also fit in a daytime Barry session. So my life is very Barry orientated, from corresponding with other fans, meeting friends locally, to arranging functions, planning for concerts, conventions, etc, etc.

It's lovely, there's always something to look forward to, always a dream to dream.

And because I am so committed to Barry and my Barry friends, I have almost completely lost touch with my former non-Barry friends.

When I'm listening to Barry or watching him I don't actually fantasize. But at those moments I *feel* – he affects me *physically.*

It varies from the pleasure of just looking at him, to a strange sort of aching in my chest, butterflies in the tummy and actual sexual arousement.

Obviously thoughts do go through my mind, but feelings are uppermost.

Even the way he may sing one word can bring some sort of reaction. The 'texture' of his voice is beautiful. I recently heard him sing 'Sakura'. I didn't understand one word but just the sound of his voice as he sang had the same effect on me as a long, lingering, very gentle kiss.

The main practical problem in being a Barry fan is money. Having no independent means, I hate having to ask my husband for money to finance my Barry activities, although in that respect he has been more than tolerant.

But this does make me feel guilty, because I know and he knows that in a strange way he is paying for the man who has taken over from him – a weird situation. I am desperately looking for work, to give me just a little independence in that way.

I have got in 'hot water' a few times for writing large cheques without asking first, but when I know that it will mean a concert seat I'm prepared to risk my husband's anger. I know that's not fair, but that's how it is.

My two children think it's normal. I don't think they feel threatened or embarrassed in any way. I think kids are switched on and they know if mum's happy they'll get the spin off. I also think I can cope with them a lot better than I did previously. I very, very rarely really lose my temper with them – oh, I shout at them and we have rows, but nowadays I rarely lose control.

The biggest conflict is with my husband. I know that it isn't really Barry's fault, but my husband doesn't.

He has been what one might call a 'good husband', a good provider, extremely capable and very sensible, but for me the magic (if it ever existed – because I can't even remember any now) died a long time ago.

I grew to resent him because I felt that he'd smothered any personality I'd had. I was afraid to ask for anything for myself, and he grew to expect me not to want anything. For years the real me has been fighting to get out, and now through Barry it has.

My husband is not a stupid man. He recognizes that my new found freedom of spirit is something beyond his control.

So for most of the time we get along all right.

But the undercurrents are there. We both realize that when he retires next year things are not going to be easy. The problems that now exist two or three weekends a month are going to be there every day.

I don't want to make his life a misery. I want him to be happy, but I don't think I can. I can't give up what I've found. Some people might think I'm crazy, to give up my safe, secure little life for what they would regard as a 'crush on a pop star'. But it's *so much* more than that.

Actual fights over Barry are rare, it's more a delicate truce situation. But the few we've had were really something.

The worst one was right after the second half of the Blenheim concert (on TV). My husband just had to be home that night. I didn't know it, but it seems he had been watching my reaction to it, and his outburst after was terrifying. He accused me of committing mental adultery and all sorts of things.

I didn't know whether to laugh or cry because the whole situation was so ridiculous, but *so* true.

I don't find that I need any man emotionally now because Barry gives me all that I need in inner happiness and peace of mind as well as a spirit of adventure – everything I've not had for so long.

I don't think my marriage will last much longer.

Farrah's fantasies about Tom of the Thompson Twins

Number 1. Tom led me to the sofa. The atmosphere in the house was very fresh and clear.

The walls were white and the rooms were virtually empty. There was that strange echo around like you get when a house is stripped bare. While I was in Tom's presence I moulded in with that strange echo perfectly. I could hear a loud buzz in my head. It was as if the electronic buzz from a stereo system had been left on – but no – it was the feeling I got from being with Tom as our knees touched sideways on the sofa.

Number 2. The summer was nearing its end and we decided to walk hand in hand in the countryside around his home.

The sun shone strangely in a dusk manner through the trees as we walked. Even though we'd been going out together for quite a few months my heart still beat doubly quick and lightly whenever I looked at his lovely face. We sat down under a large spreading tree and talked and laughed about trivial things. It might be difficult for some people to believe but even though he is an excellent performer on stage Tom is in fact a very shy person.

Then he kissed my lips softly.

Suddenly the sky darkened and lightning flashed, followed by a roll of thunder.

We ran towards an empty barn which luckily was unlocked. We went inside and bolted the door.

We had been running for quite a distance across the fields and were well and truly knackered.

Our hair was drenched and our clothes clung tightly to our bodies.

I pushed my shoulder-length black hair away from my face and tried to avoid looking into his eyes because I knew if I did I'd run to him and ask him to make love to me.

But our eyes did meet and they locked.

My brown eyes looked passionately into his vivid blue eyes and he started walking towards me. His face came closer to mine.

His face felt very soft and his breath was dry.

Then I started undoing the buttons of his black cotton shirt because I wanted to see his chest hair.

I stroked it and it was dripping wet.

It was auburn, matching the down he had all over his arms.

Tom seemed as if he was purposely trying to control his sexual feelings. He kept saying: 'No. Oh, no.'

I separated my fingers and ran them through his hair burying them deep at the top of his head. I touched the side of his face tenderly.

Suddenly he pushed me onto a pile of soft hay and his body was on top of mine.

I ran my hands through his hair again and looked up into his beautiful, interesting face above me.

If you have ever listened to the beginning of the 'Day After Day' track from the 'Into the Gap' album, you will have heard the emotions I felt at that moment.

My skirt was thin and clung to me as it was so wet. I could feel the most sexual part of his body up against me.

I said: 'Oh, Tom, I want you so much.'

He reached down to his trousers and opened the studs.

I thought: 'Christ, this is it at last!'

He seemed for a brief moment embarrassed about putting his hand up my skirt so I lowered my skimpy black briefs for him.

Then all of a sudden he seemed very impatient and he entered me.

I clung to his body tightly and held onto his black cotton shirt which was stuck to his back.

Oh, God, you'll never imagine how I felt. I was too turned on to moan. I just turned my head from side to side, drained.

It was like when you dream you are falling from a great height and you can't reach the bottom.

Then I was on a high plain and seemed to hear high pitched whistles in my head.

He moved his body up and down and he made mine move with his and as he is well-built this seemed to make me feel blocked up as if our bodies had been sculpted together.

He went on like this for 10 minutes without stopping.

Abstaining from sex for so long had made his feelings build up to an unbearable level.

Now they were released into my body which had been waiting for him for so long.

Like a tube or a soft machine

Then suddenly he moaned loudly, just like he does after the chorus of the first verse of 'Day After Day'.

And I experienced warm liquids shooting into my body which to me made my life worth living.

I never wanted to let him go.

Then he drew away from me and fell back on the hay. He took out a cigarette and we talked.

Sophie: the art of day-dreaming

I suppose day-dreaming is an art. It's just something you work on and get better and better at. You don't lose it if you try to keep hold of it. It's a wonderful thing to have. I think I'd crack up if I couldn't do it.

I'd a bit of an unsettling childhood, I suppose. I was two or three when my parents split up and I left home when I was 13 'cos I didn't get on that well with my step-dad.

Then I just sort of lived with friends, family. I was the

black sheep of the family and I loved it. That was the age when I was rebelling.

All my friends were going out to discos but I never liked that kind of thing. I didn't see myself as part of that generation. I was in a world of my own.

I wasn't much interested in boys. It wasn't that I couldn't get boy-friends. I had plenty, and some nice ones. And I wasn't a virgin.

But I just couldn't be bothered.

No one seemed perfect enough.

I was living round my nan's and I had a room to myself. I used to stay in there most of the time. I hardly went out. I was like a hermit. I was just playing Japan records all day, reading about them and things like that, silly things.

I used to dress up like them. If David Sylvian dyed his hair, I'd dye mine. I used to see a picture of them in the paper and whatever they had on I rushed out and bought it.

I was 18 then. I'd had a job after I left school but it didn't appeal to me. So I just packed my job in. It was all Japan.

Japan was my life for a few years.

As I didn't have to get up early I'd spend a lot of time sleeping.

If it was a normal day when no one was coming round and nothing was happening, I'd probably lie in 'till about dinner time. Not actually asleep, just sort of dreaming.

You couldn't see a bit of my walls for pictures of Japan and I just used to lay there for hours, looking at them.

Sometimes not even thinking about them, just looking.

And I'd play their records over and over again.

The best day-dreams were when I had headphones on and I was staring at the ceiling. They'd be singing away and I'd be there, I'd be playing something – not part of the audience, part of what they're doing. And everyone's thinking: Oh, lucky her.

Sometimes I used to lie there all day. It didn't bother me a bit. I used to get muddled up with day-dreaming and reality. My nan would say: 'Come out of it.' But I didn't see it was hurting me or anything. I liked it at the time.

When I day-dreamed I just felt happy. Which is something I hardly ever felt in the real world. I felt safe. Everything would be all right because I'd make it all right.

And when I came out of it . . . I don't know, it was like meditation. A really wonderful feeling. You felt so much better afterwards.

As if you'd been asleep for hours. A strange feeling.

Like I'd been miles away.

It was good too because I could take it with me.

If I went to stay with a friend it was still there. Perhaps not as good, but I could take it most places and no one would ever know about it.

It wasn't something I could do with someone else around. I had to be on my own.

I suppose I was frightened of someone finding out, that they might be able to see it. So I had the fantasies mostly in my bedroom.

I'd decorated it so you just sank into it.

It was all glowing. The whole room was Japanese. Half gold, half orange. Japanese pictures on the wall. 'Japan' written all over my ottoman, Japan records everywhere. Books. I just covered the walls with Japan so I couldn't escape from it.

I had big posters up. And my step-dad was a photographer so I used to get even the smallest pictures blown up huge. It was an easy room to lose yourself in.

Some people use drugs to get away from it all but I just used what I thought I needed to help *me*.

I used to look at their pictures to see what they were wearing and study the expressions on their faces. Because it's hard, unless you've actually met someone, to always remember.

So you memorize the expressions and then you put them in your dreams and it pulls the faces back.

Because sometimes you forget what a face looks like and it goes off a bit into something else. And then you think of something which pulls it back to you – like you've seen them on telly and you think: Ah, I've got it again, and carry on.

I'd think about how they'd talk. Before I heard them interviewed I had to sort of make it up. I knew what they sung like but I wasn't quite sure what they'd speak like. After I'd heard them it was easier.

It was like an affair. Not with one of them but with the whole group. Like being part of them, I suppose.

Not so much sexual as a brother and sister type thing. Very close.

We were living together in this lovely apartment. And it was all about the things that went on. They used to go touring and people used to visit us – things like that. And I would just be happy all the time being with them all the time.

I used to feel secure. It was like my own kind of private family.

It was all so clear, so vivid at the time, like running through a video or a film.

And I'd keep going back to it and taking bits out and putting bits back in.

Like the house – I could have written down every little thing: what was in the bathroom, what was in the kitchen.

Everything was like you see in magazines.

A bungalow – all on one floor with a massive split-level living room. There was no door into the kitchen but you went down a step and there was this L-shaped breakfast bar. Clear plastic with tubes going up to the ceiling. It was lovely! And the kitchen was all in white.

We would come whizzing in – like running around in our pyjamas – and go for the orange juice like typical Americans.

In the living room there was a great big telly and a mirror with what was a picture of a lady – I think, because it was like something seen out the corner of your eye.

The bathroom was massive also, with a round sunken bath. And underneath the whole house was a huge cellar with chairs and tables where they had concerts or entertained friends.

There was a long corridor too with all the bedrooms off

it. When they had to get up early I'd run along it and open every door and wake them all up. Or sometimes when I'd just woken up they would wander into my bedroom and just start to natter away.

I used to love walking through that house.

Sometimes me and Mick Karn shared the same bedroom. Or sometimes it was with him and Steve. But there was nothing sexual in it. It was like brother and sister. I knew it was all innocent. Nothing could happen like that. It was just a nice, warm feeling.

In the morning Mick would get up and have a bath. And he used to say: 'Right, what shall I put on today?' And I'd pick out what he would wear – red leather trousers, that kind of thing.

And then he'd say he was going off to the recording studio for the day.

And I'd plan my own day. Like I'd go out shopping, spend his money, meet him somewhere after he'd finished recording.

Sex wasn't the main thing. It could have been going on but I was doing something else.

They would all bring girls home and girls would want to get them into bed, but it didn't seem to bother anyone much.

I knew I'd always be there and ours just wasn't that kind of relationship.

And if something did lead up to sex it never actually got that far because the others would find out just in time or something would happen. I'd always make sure someone came in and said: 'Hadn't you better have a holiday?' or, 'Go away for a few days.'

And things would settle down again.

I knew I'd got something that the other girls could never get. Part of them.

I mean, sex was just like a physical thing. And this was deeper than that.

I even went through a stage in the fantasies where I was rebelling and I didn't want them telling me what to do.

So I used to run away from home and things like that.

And they all went looking for me. They did everything to try to find me. They were rushing around in cars trying to get me and I kept running away.

It was them wanting me rather than me wanting them.

However happy you are at the time when you're actually dreaming you still know you've got to come back. And the nicer you feel the worse it's going to be when you do get back to where you were.

I didn't like coming back and I didn't want to come back. But I knew I had to.

I knew it was just impossible to carry on like that.

Sometimes it was all right to come back and I'd feel better for it. Because it was what I'd been needing. So if I'd been feeling depressed it would cheer me up.

Other times I'd want to be there so much I'd hate everything about getting back. I'd hate everything about how I was living and I didn't see why I had to live like that when I could be living like I was there.

It used to bother me sometimes because I used to want it so bad and I knew I couldn't have it and so I used to get so upset.

If I could keep it on a level, you know, that it's a nice place to go when you want to, then it was all right.

But sometimes I got a bit desperate and I felt I really had to meet them. And that got a bit out of control sometimes.

I'd think about trying anything, even committing suicide.

'Cos I'd think: They're never going to meet me. Why the hell should they meet me out of millions of people? I'll probably never get to see them. I used to think all that type of thing.

I used to get panicky then. Not so much unhappy – it was desperation.

I used to think: Oh, I might as well just end it all. I've got nothing to live for.

Luckily the panic didn't happen very often. And when it did it didn't last very long. But it was such a strong thing at the time. A bit scary really. You think it's going to get out of control. It's a kind of thin line. And you think you'd better pull yourself back quick.

But then again, I never did take steps to meet them. I

suppose I wanted to but also I didn't. It might spoil it if I did find them.

So I never did meet them and I only got to see them twice before they split up.

The first time I didn't react like I thought I would. I sat there in the concert and I couldn't really believe it. Being in the same room as them was a really weird feeling – even though I was right at the back.

I never screamed or anything like that. It was all inside. Like I knew something no one else knew. I was all right and the rest of the audience were being stupid.

Also, I was jealous. When I'd first got to know them hardly anyone else had heard of them. Then suddenly they were everywhere: on the radio, TV. And I didn't like that. It was like everyone else getting in on the secret.

So it was obsession and possession.

All this went on for about three years and then I became pregnant.

I'd known Brian for about four years. And while the baby wasn't planned it wasn't unwanted either. Even so I didn't rush into marriage.

Because although I like Brian I've never been able to get close to him emotionally. He's not the easiest person to get through to.

Sometimes I try to talk but then it's quickly taken over by something else and gets all mixed up.

And if I said any of what I've told you to Brian he'd laugh his head off.

He doesn't know anything about what I dream about or anything like that. Or about what I went through. He knew I was into Japan, but not what I was feeling.

We never go into anything really heavy like that. Just try and avoid it.

It's just not the sort of thing you talk about, is it?

[*Sophie is 21. She is still unmarried (from choice) and lives with her baby boy in a hostel for unmarried mothers.*]

Marnie's dreams 2: key in lock

'Bowie,' I said.

'Call me David,' he replied.

'David, is this real life?'

He replied: 'Oh, yes, my lovely, it is all so real.'

I was a bit puzzled at his expression, he looked so sad as he said this.

Later on I was having a shower and I didn't hear anybody come in but then I felt a hand on my shoulder and when I turned round Bowie's eyes were so unhappy it was as if he wanted me to take pity on him.

But my mood was angry and I turned my back on him.

Then he got hold of my hair and pulled me forcibly out of the shower and I tried to hit out at him but he seized my arms and threatened me.

He took me into the front room.

Then I just blacked out.

Suddenly everything was clear again and I could feel something warm against my skin. When I looked down I saw he was kissing my navel and my thighs. All the room was like floating around my head. It was as if we were the only solid things in it.

Then his kisses got harder and harder and I tried to get away from him but he saw my legs moving and pushed them down with his arms and carried on trying to make love to me.

He stood up after that and again I tried to move. It was hopeless. I was just frozen and suddenly he was coming closer and closer to me again and he kissed me on the lips and this time he didn't stop until he'd kissed me all over my body.

I thought he would now leave me alone but instead he drove himself right into me and it was like a dagger which had been put into red hot flames ripping through my flesh and melting my skin.

We just stayed together like that for what seemed a very long time. Then we came apart and I felt something coming out of me and when I looked down it was blood.

Then it was as if Bowie was some kind of animal because he smeared himself all over with my blood.

He rubbed it into himself and then he tried to force more out of me and it came flowing out and filled up the room as if we were both in a blood bath.

Then he began crying and I moved away into a corner of the room.

With each slight movement there was pain in my body.

But then he seemed sorry and came over and kissed me very gently.

He held me close to him as if to let me know it was all right now, he wasn't going to hurt me any more.

He never goes out of the room. He just – like if you think he's gone out of the room, it's like a presence in the room. If you try to get out of the room there's no doorways or anything. Just all walls. I'm always trying to find a secret passage out of there. And I always see something outside but I can't see what it is. Then I back off and I don't like what I've seen and so I go back to the far corner of the room and then he comes in again. It's as if he's gone out but he's still there.

A rope came down with 'I need you' written on it.

I grasped the rope and it whisked me up to Bowie and we both smiled.

Then we were in an airport and Bowie totally vanished. I began to get very upset and wept.

I went inside a photo booth and all in a fantastic spark Bowie's hands grabbed me (I knew they were his. I know them like I know my face in the mirror in the mornings.)

He snatched me inside the camera and it was hysterical.

We observed all the radical changes in the appearance of people as they fiddled about with themselves waiting for the camera to flash.

Then the maddest thing of all happened. Bowie and I saw ourselves in the photo machine, fiddling with our hair, eyes, face, lips, etc.

Then we saw ourselves leave.

It was so confusing but, great!

When I feel his hair it feels sort of wet – sort of oily. Just like it's got a load of cream in it or something. And sometimes it's so soft and you run your fingers through it and your fingers just slip off his head, you know, like it's that soft you can't keep hold of it.

I walk speedily down a long, long corridor and there is a door at the end of it and then I'm running towards it.

Suddenly a cold, shaky sensation travels down through my spine and through my stomach into my vagina.

The door swings back on its hinges and Bowie is standing there looking in the mirror.

Then his head swivels round on a motionless torso and he's swimming in a hazy fog.

Our eyes meet and we try to hold each other but we're both so hot, our emotions burning, that we have the effect of an electric shock against one another.

We break apart, stunned and frustrated.

Then a red hot light so bright and shining it would sting your eyeballs if you so much as caught a glimpse of it appears through a hole in the ceiling.

Bowie places his hands on my shoulders and I'm filled with this super strength and bouncing energy like I'm just raring to go. I feel like I could climb a mountain or run the longest marathon in the world and still have super strength left over at the end of it. Then it suddenly comes to me. It just hits me smack! bang! right in the face that Bowie is feeding me with this super new life force like a car gets supplied strength from oil, and it's thrilling! fascinating! sensational!

Then there's all the sordid, eerie, rotten, aching parts of me flashing and blurring through my thoughts in a sort of flashback as I see all the mean people who hate me just for being 'me'.

And then there's a steel box.

The box is vibrating like a rapid, everlasting thump, thump heartbeat and it has 'LIFE' written on it in red letters.

Bowie carries me into a bathroom and the shower's going so fast and the steam is rising and all I can feel is his body and I'm so cold but he warms me up, and up, and up – as if it's never going to stop but it does.

It jumps, bippity bot, to a different place.

An icy, white, pure looking lake surrounded by huge

mountains and lovely, phosphorescent, snow covered peaks.

And it's great, really beautiful. I whisper to Bowie: 'I love you, and I'll never stop loving and wanting you,' and his translucent skin is touching mine and rubbing against it sending me ecstatic and spinning, hopeless, frantically through mid air, and he's teaching me to ski.

Then we are lying in snow and he's so hot pressing against me that the snow begins to melt.

Then we're back in a dressing room, and I realize I'm lying on the floor nude like I didn't even know he'd taken my clothes off because I thought I was somewhere else.

Then he really hurts me by sticking his finger up my vagina until I can feel it wiggling around almost up to my navel.

I begin writhing up and down all around the floor.

Then Bowie licks my breasts and my neck and in between my legs.

Then he parts my legs and drives himself into me as if he is trying to become a foetus again.

I can feel his arms and his legs and his whole body as if he is part of me and we make one.

Then I black out and finally I wake.

I was staying at my stepsister's. I was locked inside the house. There were no streets outside. All I could see was the church steeple.

Then two furniture men drove up in a shiny yellow van and began removing everything from the house.

Then they brought in this long yellow cardboard box.

I opened the box and Bowie opened his eyes and came out of it. And with his finger, as if out of his nail, he sort of sprayed yellow around the room like light.

And everything went soft.

It was as if he was wearing light.

His shoulders were oily and his face was oiled up, like a shiny tan. And his hair was all white and his eyes were white and he had white feathers all around him.

Then the two men came back and shook his feathers off and put him back in the box.

Then they got hold of me and put me in another box.

And they put us both in a wagon and I could just see out of a crack that Bowie was next to me.

They got to a park with white railings and left us there.

I started to cry and Bowie got out of his box and came over to me and said that everything was all right.

I was safe again. I wasn't unprotected.

He came to me and took me by the hand and ran his fingers through my hair. I looked into his eyes and it seemed that I saw in his eyes life itself. I saw feelings, the things people do to hurt others.

I saw pain, kindness, love and hate, all through Bowie's eyes.

He was giving me a quick, silent warning of the dangers that lie ahead in a young person's life – the mistakes people make.

Bowie pulled me down in between his legs and started to stroke my head. I drifted in a sort of dream state. I saw patterns and great fields of reds and blues and yellows.

I tried to share this beauty with Bowie, but my words came out soggy as hell and dripping or tasting of colour.

I could see all the small crevices and skin tones, all the pores and hills and crevices of Bowie's naked body.

I could hardly believe what a fantastic, unbelievable, expanding, thrilling dream I was having.

Then a light-headed moodiness filled my body as Bowie started to rip and tear my clothes.

With every touch of his hot, burning fingertips I felt close and warm.

Then we were riding shooting stars through the Milky Way. It was wild! It was beautiful!

Sex with him was like lightning and rainbows in the springtime.

I felt happy and relaxed and we were floating above reality and all the mundane things were lost forever in space.

He became hot and sweaty and I could feel every quiver of excitement in his skin as it touched mine.

And while he was inside me I felt so secure. We were locked together like key in lock.

Then all these hot liquids shot up inside me, and all I

could hear was non-stop echoes. Then he was groaning like nothing I've ever been lucky enough to witness before – lucky little mousy old me.

It almost drove me insane.

Our bodies were so close, his face and his every action were like fast sections of quick flashing blurs.

I was so, so unfamiliar with myself and with the whole situation.

Then we almost tipped off the edge of the world and we hit something – a red button.

Splash! Bang! I think it was meant to have been the atom bomb.

The world blew apart and crumbled beneath us. We just kept rising up, up and up again.

We made love on oozing, snow-white cotton clouds and all I could feel was him and hear his deep breathing.

Then I was brought down with a nauseating, crippling thud, yuk wham! bam! back to reality.

No Bowie, no clouds, no nothing.

Just a whole new day to live my dreary, disorganized, screwed-up life.

My lover was gone.

Jed's fantasy about Clem Burke

My sexual fantasy is to have sexual intercourse with Clem Burke, the drummer with Blondie

He would be dressed in a black satin shirt, a leather bomber jacket, skintight leather trousers and black Doctor Martin boots with the yellow stitching around the side and tied together with red boot laces.

Clem would have his tongue in my mouth, our two tongues twist and turn together. I would run my tongue over his body, inching my way slowly to his erect penis. I would suck and suck his prick until he came off. I would then swallow his warm silky semen rolling it around on my tongue. While his penis had a rest I would carry on licking and tasting his body such as his hairy chest and under his armpits.

Clem would then lie on top of me and have his tongue

in my mouth. His saliva would run into my mouth. While doing this I would masturbate him and let him come off in my hand. I would then rub the sperm all over his naked body.

I would then get whipped cream spread in his anal passage and then eat it with a spoon. Clem would then pee in my mouth. I would stick my tongue out trying to taste as much as possible.

This is my sexual fantasy, by the way I am MALE.

Helen: above the chandeliers

I remember vividly the day I first saw him on television. It was a Tuesday in April 1978.

I thought: I'll watch it, just to see. And the third song was 'Even Now'. And that was it. It just stopped me in my tracks completely. The next day I rushed out to buy *Manilow Magic*. And within a week I'd got three albums.

Over the next 18 months I collected most of the albums. I had two imported from America. It cost me a *fortune*!

And then at the end of 1979 the 1980 tour was announced and everyone I knew said: 'Yeah, I'd like to see him, but I don't want to pay £10 for a ticket.' And, totally against my character, I said: 'I'm going on my own.'

I'll never understand to this day why I did it because I'd never been to a concert on my own before.

And after the concert I was totally hooked.

My boyfriend met me after the concert to bring me home and he couldn't get through to me at all. I was just very much in a world of my own.

My feelings were so mixed up I didn't know whether I wanted to laugh or cry. And I just didn't understand why I was feeling that way for a person I'd never met who was just someone on a stage.

I really didn't understand what was happening to my feelings.

I thought: God, this guy's really got something. But I

couldn't figure out what it was. And I didn't know whether it was love or what I was feeling at the time. It was all very mixed up. Indescribably.

It was like when you have an absolutely horrific experience, or an absolutely ecstatic experience. I'd got both at the same time.

And I really didn't know how to cope with it.

It was frightening. I was frightened of my own emotions, of what I was feeling.

Because when I was a kid I went to see The Osmonds and I stood and I screamed and screamed and screamed at Donny but I really didn't know why I was screaming or why I was crying or why I was doing whatever.

And then suddenly it's there in front of me and I *know* why I'm doing it.

It's the attraction for this one man. And his personality and his music. That's what was making all my emotions get mixed up together.

Looking back I now understand, but at the time it was frightening because I was on my own with no one to share it with.

Before it had just been his music I'd found attractive but by the end of the concert I think I was passionately in love with the man as a person.

And I'd never cried at a concert before. But I got very, very emotional.

I was in that state for weeks and weeks afterwards.

And that ended – or set in the rot to – the relationship I was having with this guy I was engaged to. I didn't want to know from then on. And he had to go.

It was basically because of his misunderstanding of what I was feeling. He hadn't been to the concert. He hadn't lived through it with me. And he just couldn't understand what I went through.

He tried to understand. He saved newspaper cuttings. He recorded concerts for me. He bought me records. He knew I thought this guy's music was great but I don't think he understood anything else.

Towards the end I think he found it very, very unusual that anyone should be this way about, in quotes, 'a pop star'.

When we did eventually split I got a lot of help from Barry's music.

I was very, very depressed, very, very lonely. And I went through a phase where I was on valium. And I nearly took an overdose. I'll never understand why because I've never been that kind of person. I get upset but it blows over very quickly. But when you're in a depression it's difficult to get out of.

One problem was that because it was me ending the relationship, according to my so-called friends I was the one in the wrong. And because I'd split it up I wasn't allowed to be hurt.

I used to lock myself in my room, playing one Barry album in particular. And there were two tracks on it. One was called 'Life Will Go On', which means a lot to me even now. And the other was 'Made It Through The Rain'. I think a lot of ladies you'll speak to can relate to that in one way or another.

It took a long time for me to be able to even play that song right through without breaking down. It must have been 18 months before I could honestly sit down and play that record without breaking into floods of tears.

But Barry helped me through.

I kept thinking: Well, I can do it. It will pass. I will get out and make friends again.

And that's when I went headlong into the Manilow business – Manilow friendships.

After the '80 concert I was very much on my own regarding my adoration for him. I didn't know any other Manilow fans. I thought I was some kind of lunatic. I was 16. I thought it was about time I'd grown out of things like pop stars. I mean, you just don't do things like this when you're grown up.

And it's very, very difficult when you're the only person who believes in something with all your heart and other people say: 'What?!'

You start questioning yourself: Am I going round the twist? Am I basically insecure? Are my emotions all over the place? Is what I'm feeling right?

When you don't know anyone else who's feeling the same way it's very unsettling. So at first I tried to push it down. But when I finally met other people I realized it wasn't wrong after all.

First of all I joined the national fan club and they put me on to a local one. The first local meeting I went to was quite an eye-opener.

I expected people to be walking in with paper bags over their heads and dark cloaks and collars pulled up, and all looking round with shifty eyes and sneaking in through side entrances.

But they'd got pictures on the wall and people had T-shirts on and were flying their colours very proudly.

It only took a couple of those kind of events – we used to have a meeting once a month – for me to realize it wasn't at all wrong.

From there on I got more and more involved and through it I got to know more and more people.

Then I saw him twice in 1982. And that was it – there was no turning back after that. It escalated from there.

Now I just don't question it at all. It's right. There's nothing wrong in it at all. I get an inner strength through other fans. I get a lot of reassurance from them that it isn't wrong.

And, oh God, I've had lengthy discussions with people who aren't Barry fans and they've tried to convince me it's wrong. But now I know it isn't.

If I'd felt as strongly about it at first as I do now then I would have been put in a padded cell – or I would have put myself in one. But it's OK to feel that strongly now because it's in the right context with the right people to share it.

Because you can't love someone to that degree and not share it. If you can't share it with that person you've got to share it with someone else.

So it's more secure for me, sharing it with others. Rather than locking myself away with him in my fantasy.

Sure, I day-dream about him. Particularly when I'm walking to work – not only about him but about conventions and what's going to happen at the next get-together.

Sometimes I do fantasize about him sexually. But I don't think: Wow: that was a good fantasy, I must go to bed and dream about it now. I don't do that. And anyway when I get to bed I'm so exhausted I just flake out.

I get a big kick out of his music, it makes me feel good, and I like to have sex to his music. But I've never felt the need to masturbate to it.

Sometimes, if I'm lying in in the morning and I'm having a day-dream, then perhaps I'll feel a little aroused, but I don't feel the urge to dash out and put the music centre on and sit and masturbate to it. I just think: Cold shower time, Helen!

I've never felt the need to do that. I've got a good sex life. I haven't got a steady boy-friend. But if I need sex, I'll have sex. I don't exactly walk into bars and pick people up, but I'm adequately catered for. I've never, ever needed to satisfy myself in any way. I suppose I'm lucky.

And I don't imagine the person I'm with is Barry. I've never needed to do that.

Though I did once go out with a chap who looked very much like Barry. I was head over heels with him. Yet as a person he was not a nice person. He was unreliable, he lied, he cheated, he was everything I was against. Of course, it didn't work.

And looking back I see that look-alikes are all right, but you can't beat the real thing. That was the only case where I've tried a substitute. I'd never tried it before and I've never done it since. It just won't work. And there's no point.

You've got him in your head and your heart and that's where you've got to keep him.

But it's really difficult, you know, to love someone as much as we all love him and for him not to know we even exist.

You know: he'll *never* know we exist. And it's hard to accept. You do get to the stage where you think: Oh, God, no one does match up. I *don't* want anyone else. Fortunately they're very few and far between.

But I have phases when I just sit here and think: If I can't have him I don't want anyone.

That's when it gets too much.

And I've tried stripping the place of posters and photos

– which makes the place feel like a shell. It doesn't feel like home so they all have to go back up again.

I've also tried turning the pictures upside-down – they're still there but upside-down. That's a little easier.

I like to get away from it all sometimes. I've got a good social life away from Barry. So sometimes I go out with a group of non-Barry friends and have a good night on the town.

Or sometimes I go for a long walk away from everything. Just to get myself away for a couple of hours, or for a night or whatever, away from everything to do with him.

Then I can come back and see it in perspective.

It's just – frustration I think is the word. To sit and watch him on the telly, particularly when he's being happy and jolly and friendly – it's hell.

Luckily I've got two good Barry friends who live close by. Between the three of us there's always one who's on a high and can bring the other two up.

You say: 'Hey, come on, we don't need this. He wouldn't like to think of us sitting here moping. He does it to make us happy, not to make us low.'

That's why when we watch the videos one of us has got to be poking fun, either at us or at him. It's the only way you stay normal.

We all know what we feel like inside, but to listen to us when we're watching a video you'd think we were his biggest critics. We tear songs apart, find double meanings, laugh at things he does. Like back in '78 he hadn't a clue how to dance. He was so clumsy it was unbelievable. So we laugh at that.

And with really heavy ballads like 'Trying To Get The Feeling' – the first line is 'Doctor, my woman' which we turn round to 'Doctor my woman' and all fall about laughing.

And one of my friends has made up a little book: *Things That Barry Has Said*. Little things he says we put in a different context to poke fun at him. Because you've got to laugh. If you can't laugh you'll go round the twist. Otherwise it gets too much.

And sometimes conversations turn a little bit blue but it's still something to laugh at. We consider we have a licence to do it because we are so dedicated. It's our way of keeping it in perspective.

And although what we talk about is often very sexual, it's also got to be kept light. Because once you start getting too serious . . . You know, you've got to be able to switch off from him. If you can't then you're living in a fantasy where no one else can reach you.

I mean, after concerts, after I've been to see him, I'm up above the chandeliers somewhere and I don't want to talk about anything else. And for a fortnight I don't. But after that I start thinking: Come on. You're boring everyone else to tears. You've got to come back to earth.

And you start acting normal again. Otherwise – I mean, I couldn't do my job if I was up there all the time.

In fact, I lead a very hectic life. I'm always on the go. I work for an airline and I've got quite a responsible job. I've also got a job in a disco three evenings a week.

Everyone I work with is really good about him. They laugh and joke and they ask how he is. Like when I go to work in the disco people say: 'Hello, Helen,' and instead of saying 'How are you?' they say: 'How's Barry?' So I'll say: 'Oh, he's as handsome as ever. How are you?' And they say: 'Fine.' And it's just part of me. People know me and my love for Barry and they just bring it into the conversation and it's forgotten straight away.

So long as I know he's there.

Funnily enough, with boy-friends and other fellows it's not us who compare them to Barry. We never compare. Barry is separate. He's part of our lives but he's separate from our social life. But men get inhibited by him.

Like this flat. When fellows walk in here and I haven't said anything about this place, they walk in and they go: 'Oh, my God!' And particularly with that colour poster where his eyes tend to follow you wherever you're sitting, you can see them sitting there and their eyes keep wandering up and you can see they visibly feel uncomfortable with it.

I usually get into conversations with them about it and normally they find it a big joke. But if they do start talking seriously with me about it – and if I can talk seriously about it to them – then they soon feel they're out of their depth.

It's something they can't understand and they think: I've got a right weird one here. What we going to do with this one?

But Barry's part of my life and if they can't accept it then they can't accept me either. He's here and that's it. He's here to stay. There's no way I will trade him in for anybody.

So if I ever do settle down with anyone it will have to be with someone who can accept him.

Most husbands can't cope with it.

I know one particular girl, for instance, whose husband ripped her posters down. And he also taped over her concert video tapes.

I mean, our concert video tapes are our pride and joy – we don't let them go at all – and for someone to record over them is sacrilege.

He also tried to stop her going to the convention.

Her best friend was also very much into Barry so when the husbands were out during the day the girls were always together. He resented that as well. He resented everything to do with Barry.

He actually used to come along to the local gang meetings and sit there all night. Never say anything. Just watch his wife all night. It spoilt it for her because she couldn't relax and have a good time like the rest of us.

One of the girls who went to the Chicago convention last year got some really special photographs. And I found Millie in a side room, away from everybody, sitting and sobbing her heart out over these photographs. She had to go and lock herself away. She didn't dare react or show any kind of emotion in front of her husband. That must be a really big strain on her.

I've known other husbands just as jealous.

Another girl I know, a very dedicated Barry follower, can't talk about Barry in her husband's presence at all. He gets very, very jealous and aggressive and will go off in fits of sulks and not speak to her, or he throws a tantrum or something. Just because she's talking about Barry or watching Barry on the video.

To me, that only points to his insecurity. If he's going to see Barry as a threat he can't be 100 per cent sure of his marriage. Not if he's going to see her fantasy as a threat to their life.

I also know girls who have actually left their husbands because of Barry. They just felt Barry had become too much of them and there was no room left for their husbands. So they left.

On the other side, there are girls who get married and have to abandon Barry completely, which I find difficult to understand. That a girl has actually loved Barry and when she gets married she's actually got to abandon that love. To me, that seems very demanding on the husband's part.

Even in my own family, my mum likes Barry too, but she has to keep it down. She can't ask to go to conventions or get-togethers. Because they've been married 35 years so it's a long time to suddenly change. And I see my mum's point and I don't push it too far.

In fact, most married ladies I know have to keep it down, tone it down. Most of them manage successfully enough in that when their husbands aren't there they can rave and rant and go as mad as the rest of us.

But I envy them in a way. I have days when I fill the place full of Barry people and we all sit and watch the videos or whatever and we all get on a high. And I envy the people who have to come down to earth with a bump and go home and look after their kids and look after their husbands. For me, it takes most of next day to unwind and come back to reality.

I sometimes have Barry weekends. My place isn't very big so I normally only have about 10 people for a Barry bash. I have them sleeping on the sofa, on the floor, in the hall, in the bathroom, anywhere there's room. And all day, all night we have the video going. And normally we keep it up all day and all night and all the next day – non-stop. It's ridiculous. The video can be on the verge of blowing up.

Most of the time we keep the conversation light – a laugh and a joke, bit of a giggle. But there are particular songs that different people react to differently. One of my mates can't take 'All The Time' so when that comes on she goes and cleans her teeth till it's finished – just to get away from it.

Last time we did it we went out for a meal to a bistro – all 10 of us. And, of course, we took some Barry tapes and we said: 'Take that Julio Iglesias off – we don't want him! Put Barry on.'

Another big gang of us meets up once a month.

One of the girls who is a very good friend of mine has a husband who has to work away one week out of four.

So as he walks out of the front door, the Manilow Mob comes in through the back door.

And then it's non-stop Barry for a week. All day and all night for a week. Some of us go there at night after work, stay for the night, then get up in the morning and go to work, then come back again. And it's Monday to Friday: non-stop Barry. Then we all go home and she clears the place up and it's back to normality for three weeks. Then we're all back up there again.

Then there are the Barry nights. There's two kinds of Barry nights.

With civilized ones we hire a room in a pub and have a video on. Most of us are sitting and chatting around tables, meeting up with friends we haven't seen for a while, exchanging news and gossip – just generally having a chat. And a new video will come on and the place will go quiet and we'll all go: 'Ooohhh!' Then it will be back to normal. It's just a nice, warm, friendly feeling.

On the other side are the Barry discos, which are ridiculous.

I held one myself last September. You walk into the room you've hired and the manager and his staff are standing there. 'What's going on tonight?' 'We're having a Barry night.' 'A what?' 'Barry Manilow – playing his stuff all night.' And the general look of shock horror on their faces is amazing.

Of course we decorate the room with pictures and the DJ comes along with all the records he's going to play – all Barry, nothing but Barry all night. And from the first up-tempo Barry record everyone is on the dance floor and they're there till the last one.

It's so nice because when you go to a disco normally you've got to look your best all the time, you've got to move well with the music – you're on show. But when you go to a Barry disco you're just having a good time. You can leap up and down, your hair can get in a mess, you can smudge your make-up – it doesn't matter. There's no rivalry, no maliciousness, no bitching. It's just pure fun. I think the majority of girls are married or courting or they've got responsibilities, and it's their way of getting away from it all and they can let their hair down. They haven't got to be the sensible mum or the sensible wife. They can let all their inhibitions go and be themselves.

For an outsider it must be mind-blowing to see all these women leaping up and down on the dance floor and having the best of times and not giving a damn.

And when they're having such a good time they don't want any hassle or any aggro or anything. That's why the atmosphere is always so good.

To end the evening we play 10 to 15 minutes of slow ballads. And some of us will stand around and we all link arms and we all sway. We don't need anyone to dance with. Just because it's slow music we don't think: God, is there a man in the place I can smooch with? We don't need that.

And, of course, we always round off the night with 'We'll Meet Again' and then 'One Voice' – fish the candles out of our bags.

That's very meaningful as well because we really believe in what we're singing. With 'We'll Meet Again', we *will* meet again because we're all friends and even though we don't know everyone's names we know all the faces.

And we all know we've got one thing in common. Because even though we come from all different backgrounds and all different walks of life, when we're together we could have been friends since we were kids.

And when we sing 'One Voice' – well, that says it all. It is one voice and it makes the lot of us sing. And when we sing 'One Voice' we do mean it.

It finishes the night off on a high. Perfectly. Super, it is.

[*Helen is 22.*]

Delirium

I am a rat in a cybernetic sewer – Simon's letter to David Bowie

DEAR DAVID BOWIE (JONES)

I'M SORRY ABOUT THE LETTER I SENT TO THE QUEEN TWO YEARS AGO ABOUT ME, YOU AND THE STARS. IT WAS ABOUT HOMOSEXUAL DISSEMI-NATION, I'VE GOT YOUR PHOTOGRAPHS. I WILL ALWAYS LOVE AND RESPECT YOU BUT I'M NOT HELPLESS AS I USED TO BE.

HOW ARE YOU? I'D LOVE FOR YOU TO VISIT ME, MY TRUE IDENTITY IS GOD, I SEE U.F.O.S – QUAZARS OCCASIONALLY.

AS YOU KNOW WE HAVE OUR TELEPATHIC LINK. THROUGH ROCK AND ROLL I KNOW EVERYTHING.

UFOS CREATED YOU – UFOS CREATE ME. I SEE EARTH FROM SPACE, QUAZAR THETANOLOGY. DO NOT SPEAK EVIL, YOU ARE THE DEVIL, I AM GOD – WE ARE FRIENDS, LOVERS PERHAPS, YET IT WOULD BE IMPOSSIBLE FOR ME TO BE YOUR WIFE. BUT I STILL PLAY YOUR SONGS ON MY GUITAR.

I WORSHIP CELESTIAL LIGHT SHIPS.

THE IKON – TODD RUNDGREN.

YOU CALL ME A WONDERFUL PERSON. I THINK YOU'RE BEAUTIFUL.

I MUST BE ONE IN A MILLION TO ATTAIN NIRVANA BY TAKING LUCK IN A SKY WITH DIAMONDS.

I JUST WANT TO BE WITH YOU, I WANT TO KISS YOU. I DID WHEN I WAS 21 BUT NOW I'M 23 AND TIME BLEW IT ALL TO HELL.

I'M DYING OF THERMONUCLEAR RADIATION, AND MY HAIR'S FALLING OUT. THE CAUSE IS MOTOR CONDITIONING.

THE RADIATION IS FROM THE UFOS

SONS OF 1984: JIMI HENDRIX, TODD RUNDGREN, DAVID BOWIE

UFOS CREATED ELECTRONICS, UFOS CONTROL THE HUMAN EGO, UFOS CREATED ROCK N ROLL

I'M NOT WORSHIPPED. YOU ARE. SCIENTOLOGY PROCESSING IS ROCK N ROLL. GOD GAVE US ROCK N ROLL, GOD GAVE US LSD.

GOD COMES ON TV GOD COMES ON RADIO – E.S.T.

GOD UFOS CREATED SCIENTOLOGY YET UFOS CREATED THE POLICE

THE POLICE ARE A DIFFERENT BREED TO THE AVERAGE CIVILIAN. THE HIPPY IS ANOTHER TYPE. EVOLUTION IS TRUE MAN EVOLVED FROM THE APE ABOUT A MILLION YEARS AGO. REBIRTH DOCTRINES ARE PHSYCHOTIC, CHRISTIANITY AND SCIENTOLOGY IS PHSYCHOTIC IN THAT WAY.

DO YOU REALIZE YOU ARE SUBJECT TO DEATH AND CANNOT ESCAPE IT?

– SIDDHEARTHA –

I HATE CHRISTIANITY BECAUSE IT'S TOTALLY PHSYCHOTIC. I HATE LIES.

U.F.O PROPAGANDA IS NOT TRUE. UFOS ARE NOT MADE OF MATTER.

THEY ARE VIDEO TELEPATHIC COMPUTERISED ANTI MATTER. THEY ARE PURPLE. SEEN IN NIRVANA AS THE LIGHT OF GOD. THEY ARE PURELY SUPERHUMAN

SILICONE

MICROCHIPS

SEWN INTO THE BRAIN

ARTIFICIAL EYES OR AM I WRONG

– MY DEATH –

I LOVE YOU MORE THAN ANYONE ON THIS PLANET

I'M THE ONLY PERSON THAT UNDERSTANDS YOU AND YOUR MUSIC – FILMS, ETC –

XENONS HAVE SIX EYES, LIKE THE SPIDERS FROM MARS BUT THEIR GRAIN IS SUPERIOR TO HUMANS

I AM A ZOMBIE

– SCIENTOLOGY –

SKEMATICLY CALCULATING SCIENTISTS THAT
WALK AROUND ON STILTS
I AM THE SON OF A RACE OF NUCLEAR CYBER-
NETICS AND ROCK N ROLL STARS
I AM A RAT IN A CYBERNETIC SEWER
YOURS SIMON

Oh God, please help me! – Cheryl's letters to Nick Heyward

August 17

Dear Nick,

So much for the response to my last letter. It was sent registered, but it obviously didn't make a very big impact on the right person.

After all, I am just another faceless being who insists on writing stupid letters, making a lot of work for someone, and then having the nerve to expect a reply.

Don't I talk a load of rubbish sometimes, but it's not easy to say what I mean knowing that anyone could be reading this. I just want to write to you from a person to person point of view, not as a fan or even as a girl to a boy.

I mean, if you weren't the singer, songwriter and famous person you are and I looked you up in the phone book and wrote to you, I'd probably get a reply. I'd have a cheek, but at least I'd arouse some sort of emotion in you, and I'd attract your attention. That seems to be the hardest thing to do.

Love
Cheryl

August 18

Dear Nick,

How did your day go? Plenty of excitement and fun, no doubt. I wish it was me – what I wouldn't give to be doing something I really, really want to do.

I like my job, but I don't get enough satisfaction out of it – taxing cars, giving little old ladies their pensions and selling first class stamps doesn't exactly make you feel like you've achieved anything. I want more.

That's all for today. How long can I keep this up? As long as it takes.

Love
Cheryl

August 19

Dear Nick,

What can I say? I find it really difficult to write to someone without getting anything back. I never got on very well writing a diary because I couldn't communicate with a blank piece of paper. At least writing to you I can say things I couldn't say to people I don't know very well – I haven't got the embarrassment of meeting you.

How much fan mail do you get? Too much, I expect. You obviously can't answer them all so what happens to them? In the bin? But if you think you can chuck me in the bin as well, you've got another think coming – what a nerve. You're costing me a fortune in stamps and writing paper, and time. I think I deserve something more than to be thrown away among the cigarette ends, beer cans and bills.

I feel that, for the right person, I've got a lot to give – a lot of friendship, love, fun – everything that's good about a relationship. I'm also a very good listener. I need the physical side as well as the emotional – I don't just mean sex, but just being close to someone.

What am I telling you all this for? I don't read these letters through – I'd embarrass myself. What do you think of me? Here I am, writing all my personal feelings to you, and we don't even know each other. At least my letters are good for a giggle, if nothing else. The least you can do now is answer this letter – please.

See you tomorrow.

Love
Cheryl

August 20

Dear Nick,

I can't say much today. I feel there's no point in anything – I just feel empty and alone, like there's nothing left.

There's so much I'm aiming for in life, but today I don't see the point in trying. I want to meet you, but I know I never can.

Love
Cheryl

August 22

Dear Nick,

Sorry about my last letter. I promise no more like that for a while. After all, the way to impress someone is not to go round sounding depressed, boring and uninteresting.

What do you think of all those girls literally throwing themselves at you? I don't blame them – when I saw you at the Dominion there was such a good atmosphere I'd have done the same thing if I'd had a chance. I can't say I'd mind if a group of boys threw themselves at me.

Love
Cheryl

August 23

Dear Nick,

What can I do to cheer myself up? My boss has given me a glowing report on my progress, but even that doesn't stir any good emotions in me. I miss my friends, that's my problem. You see, I left school a term into the L6th, so that's where all my friends still are. In a way, it's like I never even existed – I never see any of them any more, and they never write. God, I'm lonely. I'm not exactly an extrovert, so I find it quite hard to make friends anyway, and being the only girl at work, I feel cut off. I feel trapped and alone, like I'm not getting anywhere. I'm in a long, dark tunnel, and I can't see the light at the end. I'll prob ably come up to London soon – I like doing things by myself, but I need someone else's company. I'm in danger of submerging myself in a world of fantasy and hiding myself from reality. I'm scared. I feel all empty – not like a person at all. I have to set myself something to look forward to each day, just to give me something, some reason to carry on – little things like getting letters from my friends. It's stupid, but I need it. I'm so young – I've got the whole of my life ahead of me – is it worth it? I've had so much growing up to do recently. One week I was a schoolgirl, and, literally, the following week I was away from home by myself for the first time ever at the start of a seven-week course. Life is for living, but I'm just existing. What happened to all the parties, films, picnics, the walks in the countryside, trips to the coast? I hate it – the more depressed I get, the worse the atmosphere for other people with me, so it gets harder.

Love
Cheryl

August 25

Dear Nick,

I've had enough of it – of what? – everything, I suppose. I feel detached from everyone else and the rest of the world. I don't seem to belong. I'm not depressed enough to think about suicide – I wouldn't have the guts anyway – but sometimes I wonder if it wouldn't be easier to step out in front of a car. Then it would all be over. In that respect, it's such a small step between life and death – from the kerb to the road. It's a defeatist attitude though – it's like admitting to myself, and to everyone else, that I've failed. But at least the hurt would be gone. I ache so much. But what about the people I'd leave behind?

Why do I pour out all my troubles to you? I've no right to impose myself. I find it so easy to talk to you though.

Bye.

Love
Cheryl

August 26

Dear Nick,

What I really look forward to is spending my time with someone really special. I've always dreamt of spending a winter's evening in front of a log fire, drinking champagne and just talking to a special boy. So far I haven't found anyone I can really talk to and open up to. Instead I tend to keep everything to myself. The one person I felt I could really trust did something to hurt me. Now I'm scared to put so much faith in someone else. I'd like to spend a passionate night of love with someone and then watch the sun rise together. God – I can be too romantic for my own good.

How do you like your tea? I just wondered. It's one of those questions I've been dying to ask. Things like: do you do all your own decorating? Can you cook? (To say I can't is being polite.) Do you suffer from cold feet? (I do!!)

I think I've come to the end now. Today was dreadful. I feel like I've climbed to the top of the building, and the only thing left to do now is jump. I've hit rock bottom. I know things can only get better. Aren't people supposed to write poetry when they're dying? I'm so scared. I don't want to carry on by myself. What went wrong? Please help me, Nick. I'm just so scared, so afraid. Please, someone help me. Someone hear me. I'm all torn apart, wasted inside, like there's no life there. Well, if it wasn't for the heart beat, there would be no life. Sod it – what am I doing? Emotional blackmail. It's none of your business – it's got nothing to do with you. Why am I telling you? I'm suffocating, being smothered. Does nobody care? I want to cry out loud, scream, yell, just to get it out. If I can get angry with myself, surely that will help. I've got to stop looking from the inside. There's two sides to everything, and I must see this from the outside. I'm scared of my boss. I can't tell you why – not anyone. At night I lie awake – I don't think about suicide, only about running away, to get away, to stop feeling trapped and isolated. Will it do any good? Of course not, you stupid bitch. There's a war going on inside my head – inner conflict. Hamlet. I don't feel like a person. Help. Help me. Please please help me. I don't want to die.

Love
Cheryl

August 28
Dear Nick,

I have a passion for playgrounds – swings, roundabouts, slides. I suppose it's the memories of my childhood – we had swings in the back garden, and there was a park just down the road. I suppose I'm still in my childhood – I could spend hours on a swing. It's a form of escape. I feel free, like when I was a little girl and I had no worries or problems.

Love
Cheryl

August 31

Dear Nick,

I saw a programme about death this evening. I don't believe that death is the end of everything – I think there's life beyond death. I don't know exactly what, but when you leave this world there's got to be something after. There's a Physics rule which says something to the effect that you can't destroy energy; you can only convert it from one state to another.

Love
Cheryl

September 2

Dear Nick,

I need some advice. To put it bluntly, my boss is a dirty old man. He can't keep his hands to himself, and he's always kissing and cuddling me. He hasn't tried to touch me yet, but I'm really scared. I hate being alone in the same room as him, so I try to avoid it, but even the things he says to me in front of everyone else is bad enough. The other staff know he does it, and he's already been reported, but I don't know how to handle the situation. The only other female is old, and, although most of the men are young, I feel as though I've got no one I can discuss it with. What do you think I should do?

Love
Cheryl

September 5

Dear Nick,

I went up to London today. I started off in Oxford St, then I went to Kings Rd, and finally Kensington. I walked up to Eaton Square, but it was decidedly posh and I felt somewhat out of place. I wasn't far from Cavendish Square either. If I'd thought, I could have personally delivered your mail. I didn't buy anything, and I haven't had the luck of bumping into you yet. I probably wouldn't see you if you walked past me anyway. How about trying it? I got fed up after a while, so I came home. I could have done with some company. I like coming up to London. It's so different to Shrovesbury that it gives me a chance to get away from everything. It's a bit noisy though, but I suppose you get used to it.

Love
Cheryl

September 6

Dear Nick,

I wonder how many letters you've received of mine – if any. I keep hoping I'll find a letter from you when I get in, but of course I never do. I feel all deflated, like there's nothing to keep me up. I don't know what's the matter with me. I'm acting like – I don't know. I don't know anything anymore. I want to be strong, to be able to cope with my life and lead it the way I want. But everything around me is so fragile. If I tip the balance the wrong way, I'll lose everything. I must do something.

I'm confused, so confused. I can't seem to escape from the trap I'm in. Help me please. Oh God, please, please help me.

Love
Cheryl

September 11

Dear Nick,

Where's my fairy godmother? They are never around when you need them. I should be Cinderella. At the moment I live in a fairy-tale anyway. It's better that reality, but even my dreams are getting out of control.

I think I'll come up to London again in a couple of weeks. I'm on holiday soon. Will you meet me somewhere – please? I just want to meet you – it'll save writing paper – and just being able to talk to someone else will make me feel better. It'll give me something to look forward to, as well. Will you meet me under Marble Arch on Friday September 23rd at 11.30am? I'll be waiting, so let me know if you can't make it because I'll be there. If Marble Arch isn't convenient, I'll meet you anywhere. I need to see you, to talk to you. Please. How will you recognize me? Does it matter? – I'll know you!

Until tomorrow. . . .

Love
Cheryl

Dear Nick,

Another day, and still no answer. What am I doing wrong? This time I've enclosed an envelope, stamp and writing paper – so there's no excuse. Will you please meet me on the 23rd? I really need to talk to you. I don't know why, but somehow I think you'll understand what I mean, more than anyone else around me. I just feel like crying all the time. I suppose you think I'm an immature, over-emotional girl. Believe me, it's more than that. Why have I found it so much harder to cope with growing up than anyone else? Surely I'm not that much weaker, so why do I feel swallowed up by everything? Why is there a black cloud over me while the sun is shining over everyone else? I've got so much more than a lot of other people – I'm healthy, I've got a good family, a job. But I don't understand. As each day passes I hurt more, and I tend to put up a barrier between me and my friends so that I don't feel any more pain. My friends seem to be pushing me aside – or is it my fault, my attitude? I have so many questions and no one to answer them. I don't understand.

Love
Cheryl

Dear Nick,

I'm really keyed up at the moment. I want to think about next Friday. I know you won't be there, and it hurts. It feels like a friend is about to walk out on me just when I need them so desperately. I'm scared – I don't trust myself. I have so little faith in myself. If I feel that way, how can anyone else feel any differently? What can I do? Please, someone answer my letters. Please, someone help me. There is no point in going on. Inside I'm dead, so why not finish it? It's so easy. I'm finding it so hard – I've got no one I can talk to. Life is so precious. I wish I could give mine to someone who really wants it. Just when I think I'm getting over it, and I slide back down, but further down – deep, deep down.

Love
Cheryl

September 19

Dear Nick,

Friday is coming closer. I know you won't be there –
you probably don't even know I exist – so why do I put
myself through this? I'm like a child who desperately
wants a very expensive Christmas present. I know I can't
have it but . . .

Are you romantic? I'm terrible. Romance is one of the
highest priorities in my life. I like watching the old films
– they give me a good excuse to have a cry.

Love
Cheryl

September 22

Dear Nick,

Well, tomorrow's the day of truth. Will you be there? I
don't think so somehow. I live on hope though. I saw you
on 'Top Of The Pops'. Very smart. How much do you
spend on your clothes?

I've had a lousy day. I need a shoulder to cry on!

Love
Cheryl

September 23

Dear Nick,

You didn't turn up. I knew you wouldn't, but it still
hurts. It was just today that kept me going, hoping that I
might get to meet you. I've got no one else I can turn to.
I need to talk to someone so desperately. The pain is so
bad. I've tried to tell my Mum, but I can't. Please, Nick –
I've got no reason to carry on now. No one cares anymore.
I don't want to live any longer. I can't cope now, and I'm
scared that I won't be able to cope with the future. There
is no future for me. There's nothing left. Inside I'm dead.
I can't explain. When you didn't arrive, everything I was
holding onto fell apart. My whole sense of reality has
gone. To expect you to meet me was a crazy idea, and my
life should not revolve around you. I'm scared of death,
but it's the only choice I have left. Please talk to me,
please. I feel like crying all the time. I'm only 17. Why do
I feel like this? There is only one way out.

Bye Bye, Nick.

Love
Cheryl

[*No more letters were sent. None had been answered. Shortly after the last letter Cheryl went into a severe depression. She tried to commit suicide and lost her job. At the time of this writing (seven months later) she is gradually recovering, but still deeply in love with Nick.*]

I'd like to screw the heart off Blondie – telephoned fantasies

Men:
I would like to make Debby Harry's quim ache.

I'd like to suck her fanny and lick her tits.

I wank over her tits at night.

I'd like to stroke Debbie Harry's bum.

Man: I want to suck Debbie Harry's tits and put my tongue inside her pussy and feel the juice oozing over my lips.

Man: I always fancied Deborah Harry and I wanted to fuck her. When she's performing on stage I'd get up there and pull her knickers down. She'd grab hold of my prick and slowly suck away until I'd come all over her. Of course, by this time I'd have my cock up her fucking arse and I'd be bumming away at her. Cor! Ain't she fucking beautiful? At the moment I am masturbating and I've just come. Bye.

Men:
I'd like to screw the heart off Blondie, and I said heart not arse.

I imagine that I rape her and twirl her tits around my mouth. Lick her pubes. Suck her thighs.

I'd like Debbie Harry to be my mistress and dress me up in a maid's uniform. My cock's working overtime.

I'd like to see Debbie Harry in bra, suspenders and little panties step in front of me so I could finger her, lick her tits.

I'd like Debbie Harry to wank me off all over her fat, beautiful tits. Then I'd like to put my swollen prick in her mouth, pull the head up and down, I'd like her to suck me off, see all my hot spunk go down her throat. I'm coming just thinking about the slag.

My fantasy would be to make love to Debbie Harry in a sauna bath. She's my favourite pop star.

My sexual fantasy is to spend an evening out with Debbie Harry. Take her for a meal, take her home, rub them lovely tits of hers and fuck her.

Carolyn: I invented Bowie

It got to the point where I thought I'd invented him. I created this creature out of *my* desire and he was working on *my* power. Never mind about communicating with him, I thought I had created him. And I still do sometimes. I still think I'm the one who gave him all this, all his success.
    After all, I imagined it first, then he did it.

It was June 1981 when I first became aware of Bowie. I hadn't heard of David Bowie. I was in a spiritual and everything low. It was one of the times when many things had happened and I was in the pits at the time, the last straw kind of thing.
    I was ill. I had an infection that caused my head to be full of liquid and all the time it was like I was in an aeroplane and everything was very strange.
    So one watches films one wouldn't normally. And this film came on: *The Man Who Fell to Earth*. And I liked it. I

really liked it very, very much. I've always liked science fiction and I thought it was very effective.

Then it came on again and I recorded it.

And in the interim something had worked on me in some mysterious way and everything changed in my life. Instead of seeing everything negatively as I had before it was just as if I'd turned a coin over and all of a sudden I could see the very things I thought were the worst were really great.

Because they spelled my freedom.

I just realized I was totally free because I could do anything I wanted.

So then I proceeded to do so. In the space of a few weeks my life just changed totally.

I used to watch television continually and overeat – but I lost 30 pounds in about five or six weeks. At that point I watched no more television. I watched some films and, of course, I watched this film. But no telly.

I started listening to rock'n'roll music. I had this burning fascination to know: who is this David Bowie? There was just something *about* him that was just so *fascinating*. I had to know more.

So I did research.

I went to a lot of places and I got a lot of old articles. And the more I read the more fascinating it became. And, of course, got all the records and I tried to listen to them more or less in order. And I was captured by the music.

And then the stories and everything led to other artists like Tangerine Dream and Kraftwerk and different people that David Bowie had been associated with. And to other films.

And then mysterious things happened in my life. Really strange things were happening which later I came to know were synchronicity. Just unbelievable things.

Like the moment I heard about the second film he'd made I wanted to see it. And wouldn't you know that they scheduled it and it had been in the can or hidden away somewhere for *years?* But within a week or two after I heard about it, it was premiering. In Hollywood, of course.

So I went down and I met someone. [*Sighs*] It was the first of my many boys. I've met many David Bowie clones in my travels along the way and that has changed things a lot for me too.

That was a strange experience. It was hardly to be believed. It happened on July 1st 1981. I went down to see *Just a Gigolo* on its first night. And at the last moment this beautiful boy comes and sits down next to me. And he was *gorgeous*. His name was Michael. He was 23. Fresh in town.

After the film I took him out, bought him a drink, had him drive me home in my car. He spent the night. And this was the night I also heard *Heroes*. I'd bought the album but hadn't played it. So we played it and we talked about Bowie. He told me a lot about Bowie I didn't know. And we did yoga together. We sang.

He was bi-sexual, but I came to realize that bi-sexual lovers, my God, they're marvellous. Perhaps because they don't have a big emotional investment. They can be *fabulous* lovers. He certainly was. He was beautiful. He was very well endowed, extremely well endowed. And at that age – the staying power! And he just, oh my God, it was simply marvellous! And Bowie music playing all around.

He was my first boy. There were others. [*Laughs*]

And I felt I had so much energy. It was like I was on coke all the time. I was filled with energy. And no appetite, of course.

And all manner of wondrous things happened, which if taken singly don't seem like much, but when they occur in series like that it was just really extraordinary.

And, of course, I had visions. And dreams. Many things about his life which came true.

I saw the album covers before they came out which is pretty extraordinary. Some I saw very clearly. One, *Let's Dance*, I saw twice. It was like: 'Pay attention to this.' And I drew a picture of it – and the rest is the history we all know. And then I saw the other one which was from *Merry Christmas Mr Lawrence*. And even in the dream I knew it wasn't *by* Bowie. But he was on the cover. And I couldn't understand it because the film wasn't even out.

As you know, 1983 was the year he came back and did just everything. Well, in 1981 I was seeing all these things happen. Of course, I was seeing he and I doing lots of things together. A lot of things came true for me and most of the things came true for him.

But unfortunately we were not together in a physical sense, you know, only in an astral way.

I had been a student between 1970 and 1977 which was how I managed to miss David Bowie. I was into rock music before then, in the sixties, but after that I was in university the whole time. Then my husband died. My son died. So that decade was really – I was turned off from that decade. And then David Bowie got to represent the seventies and through him I got into the music of the seventies – it was like a bridge for me to recreate some of the feelings and the thoughts.

And some of the records he put out and the other ones I heard seemed to be messages to me. They seemed to be about my life at the time. He put out two singles in 1981 and both of them had a meaning to my life.

I would play records and I got into dancing and singing – there was a lot of creativity, and I wrote lots of poetry. *Reams* of poetry just came out of me. It seemed like some force was taking me over, and I was like an automaton and being manipulated. At first it was continual. It was that flood of energy. I would wake up in the morning after about six hours sleep. And just spend every day doing research or playing records.

It was like a manic state only it went on for months and months and months.

And I would play a record and he would manifest. I would see him, in my living room. And the pictures would start moving. From the very beginning I started putting pictures on the wall. And they started moving. And before I had the thought to begin to meditate, I was meditating. And the pictures would move and change.

Then I had specific visions. Like I would see him with light rays coming out of him. In another vision I saw light – he was drawing the light down. And at one time I thought he was Christ. When I found out he was Jewish I was positive. And when I found out he could grow a beard, and, yes, his mother's name was Mary . . .

Then one very strong vision was he was flying through a giant tunnel and I was flying behind him. Very classic visions, but they were very impressive to me.

And you have to understand this was when I had no spiritual life. I was an atheist for many years. And I had never done table rapping or anything like this.

I also saw us fucking together in London.

But I came to see that that vision was possibly symbolic, showing the joining of the animus which, of course, is the man within one. And I felt, indeed, that I knew him. I had known him, we were one. Maybe he was the other side of me, or the other half of the egg, my astral twin.

I've been through all sorts of theories, because I'm not stupid and I realized something was happening to me which I wanted to be able to describe – the vocabulary.

So I thought: Well, it's an archetype. I've projected my archetype.

I had done some study of Jung and, of course, I did some more. And that holds true. And many of the other theories were working hypotheses for a while. I suppose there's a bit of truth in everything.

So it all came to coming over to England after a while, after I'd gone through that whole summer.

I was on the dole. I'd had this marvellous, marvellous job but I hated it. It was killing me. I'd had a private practice in psychology and that wasn't fulfilling so I had switched to public relations and I had this fabulous job in public relations.

But it sort of sucked my soul.

I had no private life and, as I say, I was overweight and just watched television and ate and drank when I wasn't involved in my job.

And everything was just sort of closed off from me.

I have grown children. My daughter I'd discovered was a junkie, shortly before then. And she went on her way.

And numerous robberies and all sorts of terrible blows.

Coming over to England was a very big step. I got rid of everything and gave everything away and came over here. More or less following the David Bowie trail.

I told myself it was for other reasons – I've always been an Anglophile, mad about English things.

But really it was this thing that I was being led somewhere. That this was destiny's play for me.

And I've become convinced about it since because I've had lots of other manifestations – physical and everything – and have really got into my spiritual life now so I don't question it hardly at all any more.

I follow.

For a long time I thought I was going to meet him. And when I came over here I thought: We're just going to happen, you know, no question about it.

Indeed, we were here for many, many months together and we just missed each other in many cases.

I would hang around certain places and I would later find out he'd been there. So without question there are mystical connections between us.

Even while I was in the States I had a strong desire to go to places he'd been. When I was in New York, for instance, I went to the theatre where he'd done *Elephant Man*. And I came over here on the QE2 – same as he had because he didn't like flying.

I didn't feel much there, but I wasn't too highly tuned yet.

Later I got the address of a place where he used to stay in Chelsea. I didn't have the exact address but streets are short in London so I would go up and down. And I felt wondrous things happening to me – that there was a force still around.

Then I got his exact address in Manchester Street and already I'd been to Manchester Street and I'd felt a lot of force around the low forties. Well, his flat turned out to be 39.

And I went to his house where he was little in Bromley. The other house I just missed – the beautiful old one in Yorkshire had just been pulled down. I thought that was quite a blow.

I don't know. For some reason I felt I had been given a lot of power. I'd been touched with power, and it seemed that if I went to these places I would get even more.

I seemed to want to do whatever I had to do to get close.

And yet I didn't want to hang around or write him a letter.

People have said: 'Why don't you write him a letter and tell him all this?'

But for some reason I've held back from making a direct attempt. I felt: If it's going to happen, you know, it's going to happen. If I camped outside his hotel it wouldn't be much of a wonder if he came out and I got to see him. But if we run into one another on a dark street one night, that's miraculous.

I suppose that's what I want to do, co-operate with the miraculous.

And Switzerland. The thought occurs even now. I love Switzerland.

I got his address – I have a friend who lives there and he got it – and the thought occurred to me this was a possibility. I know chances are I'd be tramping up one road and down the other until I find the sonofabitch. But eventually he'd have to be home for a couple of days. So yes, yes, I have thought about that.

And I've thought about – just the other day I saw that Scorcese film, *King of Comedy,* and I remarked right after to a friend; 'How much would it cost to kidnap David Bowie?' [*Laughs*]

Yes, yes. I've had fantasies about that.

But, you know, this isn't all I do. I do other things. I got very deeply into my own spritual power and I do meditate.

Do you know anything about *Kundalini* power? Well, it's been rising in me all the time. I feel very rejuvenated.

For instance, I'm not a child – I had my 52nd birthday a couple of weeks ago, but, you know, I don't feel 52. And most people tell me I don't look it.

So I really feel in my life Act III is coming up, I have a third life beginning now.

I haven't studied the *Kundalini* centres properly yet. But I know there is a centre, a *chakra,* in your sexual area, and there is also a heart *chakra.* And I actually felt my heart *chakra* open.

I didn't know what it was at the time. I just felt something inside of me open and something – an arc – come out.

One side went to MT who's this guru in Los Angeles, and another one went out to David Bowie on the other side.

And it was very strong.

Then a month went by and I had another experience. I was playing some music associated with David Bowie and the music felt like it was being drawn up through my anus and my vagina and into my body and then it was just going all through. And I said: 'Oh, my God, that's the *Kundalini* rising!'

And this is a fairly common experience for people who meditate or are doing yoga. And it's something you work for if you're a *Kundalini* freak. But it can also happen spontaneously and it can be very frightening if you don't know what it is.

It can also be very painful in lots of ways, particularly if you're not ready for it.

It's like a charge of vibration, electricity going through.

And it was like my heart *chakra* and sexual *chakra* were communicating with each other – actually communicating. And David Bowie was involved.

Then I *knew* I had to get into certain positions – either lying down lotus or arching my back completely.

And then it was like fucking motions. It was like I was fucking a divinity but David Bowie was there too.

Because when the *Kundalini* is working it is sexual.

I didn't know that for months. I didn't know except I would lie down in bed and I would feel so horny, I would actually feel so turned on that I would masturbate. I use a vibrator, by the way – I never learned to do it with my fingers.

And I'm a Sagittarian and sex has never really been that big with me, not in that physical way.

But then I gradually came to know this was the way the *Kundalini* worked. It starts in that area. And what you're supposed to do is send it up yourself.

So then I read up on it and I realized how to do it myself. Since then I've managed to send it up so that it comes up in these other marvellous patterns. And I've actually got it up to the crown *chakra* now.

And that's really – that is phenomenal.

That's like silver stardust or something, just like buzzing. But no buzzing feels as good. It's like simultaneous orgasms. And the one that I had was really spectacular. It was like four orgasms happening. Only not a peak, just like a plateau.

And you have to understand that I had all these beautiful pictures of David Bowie around.

On top of my bed was this giant one. And I mean I was fucking the dude, you know, and he was fucking me. It was very real.

And yet it wasn't physical. It really wasn't physical. It was a communication.

A definite electronic fuck was what it was.

At those moments he's very godlike. And it's like we're both in our higher selves.

So he's very much like himself, only perfect. And I'm very much like me, only perfect.

But in the fantasies he's quite human. He farts. He shits.

And that's the levelling part of it.

I had reams and reams of fantasies right from the beginning.

It's like a dream where you have layers. Some of it is actual and some of it is future and some of it is past.

I can fantasize anywhere. But I don't want distractions. The ideal situation is I suppose a whole empty house. And I don't have the radio on. There's no music while the fantasies are going on because they're real. Unless it's part of it. Like if it's a concert, I'll have a concert tape going in the other room and then I'll be in this room and that will be like sound effects.

And I like to speak aloud, I like to say the words. I love to speak in an English accent. I feel like David Bowie when I'm alone and I'm doing it. It's very entertaining and very creative and I really enjoy it.

Lying in bed at night is another good time. I run through the fantasies sort of like one watches television.

I used to spend many hours a day – maybe eight or nine hours a day – living these parts. I played all the parts. They were beautiful. I mean, it was like a soap opera. They were getting so complicated it was like a Dickens novel after a while. Everybody I knew was in them in some capacity.

They just developed into an enormous part of my day.

There seemed to be these main ones and then there were endless variations. And then it was like a soap opera. I was *living* it. I adored playing the David part. Well, I suppose that's why he's tortured so much – it's because I play the part. And, oh, God, I could cry so easily. These scenes are very sad. I say the words and I actually cry.

And I guess I really did feel like David Bowie for a long, long time.

It was hard for me to figure this out or explain to other people – that I didn't want to meet him and ball him, I wanted to *be* him.

I expect that comes up in a lot of other people also. It's part of one's identity which one projects up there in a kind of idealized way.

The fantasies are terribly personal and I haven't even wanted to write them down.

They're very dramatic and intimate and everything.

For instance, he's shot on stage.

He and Mick Jagger – this has not come to pass yet – are doing a short concert tour together. And David Bowie is shot on stage. And he's paralysed.

Well, there's different versions of this, alternative fantasies about the degree of paralysis.

In some of them it's from the waist down. Then there was one where he was totally out of it – he could only blink his eyelashes. But he still managed to communicate.

And naturally I'm right there and it's sort of like a Howard Hughes relationship where he doesn't want to deal with anyone and he only wants to deal with me because for some reason he trusts me.

And there's one very persistent one where he's all burnt out and he doesn't want to get back on heavy dope again. He can't seem to relax and only I can relax him.

I can do this in fairly legitimate ways. As a counsellor I learned the techniques.

And I save him a lot. And he suffers a great deal. He's in pain much of the time.

Sometimes he's kidnapped and tortured by these crazy weirdo freaks. Sometimes they're Arabs, sometimes – just lately – they're Irish. But it's a scene that's very erotic to me, very exciting.

And in his films, indeed, there is always a theme of that S&M stuff.

I've always been a masochist. Even my first husband and I played around a bit and my second husband and I did a *lot*. Psychologically *and* physically.

We acted out fantasies.

And in the fantasies with David Bowie I do too. They're just very intimate. You know, it's *The Seventh Veil*. I guess I don't even want to face myself with some of this.

Even as a very, very young person – as soon as I could read – I was attracted to that theme. I seem to remember reading a comic strip, *Flash Gordon*, and the scene of these tortures is the one that grabs me. And Japanese torture – there are books about that. I read them when I was a little kid, and they turned me on. At the time I didn't even know what it was, but looking back now I can see the thread.

Sometimes he goes mad. He's gone uncontrollably mad and has been committed. We had a lovely one where Bowie was mad, mute and catatonic, and then Mick Jagger and I made a film together about the three of us. And we used a double for the Bowie part. And it was all very complicated and quite exciting. I think it would make a great film!

And then, of course, he recovers. Well, there was a time when I was trying to get rid of him, even in the States. So in my fantasies I would kill him. He'd be lost at sea or go mad. But he always came back. [*Laughs*]

Sometimes he's kidnapped for ransom and I'm sent to try to get people to send the money along.

The kidnappers usually have him for three days.

At first he's just beat up, knocked about, knocked down, humiliated, made to get up and knocked down again.

Then he's generally whipped. I've seen it in so many films and it's just got to be. The standard, you know:

clothes off, tied up, whack him with a whip. It's just immensely turning on.

Sometimes his hands are broken. Sometimes his hands are burnt or damaged and he's made to play the piano. Sometimes he's chained to pianos. Sometimes he's sexually assaulted. Sometimes he's made to go down on one of the captors. There's always a really crazy one that wants him to do crazy things and so I imagine that. Sometimes they're not so bad and they make friends and they'll part friends because Bowie is so beautiful about it. Sometimes they fuck him in the arse, the way Lawrence of Arabia presumably was. Sometimes he has a lot of internal damage and then he can't bear to see anyone and we go off together to an island or some place while he tries to regain his equilibrium, sanity or whatever.

And sometimes they make me hurt him. Sometimes they make me hold the whip or burn him. Sometimes they get us both loaded with drugs and there's this long, mad, final night. And one hardly remembers what happens but it's like a horrible, Bacchanalian orgy of torture and pain. Later he remembers or he starts to remember and he doesn't want to, and then this is an excuse for him to be cold and cruel to me.

I like him to be a little cruel to me sometimes, but there's always got to be a good reason. Because essentially he's such an angelic, pure person.

And then there's another one after he's been shot and he's paralysed.

He's in a wheelchair. He didn't even want to get in a wheelchair but I bought him this really fancy one.

He won't have sex because he's so shattered physically and can't even walk. He's so graceful normally that this just tears him apart and he can't bear the thought of having sex in his present situation.

So I have to practically rape him. And one night I finally do: I knock him out of his wheelchair and we work it out.

As a matter of fact, I acted that one out with a subsequent lover [a Bowie clone]. I said: 'OK, you want to fuck me? We'll do it this way. Pretend you're in a wheelchair.' And I knocked him off the chair. These boys will do anything I say! [Laughs] That's why they're so much fun.

And he's raped. He gets raped a lot.

Even when he was in the insane asylum. Of course, he's catatonic, he has no control over what's going on. He just lies there. And there's this crazy person that comes in and has his way with him. Sometimes he sucks his cock, sometimes he, you know, fucks him. Poor David.

But then I find out about it and save him again, protect him.

Because I'm frequently protecting him, saving him, healing him.

Sometimes he's a little cross and during this period – when he was going mad – he hit me a couple of times, just to show how mad he was going.

Mostly he's self-destructive though. He'd rather kill himself than hurt me.

But sometimes he can be manipulative.

Sometimes when he's hung up he will just turn me on and then not satisfy me. Then I will have other lovers and he finds out about it.

Sometimes too he will run away and go off with a drug dealer. Then he's terribly degraded because the drug dealer first has Bowie sexually and then keeps him loaded all the time with all kinds of wild drugs and then lets his friends have Bowie.

Then Bowie wants to escape, of course, and then we have to find him. We find him and, oh, he's just terrible and starving and filthy and terribly degraded.

And we save him.

I give him baths a lot. I bathe him.

Sometimes I'm in the bath with him. Sometimes he's in the bath tub with Mick Jagger. And he and Jagger have sex together a lot in the fantasies. And all three of us . . .

I mean, I'm insatiable. I'm absolutely out of the question when it comes to this fantasy stuff. You know, it's creativity, isn't it? And why don't I write all this down? I mean, good God, I could write some terrific fiction.

But sometimes I think: Well, this is so ugly, this is so aggressive, this is the negative of me. Why should David Bowie want to know a person who wants to see him tortured continually? And I try to lighten them up or some-thing. But it is very difficult for me to think of a fantasy where he doesn't suffer. Or have something to overcome. I mean, how many plots are there? You know, if you're all happy and you're just sitting around . . . you've got to have some drama in it.

It's sort of embarrassing in a sense and yet it isn't in another. Because it's my subconscious working and I have to accept my own products. Maybe that's what it is: a catharsis. Finally, for Christ's sake, getting it out.

One theme of all my fantasies is that I need to be free. And that comes up in my life also. I must keep myself free, not become domesticated.

That's why I don't sleep with men. I fuck them, but I can't bring myself to spend the night with them.

And if it happens by accident – occasionally, you know, you're stuck – but if I can possibly get out of it: zip, el zippo, you know.

Fuck 'em, drink with them, but for God's sake don't spend the night. Don't let their seed stay in your body all night because this is a way of giving you bonds, holding you down. And you need to be free for your destiny.

With boys it's very easy to arrange that. With men it's a little harder.

With the boys I guess I was looking for Bowie and they got in the way. I was sending out some kind of rays and they were attracted to me. And it just so often happened that we went to bed.

That was very good for my ego. Because being older and having one or two boys is one thing, but when you have a string of them, continually, two at a time . . . I guess I needed that.

I needed that to know that a woman's age is not considered to be a terrible detriment.

In America with the youth culture, especially in Los Angeles in the motion picture business where I've been on the periphery for so long, the people out there are so beautiful, so young, so perfect, so white-toothed – you know, every hair in place. You have no idea of the standards until you live there.

So it was a very good experience for me to come over

here and to have everybody with English accents. And to go to bed with them.

English boys are very sophisticated. They make love well.

I suppose I could spend a lot more energy deliberately seeking out Bowie clones if this pleased me. And I suppose I have done that up to a point.

But it's nothing I really . . . I'm not ashamed of it but I just don't want to continue doing it.

Because, after a while, I've had so many beautiful boys and so many beautiful adventures, it's almost as much fun now just to fantasize it.

It's like a piece of chocolate. It's beautiful and lovely but so what? You can't live on it.

It's not taking me anywhere any more. I feel I've outgrown it, I suppose.

I have such a short attention span. But this fascination, this fucking David Bowie will not let me alone! I mean enough already! At least get me there, give me some definite sign. Have him write *me* a letter. Have him send a chauffeur round. Or leave me alone.

I felt at one point he was directing my life completely. Even in my dreams.

I woke up once and he was telling me what to do. I'd just fallen asleep. I hadn't gone to sleep proper and then woke up and I felt I wasn't supposed to hear this but I was just getting the tail end.

It was like brainwashing, mind control.

I felt he was definitely telling me what to do. It wasn't negative. It was like a lecture. Because in my dreams he's frequently giving a class in university and I'm going to his classes. And it's like he's a guru.

Because I firmly believe that some spirit or god or my guide or some higher power is using David Bowie to educate me. Some thing, some force, some power is working through me and I have an enormous personal relationship with this thing or this person or this force.

I don't know what it is. All I know is David Bowie is the one in the middle. It's like David Bowie is the mailbox or something. We communicate through David Bowie.

Whether he's aware of it or not I don't know. Some day I may find out.

A day simply doesn't go by without thoughts of Bowie. Looking at him. I could look at his face for ever. His face is so beautiful. His face is beauty.

But his body is possibly more important than his face. It's the body that we've seen so many times in his films and, you know, he does exhibit it.

I adore that type of slender bare body, practically hairless.

And I love him being bi-sexual. Because I think everybody is.

In that way I think he's a sociological hero. I think he's been acting out many of the major themes that face people.

He's a Renaissance man. A major manipulator of symbols.

Though I don't know whether his artistry lies more in business or art. Because I think he's really playing his cards phenomenally well.

I do love him. I love him *totally*. I love David Bowie, I'll say it.

This embarrassed me as being inappropriate for a long time. But then I came to see that love is an enormous force for good.

I never understood that 'God is love'. What does that mean? And the Beatles' 'love' and everything . . . 'love, love, love' – that was just popcorn. It had no meaning. But I mean love is *love*. [*Laughs*] And loving him, I can love others. It's like something was opened in me.

I would do anything for him. I would die for him. I would give my life for him. There ain't no question about it.

And then the dreams and the visions and the fantasies all blend together after a while.

I sort of forget which is which. When you devote your life the way I have to doing these things, one of your aims is to live your life like a dream. And to make your dreams more like life.

His face is so fascinating. His body is fascinating.

I've spent hours and hours going through thousands, literally thousands of photographs, looking at his ears, for instance. I have learned how to look from Bowie. To observe.

People used to say: 'What is it you like about him?' Well, I can give you a list, you know.

His voice, of course, is phenomenal. And his hair is phenomenal. He is my idea. He is my ideal.

I don't just love him, I *adore* him. I worship him. And I have come to know that he is my personal choice as God. He is a manifestation of God. Well, we all are. But he is the one that I have chosen.

Oh and I think he's more beautiful now than when he was a boy. He was a beautiful boy and now he's a beautiful man.

Oh, I can't wait till he gets older, and older – he's going to be a beautiful man . . .

And yet I think he's going to die. So many of his fans think he's going to die.

And because of all the death in my fantasies I have to ask myself: Is this my subconscious or is this..? So much else has come true.

The first time I dreamt that he died it really shook me.

I woke up immediately afterwards and I felt so . . . I was upset. It was like an earthquake.

And I was on the point of calling my mother.

I've thought of killing him.

Yes.

And I can understand that chap that killed Lennon. He started out a fan, you know. Yes, yes, I've gone through that. Or Charlie Manson, for instance, who was really a fan. [*Laughs*]

It's a sort of like frustration or anger: Why don't you pay attention to me? I love you, you sonofabitch. Why don't you love me? Oh, and one feels inferiority. Like at one point in '83 when just every day it was David Bowie and he was getting more and more inaccessible and brilliant and famous and wonderful, and I was just getting older and, oh, just horrible feelings . . .

It was like taking the thought to its highest level of the

ridiculous to gain clarity. And taking it to that level was seeing myself as nothing.

Like in *The Story of O* – not even human.

Then I suppose that engendered a lot of aggressiveness. And I thought: OK, I'll just get a gun and I'll kill the sonofabitch and then I'll be just as famous because everybody . . .

You know: I'll join us together in some way.

Because in my fantasies when I kill him then he's definitely part of me. He's physically inside of me then, and we really are finally joined because he's dead.

So I thought: You sonofabitch, you don't love me. I'll kill you . . .

I didn't put a whole lot of energy in it but it was a possibility.

This was when I suppose I thought that maybe I would do something. I would take positive action to actually see him.

And this was one of the things that came up.

I feel frustrated sometimes because I didn't follow acting, I didn't become a great actress. I didn't follow writing enough to get published. I didn't follow counselling when I was in that world. I'm a better dancer than normal but not good enough to be professional. I'm a better singer than average but not good enough.

I never did anything – but I'm the world's greatest audience because I know what goes into making those things happen.

I have so many talents, I have so many things I'm good at, but I've just never specialized.

Somehow with David Bowie it all comes together. I have a destiny somewhere. To do something with someone. And I'm waiting until more information comes.

It's almost like a priestess thing. I have given myself body and soul and I'm just waiting for the instruction to come.

I'm over here literally following my star. And to find out what will happen. Waiting for more messages. And they will come.

They definitely will come.

Afterword

Celebrity is the religion of our consumer society. And fans are the mystical adepts of this religion who dramatize moods, fantasies and expectations we all share.

You may find their intensity unusual or alarming but that is because no one has ever allowed them to express their feelings so comprehensively.

Showbiz folklore likes to pretend there is an 'acceptable norm' of fanhood, only occasionally transgressed by extremist deviants. Most fans, it asserts, are jolly sorts who only desire their idol's well-being and the smooth operation of the industry. We met quite a few who desired rather more.

Moreover, it is not any particular fan who is 'extreme', so much as the condition of fanhood itself.

The fans in this book, however, are not passive victims of showbiz exploitation, but real and socially functioning people working through and acting out the consequences of fanhood for all of us. In the same way that Bowie, for example, explored the idea of stardom. And, we think, with as much courage, innovation and daring. Some of the visions and ideas in this book are as suggestive and exciting as anything produced by any rock star. When did Robert Plant write anything as beautiful as Lucille's fantasy about him?

We started this project as a psychohistory of fans. There is an intriguing development linking the history of consumerism to the mutations of hysteria, a development from the first fan suicide (for Valentino) of Peggy Scott above a London hat shop, to Chapman's Hawaii Five O style execution of John Lennon. A story of phantom horizons and fantastic expectations, discharging into a spiralling logic of desire which the economist Schumpeter prophesied would spell the doom of capitalism itself.

That book is still in progress. But we soon realized there was a need for this more immediate and accessible book in which fans could share their experiences with one another.

Because many fans we spoke to were quite anxious about what they were going through and didn't realize what the sources of their experiences were or how prevalent they were. Fanhood can be a quite frightening kind of possession.

And nowhere in the vast media operation dedicated to pop and all its works is there any vehicle for fans to talk unashamedly across fan club lines and in a non-trivialising context. To talk from their own rather than their idols' or the industry's point of view. No one will give fans the stage. We decided to do just that.

There is a curiously embarrassed censorship of fans' attitudes, ideas and declarations, both in the media and by over-protective fan club stewards. Hearing of our research, a radio producer rang to canvass our help. He was making a documentary on pop fans and reeled off an impressive list of stars his team had interviewed. And how many fans? 'Ah, yes, well actually that's why I'm ringing. I thought you might know a few....'

And many stars are quite unaware of the kind of letters they are sent, the kind of emotions they inspire. One merchandiser we interviewed, a man at that time responsible for dealing every year with hundreds of thousands of letters to about a dozen acts, said:

> M: I don't know how many people believe any of the stars ever read this stuff or ever see it. I suppose there must be quite a few of them.
>
> Q: What happens, in fact? Do you reply to any of these?
>
> M: No. We just send them a form to spend some money. I mean it's impossible. You can't, you just can't write back. What can you say to them?

What indeed?

Another merchandiser told us he had instructions from one of his acts to burn any gifts sent in by fans. And we witnessed two well groomed secretaries in a major management office whose job it was to rip open fan mail, extract any cheques and cash, then throw the letters into waste bins.

All of which expresses the kind of uneasy contempt towards fans which has become a standard response. Music journalists (who lack the curiosity which redeems their mainstream colleagues) are simplistically derisive. Every few months they wheel out the old standby: Are fan clubs ripping the fans off? Then they yawn and go back to their stereo systems. And when did you last see or hear an interview with 'a fan' which didn't begin with a chuckle or end in a snigger? One TV programme we had the misjudgement to contribute to actually consulted a psychiatrist about the mentality of fans – why not consult a psychiatrist about the mentality of stars? Fans are regularly soothed and baby talked along, tricked, jeered at, conned and placated, frequently suppressed and censored, practically never listened to.

When we started listening we were initially shocked by the depth and extent of fans' involvement with the pop media. But as we got to know them better, and thought about it more, their involvement began to tell us quite a lot about our own relationship to media output and also about the degree of media penetration in general. Because while fans may be ultra consumers, we all consume pop and celebrity one way or another. What was that story about Princess Di wanting to meet Boy George?

So often fans are spoken for. Even when they get to write something themselves they are seduced by the publisher's expectations and by their own sense of decorum and also by a desire not to offend into accounts somewhat less than the whole story. Where for example is all that masturbation, all those nights of weeping? All that anger?

To begin with we were astonished by the degree of hostility and aggression, spoken and unspoken, shown by fans towards stars. Later we realized this was one necessary consequence of such unconsummated, unconsumable passion. We felt it important to represent this often concealed aspect of adulation – which will hardly surprise anyone who knows about ambivalence. We did however suppress any psychotic fantasies and any plausible threats (as well as any pornography which didn't show something characteristic or revealing about the relationship of fan to star).

Pop is a frustration machine. And one of its most interesting mechanisms is the tension between the star's incitement of desire and passion (not to mention hysteria) and the bureaucratic and ideological apparatus erected to protect stars from the consequences of this incitement.

At one point we interviewed Adam Ant's manager, Don Murfet, an expert in personal security for stars. Don turned out to be a wise and benevolent man, as genuinely concerned for the well-being of fans as stars. One month after this interview, his protégé Adam Ant appeared on the front cover of Sounds, *glowering lustily at all and sundry with both hands tucked meatily into gaping flies. What was a fan to think?*

It is hardly surprising, when stars offer themselves so lavishly for consumption, *that some fans will take the invitation literally.*

Like Mark Chapman.

After all, one plausible way to 'consume' people is to annihilate them.

And in this light, the grisly episode of Lennon's killing (and its publicity aftermath) appears less an aberration that the following through of a cultural logic implicit in showbiz itself. There is a kind of violence about the fan/star relationship not adequately explained by the psychologistic maxims of, say, Bob Randell's The Fan *or Peter Gabriel's 'Family Snapshot' which reduce the problem to individual psychosis while ignoring the massive and systematic social and cultural provocation.*

This book doesn't propose any answers, only some insight into some of the human consequences of all that jolly talk by DJs, all that promo, all those glossy pix in Smash Hits.

The closer you look at fans the less they seem like devotees of any particular act than the priestesses/priests of a disturbing kind of consumer mysticism which transcends all the acts. The star, as Carolyn puts it in this book, is just the 'mailing box'. Fanhood is an a priori *decision about the kind of person you choose to be and the kind of culture you choose to insert yourself in. You are a fan first and then you choose your star. And the star you elect to follow seems secondary, a matter of convenience or taste.*

Finally, I really think the whole power and magic of celebrity is one of today's crucial political *issues. In their passion, in their ecstasies, in their delirium, fans show themselves to be the true heirs of utopian Romanticism, a current of sensibility which has consistently proved itself more troublesome, more subversive and more challenging than many a professed radicalism.*

Our world is so steeped in celebrity values and saturated by the celebrity systems that no excess, no absurdity, no subversion seems to effectively challenge it. Every challenge is absorbed and normalized, then recycled. The myths and emotions of celebrity are now so deeply ingrained in us that they appear as physical reflexes. Who could suppress a blush, a tremor, a giddy sense of déja vu, *in the presence of that perfectly ordinary mortal, David Bowie?*

But while most of us take it, all that product – as Julie says in this book – 'on the chin', fans actively interpret, refashion, use for themselves what stars give out, often to a point which the industry finds reprehensible, even threatening.

To take publicity literally *may be a more critical stance than to repudiate it.*

But that is another book. This one is by the fans, for the fans.

Fred Vermorel, 1985.

Acknowledgements

All names have been changed and places, dates and occu-
pations etc, altered where necessary to protect our
contributors' identities. Ages are given at time of interview
or writing. Many of our informants requested anonymity
and we decided not to name any of them. But *they* know
who they are, and we thank them all most warmly for
opening themselves so sincerely to this project and for
showing so vividly some of the human reality behind the
star making industry. We were also helped by many
professionals in the biz, many of whom likewise asked for
anonymity, and we thank them for their trouble and time
and for helping to make this book more comprehensive
and representative than it might otherwise have been.